The Good Book
and
The Big Book*

*Big Book® is a registered trademark of Alcoholics Anonymous World Services, Inc.; used here with permission of A.A.W.S., Inc.

Other Titles by Dick B.

Dr. Bob's Library: Books for Twelve Step Growth

Anne Smith's Journal, 1933-1939: A.A.'s Principles of Success

Design for Living: The Oxford Group's Contribution to Early A.A.

The Akron Genesis of Alcoholics Anonymous

New Light on Alcoholism: The A.A. Legacy from Sam Shoemaker

The Books Early AAs Read for Spiritual Growth

Courage to Change (with Bill Pittman)

That Amazing Grace: The Role of Clarence and Grace S. in Alcoholics Anonymous

Good Morning!: Quiet Time, Morning Watch, Meditation, and Early A.A.

Turning Point: A History of Early A.A.'s Spiritual Roots and Successes

The Good Book
and
The Big Book*

A.A.'s Roots in the Bible

Dick B.

With a Foreword by Robert Smith
son of A.A. co-founder Dr. Bob and his wife Anne

Bridge Builders Edition

Paradise Research Publications, Inc.
Kihei, Hawaii

Big Book ® is a registered trademark of Alcoholics Anonymous World
Services, Inc.; used here with permission of A.A.W.S., Inc.

Paradise Research Publications, Inc., Box 959, Kihei, HI 96753-0959

This special Bridge Builders Edition is published by arrangement with Good Book Publishing Company, Box 959, Kihei, Maui, HI 96753-0959

Cover Design: Richard Rose (Sun Lithographic Arts, Maui)

We gratefully acknowledge permission granted by Alcoholics Anonymous World Services, Inc., to quote from A.A. Conference Approved publications with source attributions and to reprint the Twelve Steps. Permission to reprint this material does not mean that A.A. has reviewed or approved the contents of this publication, nor that A.A. agrees with the views expressed herein. A.A. is a program of recovery from alcoholism *only*—use of the Twelve Steps in contents and discussions which address other matters does not imply otherwise.

Publisher's Cataloging in Publication

B., Dick.
   The Good Book and the Big Book : A.A.'s roots in the Bible
   / by Dick B. -- San Rafael, Calif. ; Paradise Research Publications, 1995
   with a foreword by Robert Smith, son of A.A. co-founder, Dr. Bob.
   p. cm.
   Includes bibliographical references and index.
   ISBN: 1-885803-16-8

   1. Alcoholics Anonymous--History. 2. Alcoholics Anonymous--Religious aspects. 3. Twelve-step programs--Religious aspects. 4. Bible--Influence. 5. Oxford Group. 6. Shoemaker, Samuel M. (Samuel Moor), 1893-1963. 7. Spiritual life. I. Title
   HV5275.B34 1995   362.29'286

Library of Congress Catalog Card Number: 95-69696

To Frank Costantino and The Bridge Builders of America

When we became alcoholics, crushed by a self-imposed crisis we could not postpone or evade, we had to fearlessly face the proposition that either God is everything or else He is nothing. God either is, or He isn't. What was our choice to be? Arrived at this point, we were squarely confronted with the question of faith.

Alcoholics Anonymous

The trouble with the faith of to-day is that it is . . . [removed] from faith in God. It is faith in laws, and moral principles, and ways of life: but it is not faith in God Himself.

Samuel M. Shoemaker, Jr., *Confident Faith*

So then faith *cometh* by hearing, and hearing by the word of God.

Romans 10:17

Contents

Foreword to the First Edition

Before there was a Big Book—in the period of "flying blind," God's Big Book was the reference used in our home. The summer of 1935, when Bill lived with us, Dr. Bob had read the Bible completely three times. And the references that seemed consistent with the program goals were the Sermon on the Mount, 1 Corinthians 13, and the Book of James. At Anne's "Quiet Time"—a daily period held with the alcoholics in our home, the Bible was used.

The search for spirituality seems to be insatiable among those who truly seek continual growth. In this book, Dick B. has shown serious research and integrity to give us an excellent base as we seek to progress ourselves.

BOB SMITH
Nocona, Texas

Bob Smith, "Smitty," is the son of Dr. Bob and Anne Smith and co-author of *Children of the Healer*

Preface

The purpose of this particular title is, quite simply, to provide an historically accurate account of what early AAs heard, studied, and borrowed from the Bible. That they did so is clear. But *what* they did has never been researched and recorded in any detail. We hope this book will assist AAs themselves and students of A.A. history in seeing the light the Bible sheds on the reasons for early AAs' relationship with God and the resultant power and success they had.

My previous titles have led up to this work. *Dr. Bob's Library* recorded the Biblical materials A.A.'s co-founder studied, recommended, and circulated. *Anne Smith's Journal, 1933-1939* showed what AAs were hearing in their meetings and at A.A.'s birthplace; and illustrated how the Bible was the center of their faith. *Design for Living: The Oxford Group's Contribution to Early A.A.* detailed the origins, beliefs, activities, and impact on A.A. of the Oxford Group ("A First Century Christian Fellowship"), of which A.A. was an integral part in its formative years—and from which much of its spiritual structure was obtained. *The Akron Genesis of Alcoholics Anonymous* told how it all came together at A.A.'s birthplace at the home of Dr. Bob and Anne Smith in Ohio. *New Light on Alcoholism: The A.A. Legacy from Sam Shoemaker* revealed the enormous influence that the American Oxford Group leader, the Reverend Sam Shoemaker, Jr., of Calvary Church in New York, had on the thinking of A.A.'s East Coast co-founder, Bill Wilson. *Courage to Change* was a shorter work that Bill Pittman and I wrote and which set forth a view of Shoemaker's writings as they seem related to A.A.'s Twelve Steps. *The Books Early A.A.'s Read for Spiritual Growth* was and is the most comprehensive bibliography available on exactly those Biblical and religious materials that early AAs studied as they were developing the program of recovery that later became embodied in A.A.'s Big Book.

We believe this work on the Bible illustrates in detail precisely what Dr. Bob meant when he said AAs got their basic ideas from a study of the Bible. Dr. Bob called the Bible the Good Book. And Good it was. Our title shows how A.A.'s highly successful recovery program was developed from the Biblical materials: (1) covered in the daily devotionals AAs read, (2) developed by the Oxford Group to which they belonged, (3) taught by Sam Shoemaker as he instructed AAs about the Biblical ideas underlying their practical program of recovery, (4) passed along by Anne Smith (Dr. Bob's wife) as she shared from her spiritual journal with the early AAs, including Dr. Bob and Bill, and (5) used by the AAs themselves as they read widely from the religious literature of their day.

We are convinced that a knowledge of A.A.'s roots in the Bible can illuminate the pages of the Big Book, can set the stage for spiritual growth among individual AAs today, and can provide aid and comfort for those who believe, as did Dr. Bob and his wife, Anne, that the Bible should be the main source book for information about God, about His will and power and love, about prayer, and about the way to deliverance.

We gratefully acknowledge permission granted by A.A.W.S., Inc. to use the name *Big Book* as part of our title and do not, by that use, claim to speak for A.A.

Our cover uses an artist's rendering of a Bible cover and of the old "circus" cover of the First Edition of A.A.'s basic text, *Alcoholics Anonymous*, which was published by the Works Publishing Company in 1939. Bill Wilson said the original "Big Book" was made large and thick to depict something of great value. And the circus cover—apparently designed to attract attention—was later abandoned when A.A. itself published the text.

Acknowledgements

The list of those to whom the author is indebted for assistance grows longer by the day; and it is much more detailed in our other titles. Here we will list the contributors by category, and thank them once again for making our research and writing possible.

My son, Ken, is in a category by himself. He is the Bible scholar, critic, reviewer, computer consultant, and daily resource. There would have been no eleven titles, nor the revised editions of them, without his immeasurable patience and help.

Survivors of A.A. founders have had the most impact on this particular work. They are: Robert and Betty Smith, Sue Smith Windows, John F. Seiberling, Dorothy Seiberling, Mary Seiberling Huhn, Dorothy Williams Culver, Sally Shoemaker Robinson, and Nickie Shoemaker Haggart.

Oxford Group people, both former and present, in America and abroad, have given immensely of their time, treasured books, and memories. They are the Reverend Harry Almond, Kenneth D. Belden, Terry Blair, the Reverend Howard Blake, Charles D. Broadhead, Sydney Cook, Charles Haines, Mrs. W. Irving Harris, Michael Henderson, James Houck, the Reverend T. Willard Hunter, Michael Hutchinson, Garth D. Lean, Mary Lean, Dr. Morris Martin, Dr. R. C. Mowat, Eleanor Forde Newton, James D. Newton, Richard Ruffin, L. Parks Shipley, Sr., George A. Vondermuhll, Jr., and Ted Watt.

Clergy who rendered special comments, assistance, and insight are Father Paul B., the Reverend Steve Garmey, the Reverend Tom Gray, the Reverend Dr. Richard L. McCandless, the

Reverend Dr. Norman Vincent Peale, the Reverend Dr. Charles Puskas, Jr., and the Reverend Douglas Seed.

Others who provided special resources and other kinds of support were Frank M., archivist at A.A. General Services in New York and his staff; Nell Wing, A.A.'s first archivist; Ray G., archivist at Dr. Bob's Home; Gail L., archivist for Founders Day in Akron, Ohio; Paul L., archivist at Stepping Stones; Marjory Zoet Bankson at Faith at Work; Dr. Ernest Kurtz; Martha Baker; Dr. John Campbell; Leonard Firestone; Raymond Firestone; Robert Koch; the Thomas Pike Foundation; Mrs. Walter Shipley; R. Brinkley Smithers; Dr. Enoch Gordis; and Dr. Paul Wood of the National Council on Alcoholism and Drug Dependence.

There have been a host of A.A. and Al-Anon oldtimers, archivists, historians, and collectors who have responded to queries, sent books and historical items, and opened their treasures for inspection. They include David A., Mel B., Charlie B., Paul B., Dennis C., Earl H., Mitch K., Joe McQ., Tim M., Charlie P., Bob P., Bill P., Ron R., Bill R., Robert R., Dave S., Grace S., Sally S., Eddie S., Jay S., Joe S., George T., Berry W., Charles W., Jim W., Bruce W., Danny W., and Fay and Bob W.

The men on Maui whom I sponsor and the members of our Bible fellowship have helped in many ways. They are: Bob, Cody, Jeff, Katy, Nathanael, Patrick, Shane, and Tamara. Thanks also to my sponsor Henry B. and my grand-sponsee Robert T. Special thanks also to my daughter-in-law, Cindy, who has always helped and been available for endless tasks. I owe a special debt to Matt G., who, as a member of our Bible fellowship, rendered great assistance in checking footnote accuracy against the innumerable references to the Bible, to Twelve Step literature and histories, and to the religious literature applicable to this work.

1

Lest We Forget Early AAs and Their Bibles!

Alcoholism, substance abuse, and their often attendant addictions can be, and frequently are, deadly, terrifying, productive of despair, financially devastating, and morally destructive. A recent annual report from the Center on Addiction and Substance Abuse at Columbia University declared, as to the American people alone:

- 18-and-a-half million are addicted to alcohol or abuse it.
- Some 12 million abuse legal drugs, such as tranquilizers, amphetamines and sleeping pills.
- Two million use cocaine weekly, including at least half a million addicted to crack.
- Up to one million are hooked on heroin.
- Half a million regularly use hallucinogens such as LSD and PCP.
- Some 1 million, half of whom are teenagers, use black-market steroids.
- The financial costs of substance abuse approach a staggering $400 billion annually.[1]

To these figures, the National Council on Alcoholism and Drug Abuse has added that some seventy-five million American lives are

---

[1] 1992 Annual Report, CASA, 152 W. 57 Street, New York, N.Y. 10009.

impacted by the disease of alcoholism.[2] Technical reports and newspaper accounts of the day make it clear that interdiction, prohibition, prevention, punishment, intervention, treatment, therapy, counseling, and "self-help" groups are not even close to eradicating these problems.

Such was not the picture as it looked on June 10, 1935, and continued through the early 1940's. In that period, an age-old solution had been rediscovered out of the helplessness of medicine, the message of assured deliverance in the Bible, and the desperate experimentation of a handful of drunks who sought to rely exclusively on the power of God.

If one is prepared to accept the following verdict from a staff member of a world-renowned hospital, many doctors and psychiatrists agree to the following:

> What you [the staff member said to several AAs] say about the general hopelessness of the average alcoholic's plight is, in my opinion, correct. As to two of you men [in Alcoholics Anonymous in the 1930's], whose stories I have heard, there is no doubt in my mind that you were 100% hopeless, apart from Divine help. Had you offered yourselves as patients at this hospital, I would not have taken you, if I had been able to avoid it. People like you are too heartbreaking. Though not a religious person, I have profound respect for the spiritual approach in such cases as yours. For most cases, there is virtually no other solution.[3]

The spiritual solution was most definitely the power of God Almighty. A.A. co-founder Bill Wilson said the following:

---

[2] 1992 Annual Report, National Council on Alcoholism and Drug Dependence, Inc.

[3] *Alcoholics Anonymous*, 1st ed. (New York City: Works Publishing Co., 1939), pp. 54-55. Unless otherwise indicated, A.A.'s basic text will hereinafter be referred to as the "Big Book," the name AAs have affectionately bestowed upon it. Except where otherwise indicated, we too will be referring to this basic A.A. text as the Big Book. *Big Book** is a registered trademark of Alcoholics Anonymous World Services, Inc.; used here with permission of A.A.W.S., Inc.

God knows we've been simple enough and gluttonous enough to get this way, but once we got this way [became real alcoholics], it was a form of lunacy which only God Almighty could cure.[4]

A.A. was not invented.[5] Nobody invented Alcoholics Anonymous.[6] Who invented AA? It was God Almighty that invented AA.[7]

What is this but a miracle of healing? Yet its elements are simple. Circumstances made him [the real alcoholic] willing to believe. He humbly offered himself to his Maker—then he knew. Even so has God restored us all to our right minds.[8]

We never apologize to anyone for depending upon our Creator. We can laugh at those who think spirituality the way of weakness. Paradoxically, it is the way of strength. . . . All men of faith have courage. They trust their God. We never apologize for God.[9]

A.A.'s other co-founder Dr. Bob was equally explicit in his personal narrative in A.A.'s Big Book editions:

If you think you are an atheist, an agnostic, a skeptic, or have any other form of intellectual pride which keeps you from accepting what is in this book, I feel sorry for you. . . . Your Heavenly Father will never let you down!

---

[4] From a transcript of Bill Wilson's December 12, 1954, interview of T. Henry and Clarace Williams in their Akron, Ohio, home. Transcript located at the archives of A.A. General Services in New York.

[5] *As Bill Sees It . . . The A.A. Way of Life . . . selected writings of A.A.'s co-founder* (New York: Alcoholics Anonymous World Services, Inc., 1967), p. 67.

[6] *The Language of the Heart: Bill W.'s Grapevine Writings* (New York: The AA Grapevine, Inc., 1988), p. 202.

[7] From the notes of the Rev. Samuel M. Shoemaker, Jr., on Bill Wilson's address on November 9, 1954, at the Grand Ballroom of the Commodore Hotel in New York, p. 5. Notes located at the Episcopal Church Archives in Austin, Texas. Copy in author's possession.

[8] Big Book, First Edition, p. 69.

[9] Big Book, First Edition, p. 81.

In an article published in A.A.'s official publication in July, 1951, shortly after Dr. Bob's death, the famous medical writer Paul de Kruif wrote:

> The medicine the AAs use is unique. Though it should be all-powerful, it has never been tried with any consistent success against any other major sickness. This medicine is no triumph of chemical science; has needed no billion dollar scientific foundation to discover it; does not come in capsules or syringes. It is free as air—with this provision: that the patients it cures have to nearly die before they can bring themselves to take it. The AAs' medicine is God and God alone. This is their discovery.[10]

And there is no doubt that the foregoing names for God and comments about Him were a direct product of the Bible study which took place daily in early A.A. Let's look at Dr. Bob's comments:

> Dr. Bob, noting that there were no Twelve Steps at the time [from mid-1935 to early 1939] and that "our stories didn't amount to anything to speak of," later said they were convinced that the answer to their problems was in the Good Book. . . . As Dr. Bob recalled: "I didn't write the Twelve Steps. I had nothing to do with the writing of them. . . . We already had the basic ideas, though not in terse and tangible form. We got them. . . as a result of our study of the Good Book."[11]

> He [Dr. Bob] cited the Sermon on the Mount as containing the underlying spiritual philosophy of A.A.[12]

---

[10] *Volume II Best Of The Grapevine* (New York: The AA Grapevine, Inc., 1986), pp. 202-203.

[11] *DR. BOB and the Good Oldtimers: A biography, with recollections of early A.A. in the Midwest* (New York: Alcoholics Anonymous World Services, Inc., 1980), pp. 96. Unless otherwise indicated, this title will hereinafter be called DR. BOB.

[12] *DR. BOB*, p. 228. A.A. historian Mel B. informed the author in a telephone interview that Bill Wilson had given the same accreditation to the Sermon on the Mount as Dr. Bob had. Mel stated Bill had made the remarks to him [Mel B.] on at least two occasions.

If someone asked him [Dr. Bob] a question about the program, his usual response was: "What does it say in the Good Book?"[13]

Dr. Bob donated that Bible [the one he carried to meetings] to the King School Group [A.A. Group No. 1], where it still rests on the podium at each meeting. Inside is an inscription: "It is the hope of the King School Group—whose property this is—that this Book may never cease to be a source of wisdom, gratitude, humility, and guidance, as when fulfilled in the life of the Master" [Jesus Christ]. It is signed "Dr. Bob Smith."[14]

Bill Wilson, a former atheist, was gun-shy when it came to mentioning the dominance of the Bible in the early scene. But the following is reported in A.A.'s official biography of him:

Bill [when he moved in with Dr. Bob and his wife Anne in the summer of 1935] now joined Bob and Anne in the Oxford Group practice of having morning guidance sessions together, with Anne reading from the Bible. "Reading from her chair in the corner, she would softly conclude, 'Faith without works is dead.'" The Book of James was considered so important, in fact, that some early members even suggested "The James Club" as a name for the Fellowship.[15]

Dr. Bob's wife Anne wrote in the journal she shared with A.A. pioneers:

Of course the Bible ought to be the main Source Book of all. No day ought to pass without reading it.[16]

---

[13] *DR. BOB*, p. 144.

[14] *DR. BOB*, p. 228. The quote in *DR. BOB* erroneously uses the word "sobriety" instead of the word "property," which we use above.

[15] *Pass It On: The story of Bill Wilson and how the A.A. message reached the world* (New York: Alcoholics Anonymous World Services, Inc., 1984), p. 147. Unless otherwise indicated, this title will hereinafter be called *Pass It On*.

[16] Dick B., *Anne Smith's Journal, 1933-1939: A.A.'s Principles of Success* (San Rafael, CA: Paradise Research Publications, 1994), p. 60.

Clarence Snyder, who founded A.A. in Cleveland and was responsible for its tremendous growth in 1939 and the early 1940's, said: "Everything in this program came from the Bible."[17]

Wrapping up his 1938 survey of the early recovery program, A.A.'s Trustee-to-be Frank Amos reported to John D. Rockefeller, Jr.:

> He [the alcoholic] must have devotions every morning—a "quiet time" of prayer and some reading from the Bible and other religious literature. Unless this is faithfully followed, there is grave danger of backsliding.[18]

A word or two about the Bible in our society today. The Bible still appears to stand as America's Number One authority on the matter of "divine help." A recent survey by George H. Gallup, Jr., and Robert Bezilla (issued by the Princeton Religion Research Center), which appeared in *The Maui News* on September 16, 1994, bears the headline *"Bible still best seller, but lessons being lost."* Gallup and Bezilla began their article as follows:

> It never appears on the best seller lists, but the Bible is the nation's perennial best-selling book.

And we believe that, just as the Bible still stands as America's top best seller, it stood in the 1930's as number one on the early AAs' reading and study list for information on divine help.

We believe those concerned with preventing and treating the devastating problems of alcoholism and drug dependence will want to consider two questions: (1) Is a knowledge of the Biblical roots of A.A. of major importance today in Twelve Step programs, the religious community, and in the treatment arena? (2) Is there sub-

---

[17] Dick B., *That Amazing Grace: The Role of Clarence and Grace S. in Alcoholics Anonymous* (San Rafael, CA: Paradise Research Publications, 1996), p. 43. Except as otherwise indicated, this title will hereinafter be called *That Amazing Grace*.

[18] *DR. BOB*, p. 131.

stantial, credible evidence that early AAs took most of the basic ideas for their highly successful recovery program of the 1930's from the Bible, which they affectionately called the "Good Book"?[19]

One will not understand the importance of knowing the biblical roots of the Twelve Steps without also understanding that A.A. (the Number One success group) is undergoing a plummeting *rate* of recovery while being asked to process vastly increasing numbers of alcoholics *and* addicts. Let's examine the success rate of the 1930's and compare it with widely reported failures in the alcoholism and addiction arena today.

Early A.A.'s Success Rate Compared to Today

Early A.A. claimed at least a seventy-five percent success rate among those who really tried. Early AAs, who were deemed "medically incurable" in the late 1930's, actually *recovered* from their seemingly hopeless disease at that very high percentage rate.[20] And many observers in and out of A.A. underlined, and/or corroborated the early AAs' seventy-five percent claims.[21] Bill Wilson himself contended there was an 80% success rate.[22] *Early*

---

[19] As to the name "Good Book," which AAs often used to describe the Bible, see, for example, *DR. BOB*, pp. 96-97.

[20] Big Book (3rd ed., 1976), pp. xiii, xv, xvii, xxiii, 17, 20, 29, 45, 90, 96, 113, 132, 133, 146, 165, 309, 310.

[21] See Big Book (3rd ed.), p. xx; *Alcoholics Anonymous Comes of Age: A Brief History of A.A.* (New York: Alcoholics Anonymous World Services, Inc., 1957), pp. 309-10; *A Program for You: A Guide to the BIG BOOK's Design for Living* (MN: Hazelden, 1991), p. 15; and the "4, 2, 1" program of early A.A. which was related to the author by Father J. (a priest in the Pennsylvania area), in which oldtimers told him: Four newcomers came into A.A. Two recovered. One relapsed and recovered. And one just didn't make it.

[22] Ernest Kurtz and Katherine Ketcham, *The Spirituality of Imperfection: Modern Wisdom from Classic Stories* (New York: Bantam Books, 1992), pp. 109-10.

Cleveland AAs actually recorded a 93% success rate there.[23] And in his famous 1941 *Saturday Evening Post* article about A.A., Jack Alexander said AAs claimed 100% success among non-psychotic drinkers.[24]

Yet these high percentage rates of yesteryear do not depict the A.A. success rate today—a fact to which any active AA can attest. Those of us who regularly attend A.A. "birthday," "chip," or "anniversary" meetings can observe that the number of people who rise to celebrate their A.A. birthday quickly decelerates after the first year; and very very few stand at these meetings and exhibit significant, long-term sobriety.

To be sure, A.A.'s *numbers* have increased from perhaps 100 in the late 1930's to some two million in 1996, but the *percent* who recover today is tiny compared to that in the early years. And these are facts which have been observed both within and without of the rooms of A.A.[25]

As a caveat, we need to add that it is very difficult to "survey" a fellowship which has no members as such; which claims it ought never be organized; whose attending people are not consistent in the meetings they attend or the groups to which they belong; and

---

[23] *DR. BOB* states at page 261: "Records in Cleveland show that 93 percent of those who came to us never had a drink again." See also Dick B., *That Amazing Grace*, pp. 7, 29, 66, where Clarence Snyder's widow recalled a ninety-five percent success rate. But Clarence's sponsees believe she was referring to the documented ninety-three percent rate.

[24] The Jack Alexander Article about AA [in the March 1, 1941, issue of *Saturday Evening Post*, and reprinted in full by A.A.] (New York: Alcoholics Anonymous World Services, 1991), p. 15.

[25] See Dick B., *Design for Living: The Oxford Group's Contribution to Early A.A.* (San Rafael, CA: Paradise Research Publications, 1995), pp. 5-8; *New Light on Alcoholism: The A.A. Legacy from Sam Shoemaker* (Corte Madera, CA: Good Book Publishing Company, 1994), pp. 1-2; *The Language of the Heart*, p. 252; *A Program for You*, p. 15; Joe McQ., *The Steps We Took* (Little Rock, Arkansas: August House Publishers, 1990), pp. 11, 175-78; Charles Bufe, *Alcoholics Anonymous: Cult or Cure* (San Francisco: Sharp Press, 1991), pp. 108-09; William Playfair, *The Useful Lie* (Wheaton, Il: Crossway Books, 1991), pp. 22-23, 64-71; Charles Bishop, Jr. & Bill Pittman, *To Be Continued. . . . . The Alcoholics Anonymous World Bibliography 1935-1994* (Wheeling, West Virginia: The Bishop of Books, 1994), p. xiii.

which keeps no rosters, does not conduct research, and has difficulty keeping in touch with its own groups, meetings, and the floaters who come and go. That said, there have been some creditable observations about today's success rate.

First, in its own 1989 A.A. Membership Survey and Analysis, A.A. General Services in New York stated the following:

> Half those coming to A.A. for the first time remain less than three months. . . . approximately 50% of those coming to A.A. leave within three months.

> Unfortunately there seems to be no way in which the reasons for departure can be determined. . . . It is little comfort to suggest that many who leave return later, because those who have done that are already counted in the numbers shown here. After the first year, survey results show that attrition continues, but at a much slower rate. [After providing a number of graphs, the survey closed as follows:] Individuals may rebel against this result as contradicting our time-honored statement that "half get sober right away, another 25% eventually make it," etc. That statement applies to observations made at an earlier time, and there is no reason to doubt that changes in society and in A.A. since that time could create a different circumstance today.

While the figures were difficult for this author to interpret and express in clear terms, the Survey then set forth percentages of those surveyed who have been sober for varying lengths of time. In the first year, it reported 34.5%; 13.3% in the second year; 17.2% for five to ten years; 6.8% for ten to fifteen years, and then figures for intervals of five years that move from 2.8% to .1% at 40 to 45 years.[26]

Dr. Enoch Gordis, Director of the National Institute on Alcohol Abuse and Alcoholism, delivered an address on April 30, 1989, to

---

[26] The Membership Survey was transmitted on January 22, 1991, to Enoch Gordis, M.D., Director, National Institute on Alcohol Abuse and Alcoholism, Department of Health and Human Services. Dr. Gordis provided the author with a copy and Gordis's own comments.

the Board of Directors of the National Council on Alcoholism and Drug Dependence. Dr. Gordis furnished the author with a transcript in which Dr. Gordis stated:

> I believe that much of our field's present difficulties with public skepticism is the *misleading message* that we have all been putting out. . . . The misleading message is this: that treatment is a solved problem, and that the main issue in treatment is motivation and referral—all you have to do is to get John or Mary to become aware of their problem, then go to AA meetings, to the NCA affiliate office, or to the treatment program and everything will be OK. But everything is *not OK* for most patients. And, although we all are aware of the tremendous relapse rates in our field, we continue to foist upon the public this misleading message in TV shows, in the literature, on bus and train posters, and in many other public places (p. 4, italics in original).

> Even if we were to assume that AA was the magical solution for everybody, which Bill Wilson never claimed, note first that after 54 years, *less than 5 percent of the alcoholics in this country are involved with AA.* . . . The second thing is the very high relapse rate in our field. The fact of the matter is that only a minority of people do very well. . . . I think we all know that only a minority of patients do very well, while the majority either bounce from one treatment to another with some periods of sobriety or disappear altogether from the treatment world. These are the facts! Not that some patients don't do well. And those who recover through AA must consider themselves blessed (pp. 6-7).

An article in the *Akron Beacon Journal* reporting on A.A.'s Founder's Day Weekend in June, 1995, quoted Scott Tonigan, Ph.D., deputy director of the Research Division at a Center on Alcoholism in Albuquerque, New Mexico, as follows: "It is an axiom in the field that about 75 percent of those who turn to AA drop out by the end of the first year."[27] As stated, similar facts

---

[27] *Akron Beacon Journal*, Friday, June 9, 1995, Page A6; article headlined "Times change for AA: Tenets the same, but not membership."

on the negative side were supplied to the author (from A.A.'s own surveys and from other data) by the Director of the National Institute on Alcohol Abuse and Alcoholism at Rockville, Maryland.[28]

Joan Matthews-Larson, Ph.D., wrote an article for The PHOENIX, April, 1997, issue. It was titled: "An End to the Revolving Door of Treatment." Quoting Dr. Gordis, the writer then asked:

Would you sign on for surgery that had a 75% failure rate?

Then she wrote:

In 617 independently done follow-up studies, conventional (psychologically-based) treatment has an average success of 24 percent. The Rand Corporation Report, which followed 900 males from six NIAAA Treatments Centers over a four-year period, found only 21 percent sober after the first year, and seven percent still sober in the fourth year.

Referring to a Kansas City Veteran's Administration Medical Center study of three groups: (1) those who got no treatment at all; (2) those who received anabuse only; and (3) those who got a

---

[28] At the request of the author, Enoch Gordis, M.D., Director of the National Institute on Alcohol Abuse and Alcoholism of the Department of Heath and Human Services, supplied the author with the following three pieces of information on June 23, 1995: (1) A copy of the 1989 A.A. Membership Survey and Analysis of the 1989 survey along with other surveys since 1977 (disseminated by the General Service Board of Alcoholics Anonymous)—parts of which were quoted in the text above. (2) A copy of the address by Dr. Gordis to the National Council on Alcoholism on April 30, 1989, from which remarks were quoted above. (3) A copy of an article, titled "Alcoholics Anonymous: Who Benefits," that appeared in the Volume 18, Number 4, 1994, edition of the NIAAA quarterly journal, *Alcohol Health & Research World*, which concluded: "Most of the studies found that greater AA involvement could modestly predict reduced alcohol consumption." The above information stands in marked contrast to the reports about A.A.'s success at the time of the publication of the Big Book in 1939. A.A.'s then reported success is exemplified by this Big Book statement: "Rarely have we seen a person fail who has thoroughly followed our path" (1st Edition, p. 70).

full range of treatment services, including Alcoholics Anonymous, Dr. Matthews-Larson reported:

> At the end of one year, here's how the three groups compared: 1) no treatment—37 of the 50 alcoholics were still drinking (76 percent failure); 2) anabuse only—39 of the 49 alcoholics were still drinking (80 percent failure); and 3) full treatment services—39 out of 49 were still drinking (80 percent failure).

Whatever the reasons, alcoholics who go to Alcoholics Anonymous are not coming close to achieving the successes that their brothers and sisters did in the early pioneer days when God Almighty was the cure and the Holy Bible was the guidebook.

So the question is: Should the Twelve Step, recovery, and religious communities continue to ignore the fact that something good, something dramatic, and something uniquely successful was developed in those early, heady A.A. years of the 1930's. And do they really want to forget the major spiritual tool that produced the results?

As they review the following quotes from A.A.'s own "Conference Approved" literature, people in the Twelve Step, religious community, and recovery programs may want to revisit in detail *early* A.A.'s highly successful spiritual roots and practices. We believe these people do not wish to be uninformed as to a vital early A.A. tool, nor miss the opportunity to bring their own expertise to bear with that information in mind, nor compromise their contributions by pointing to ideas that are not producing a high success rate in Twelve Step programs today.

And these are some quotes we offer for consideration:

1. To the Fellowship of Alcoholics Anonymous:

> [On the importance of learning what early A.A. ideas meant in their highly successful, experimental days:] Do not let any

prejudice you may have against spiritual terms deter you from honestly asking yourself what they mean to you.[29]

[As to A.A.'s program resting on spiritual verities, rather than treatment techniques:] THE OTHER SIDE: During a meeting one day, I remarked that I was just tickled to death with this A.A. program—all but the spiritual side of it. After the meeting, another member came up to me and said, "I liked that remark you made—about how you like the program—all but the spiritual part of it. We've got a little time. Why don't we talk about the *other* side of it?" That ended the conversation.[30]

[On the danger of A.A.'s forgetting its spiritual roots:] Whenever a civilization or society perishes, there is always one condition present. They forgot where they came from.[31]

2. **To churches, the clergy, and the religious community in general:**

[On the fact that AAs themselves bowed to the expertise of established religion when they were formulating their program:] As a society we must never become so vain as to suppose that we have been the authors and inventors of a new religion. We will humbly reflect that each of A.A.'s principles, *every one of them,* has been borrowed from ancient sources. . . . Let us constantly remind ourselves that the experts in religion are the clergymen; that the practice of medicine is for physicians; and that we, the recovered alcoholics, are their assistants.[32]

---

[29] Big Book, p. 47; also in *Came to Believe: The spiritual Adventure of A.A. as Experienced by Individual Members* (New York: Alcoholics Anonymous World Services, Inc., 1973), p. 1.

[30] *Came to Believe*, p. 6 (italics in original).

[31] A quote from historian Carl Sandburg, which is frequently used by A.A.'s current archivist, Frank M., in his talks about the origins of A.A.—a quote Frank used in a program on the spiritual roots of A.A. in which the author participated several years ago, and which Frank used again at A.A.'s 1995 International Convention in San Diego.

[32] *Alcoholics Anonymous Comes of Age*, pp. 231-32.

[On the fact that early A.A.'s religious emphasis was not on a particular sect, denomination or religion, but rather on the Bible itself:] The Bible was stressed as reading material, of course.[33]

[On the facts about the Good Book and Jesus Christ, Cleveland A.A. Founder Clarence Snyder said:] Since our A.A. program was based on the Word of God, God says there is no access to Him except through His Son Jesus Christ [See John 14:6]. That was the basis for getting the kids on their knees and meeting Jesus.[34]

[On the fact that A.A. itself could not provide enough spiritual information for Bill Wilson's own growth, Bill said:] Some AAs say, "I don't need religion, because AA *is* my religion." As a matter of fact, I used to take this tack myself. After enjoying this simple and comfortable view for some years I finally awoke to the probability that there might be sources of spiritual teaching, wisdom, and assurance outside of AA. . . . AA didn't try to answer all my questions. . . . Neither science nor philosophy seemed able to supply me convincing answers. . . . Though still rather gun-shy about clergymen and their theology I finally went back to them—the place where AA came from. . . . I here cast up AA's debt to the clergy: without their works for us, AA could never have been born; nearly every principle that we use came from them. . . . Almost literally, we AAs owe them our lives, our fortunes, and such salvation as each of us has found.[35]

3. **To physicians, therapists, counselors, and recovery center staffs:**

[On the fact that distinguished medical and psychiatric people humbly declined to trench on religion's jurisdiction over A.A.'s root ideas:] Men have cried out to me in sincere and despairing

---

[33] *DR. BOB*, p. 151.

[34] Dick B., *That Amazing Grace*, p. 83.

[35] From Bill Wilson's article "The Clergy" in *The Language of the Heart*, pp. 178-79.

appeal: "Doctor, I cannot go on like this! I have everything to live for! I must stop, but I cannot! You must help me!" Faced with this problem, if the doctor is honest with himself, he must sometimes feel his own inadequacy. . . . One feels that something more than human power is needed to produce the essential psychic change.[36]

[On the fact that AAs could predetermine their demise by the same kind of stubborn resistance to God that they displayed to admitting their alcohol problem:] Mine was exactly the kind of deep-seated block we so often see today in new people who say they are atheistic or agnostic. Their will to disbelieve is so powerful that apparently they prefer a date with the undertaker to an open-minded and experimental quest for God.[37]

The author believes it will be immensely valuable to learn the following points involved in the subject of our exploration—A.A.'s roots in the Bible:

1. If, as is commonly acknowledged, A.A.'s success rate is declining even as its numbers have, until lately, been increasing geometrically, is it not important to learn everything possible about the major source of A.A.'s ideas during the period it produced miraculous results among those who really tried?

2. We believe we can show how the pages of A.A.'s Big Book and the language of its Twelve Steps can be significantly illuminated by understanding what early AAs really meant when they used phrases from the Authorized (King James) Version of the Bible—phrases such as "Thy will be done," "Faith without works is dead," and "Love thy neighbor as thyself." Understanding can also be enhanced through knowing where AAs borrowed such ideas as "willingness," "humility," and the "experiment of faith." Therefore, why not approach A.A.'s

---

[36] Discussion in the Big Book, p. xxvii, by Dr. William D. Silkworth, A.A.'s medical mentor who endorsed the book and treated over 50,000 alcoholics.

[37] *The Language of the Heart*, pp. 245-46.

program in the light of what the early, successful AAs actually meant when they used Biblical terms instead of fashioning self-made substitutes which have no present-day success rate to confirm their utility?

3. If, as we've shown, A.A.'s own founders humbly conceded that they had learned their ideas elsewhere than from alcoholics, that they had not invented their own religion, that they were not theology experts, and that much could gained from turning to root sources, why not learn what those root sources were?

4. If, as we think A.A. history discloses, the spiritual elements of early A.A. have become subject to what A.A.'s religious mentor, the Reverend Sam Shoemaker, Jr., called "half-baked prayers," "absurd names for God," and self-made religion, why not enlighten Twelve Step people and the religious and recovery communities by showing how much can *still* be contributed to Twelve Step recovery by searching its Scriptural foundations and understanding its Biblical roots?

The Historical Evidence of A.A.'s Good Book Roots

There is an abundance of clear and convincing evidence establishing that Alcoholics Anonymous—early Alcoholics Anonymous—had its roots firmly planted in the Bible. There is also ample evidence establishing that countless basic ideas and quotes from the Bible found their way directly or indirectly into A.A.'s basic text and Twelve Steps of recovery.

But there is a problem with specifics. To be sure, Dr. Bob told early AAs that such A.A. slogans as "First Things First" and "One day at a time" came from certain verses in Jesus's Sermon on the Mount.[38] However, with such minor exceptions, neither of A.A.'s co-founders, Bill and Dr. Bob, ever really graced us with records, speeches, or writings stating this specific idea, this specific phrase, or this specific step in their Big Book came from

---

[38] Dick B., *The Akron Genesis of Alcoholics Anonymous* (Corte Madera, CA: Good Book Publishing Company, 1994), pp. 209-10; *That Amazing Grace*, p. 38.

this specific verse, chapter, or idea in the Good Book. And that has caused some doubters and critics to question whether there is convincing historical proof that A.A. took its basic ideas from the Bible.[39]

As we will see, there is a solution to the problem of specificity. To begin with, A.A.'s co-founders stated very clearly that A.A.'s spiritual principles came *either* from the Bible or from "A First Century Christian Fellowship" from which A.A. sprang.[40] Also, "A First Century Christian Fellowship" (the Oxford Group) and its writers stated clearly that their fellowship and its principles came from the principles of the Bible.[41] During the period in which A.A. was an integral part of the Oxford Group, Dr. Bob and many other early AAs referred to their society and its meetings as "a Christian fellowship."[42] And the spiritual

---

[39] See, for example, Bishop & Pittman, *To Be Continued*, Item 716.

[40] For most of the years from about 1921 through at least 1934, Dr. Frank N. D. Buchman's Christian fellowship was known primarily as "A First Century Christian Fellowship." In 1928, the fellowship adopted the name "Oxford Group" when newspaper reporters in South Africa gave it that name during the visit to South Africa of a small fellowship team which was composed mostly of team members from Oxford University. As to the details on "A First Century Christian Fellowship," see Dick B., *Design for Living*, pp. 83-86. See also Part 1 of the five-part history of Faith at Work by Karl A. Olnson, "The History of Faith at Work," *Faith at Work News*, 1982-1983. Bill Wilson's spiritual teacher in the 1930's, the Reverend Sam Shoemaker, Jr., frequently referred to the Oxford Group as "A First Century Christian Fellowship." See Samuel M. Shoemaker, Jr., *Twice-Born Ministers* (New York: Fleming H. Revell, 1929), pp. 23, 90, 95, 101, 122, 147, 148; *Calvary Church Yesterday and Today* (New York: Fleming H. Revell, 1936), p. 270. See also Irving Harris, *The Breeze of the Spirit* (New York: The Seabury Press, 1978), pp. 47, 58; Theophil Spoerri, *Dynamic out of Silence: Frank Buchman's Relevance Today* (London: Grosvenor Books, 1976), p. 79; Harold Begbie, *Life Changers* 12th ed.(London: Mills & Boon, Ltd., 1932), p. 122; Olive M. Jones, *Inspired Children* (New York: Harper & Brothers, 1933), p. ix; *Pass It On*, p. 130. The author has in his possession a number of invitations to, and programs for, "house parties" of the Oxford Group fellowship that were held during the period from 1928 through 1934; and most are issued by "A First Century Christian Fellowship."

[41] Day, *The Principles of the Group*, p. 1.

[42] *DR. BOB*, pp. 118-19. Dr. Bob's daughter, Sue Smith Windows, informed the author in a personal interview at Akron, Ohio, in June, 1991, that Dr. Bob described every King School Group meeting (of A.A.) as a "Christian Fellowship." See discussion

(continued...)

principles enunciated by the Bible, the First Century Christian Fellowship, *and* A.A. are, in many instances, an exact match. In fact, A.A.'s principal writer and co-founder Bill Wilson demonstrated the existence of roots outside of A.A. by stating with ever-increasing particularity as the years rolled by that "every" idea in A.A. came either from medicine, or from religion, or from A.A. experience. The principles were *all* borrowed, he said.[43]

To the author it therefore seemed clear that one could determine what A.A. borrowed from the Bible by simply matching up the language and statements in A.A.'s Big Book and Twelve Steps with the language and teachings in A.A.'s Biblical roots. And though this appears never to have been done, the evidence established the links almost to the point of demonstration. To be sure, there is little or no A.A. eye witness verification. There is little or no A.A. textual proof. As far as we can tell, there is no statement by either Bill Wilson or Dr. Bob that such Big Book expressions as "Thy will be done," "Faith without works is dead," and "love thy neighbor as thyself" (all exact quotes from the Bible found in the Big Book) had any relationship whatever to the Good Book. In fact, the co-founders seem rather clearly to have chosen *not* to say so in their Big Book references to Biblical phrases. One of the earliest AAs in New York, a Christian named John Henry Fitzhugh M., lost his battle to have A.A. literature *be specific* about its Biblical roots; and one A.A. historian states that "Fitz" headed up a group which wanted A.A. to espouse Christianity and declare Jesus Christ as the "Higher Power."[44] Whatever may be the precise details, Fitz very definitely lost his battle just as A.A.'s

---

[42] (...continued)
of similar remarks by Akron A.A. oldtimer, Bob E., in Dick B., *Design for Living*, p. 85.

[43] See, for example, *The Language of the Heart*, pp. 195-202; *As Bill See's It*, p. 67; *Twelve Steps and Twelve Traditions* (New York: Alcoholics Anonymous World Services, 1952), p. 16; Nell Wing, *Grateful to Have Been There: My 43 Years with Bill and Lois and the Evolution of Alcoholics Anonymous* (Park Ridge, IL: Parkside Publishing Corporation, 1992), p. 25.

[44] Wally P., *But For the Grace of God*, p. 205.

Big Book was going to press—a point of A.A.'s history that has been widely reported by A.A. itself.[45]

Nonetheless, we believe that the specifics about what A.A. borrowed from the Bible have not been lost—merely shelved. We were and are certain they could and can be learned.

What Dr. Bob and Other Akron AAs Said

Always terse and practical, A.A.'s co-founder Dr. Robert Holbrook Smith, whom AAs know as "Dr. Bob," put his finger on A.A.'s four most basic Biblical sources.

In his last major address to AAs in 1948, Dr. Bob said:

> When we started in on Bill D., we had no Twelve Steps. . . . But we were convinced that the answer to our problems was in the Good Book. To some of us older ones, the parts that we found absolutely essential were the Sermon on the Mount, the thirteenth chapter of First Corinthians, and the Book of James. . . .[46]

Then, as to four particular early A.A. spiritual principles, Dr. Bob added, "The four absolutes, as we called them, were the only yardsticks we had in the early days, before the Steps."[47] The "Four Absolutes" were the basic moral standards or "yardsticks" of the Oxford Group, of which, as we will discuss, A.A. was an integral part in the 1930's. And the Oxford Group's four standards came from the teachings of Jesus Christ.[48] Some in the Oxford Group believed the Absolutes were derived directly from Dr.

---

[45] *Alcoholics Anonymous Comes of Age*, pp. 17, 166-67; *Pass It On*, p. 199; *The Language of the Heart*, pp. 200-02.

[46] *The Co-Founders of Alcoholics Anonymous. Biographical sketches Their last major talks* (New York: Alcoholics Anonymous World Services, 1972, 1975), pp. 9-10.

[47] *Co-Founders*, pp. 12-13.

[48] Robert E. Speer, *The Principles of Jesus* (New York: Association Press, 1902), pp. 33-36; Garth Lean, *On the Tail of a Comet: The Life of Frank Buchman* (Colorado Springs, CO: Helmers & Howard, 1988), p. 76; Helen Smith Shoemaker, *I Stand by the Door: The Life of Sam Shoemaker* (Texas: Word Books, 1967), pp. 24-25.

Robert E. Speer's study of Jesus's Sermon on the Mount.[49] And
Jesus's four moral standards *can be found* there. But Dr. Speer
and other Oxford Group mentors and writers developed the
standards from *several* of Jesus's teachings (including, among
others, those in the Sermon on the Mount) and from the New
Testament Church Epistles of Paul.[50]

A pamphlet published by "AA of Akron" and written at the
request of Dr. Bob states:

> There is the Bible that you haven't opened for years. Get
> acquainted with it. Read it with an open mind. You will find
> things that will amaze you. You will be convinced that certain
> passages were written with you in mind. Read the Sermon on the
> Mount (Matthew V, VI, and VII). Read St. Paul's inspired essay
> on love (I Corinthians XIII). Read the Book of James. Read the
> Twenty-third and Ninety-first Psalms. These readings are brief but
> so important.[51]

> The Bible tells us to put "first things first" [Matthew 6:33].[52]

> Take therefore no thought for the morrow: for the morrow shall
> take thought for the things itself [sic]. Sufficient unto the day is
> the evil thereof.—Matthew VI, 34. Those words are taken from
> the Sermon on the Mount. Simply, they mean live in today only.
> Forget yesterday. Do not anticipate tomorrow. You can only live

---

[49] See, for example, the comments of Samuel M. Shoemaker, Jr., in *How to Become
a Christian* (New York: Harper & Brothers, 1953), p. 57.

[50] See Dick B., *Design for Living*, pp. 237-46.

[51] *A Manual for Alcoholics Anonymous*, 6th Rev. ed. (Akron, OH: AA of Akron,
1989), p. 8. According to A.A. historian Wally P., this pamphlet was one of four Akron
pamphlets published during the 1940's. Each was written by Evan W. at the request of
Dr. Bob that Evan write some "Blue Collar" pamphlets to simplify the program for the
average A.A. coming into the Fellowship at that time. See Wally P., *But, For the Grace
of God . . .: How Intergroups & Central Offices Carried the Message of Alcoholics
Anonymous in the 1940's* (West Virginia: The Bishop of Books, 1995), p. 44.

[52] *A Manual for Alcoholics Anonymous*, p. 7. Dr. Bob specifically pointed out that
the "First Things First" slogan in A.A. came from Matthew 6:33 (a portion of Jesus's
Sermon on the Mount).

one day at a time and if you do a good job of that, you will have little trouble.[53]

The Akron pamphlet is not A. A. "Conference Approved," but it had the statement on its cover that it "was written and edited by members of Alcoholics Anonymous of Akron, Ohio, . . . among [whose] Akron members are one of the founders, the first person to accept the program, and a large number of other members whose sobriety dates back to 1935, 1936, and 1937."[54]

Another Akron, Ohio, A.A. pamphlet of the 1940's—published by the Friday Forum Luncheon Club of the Akron A.A. Groups—summarized the following from a "lead" (address) given by Dr. Bob in Youngstown, Ohio:

Members of Alcoholics Anonymous begin the day with a prayer for strength and a short period of Bible reading. They find the basic messages they need in the Sermon on the Mount, in Corinthians and the Book of James.[55]

Still another Akron pamphlet said:

Remember this simple thing: The entire structure of the Christian religion is built on Love. The word has many synonyms, such as Charity [1 Corinthians 13], Grace, Good-will, Tenderness, Generosity, Kindness, Tolerance, Sympathy, Mercy, and others. . . . Spirituality is simply the act of being unselfishly helpful. If you will start with this simple explanation you will find that the green light has been flashed on. Christ taught that there are two great commandments: to love God; and to love your neighbor as yourself. If you can follow these you will have no trouble.[56]

---

[53] *A Manual for Alcoholics Anonymous*, p. 13. Dr. Bob often pointed out that this verse was the origin of the A.A. slogans "Easy does it" and "One day at a time."

[54] *A Manual for Alcoholics Anonymous*, quote from cover. See Wally P., *But, For the Grace of God*, p. 37.

[55] Wally P., *But, For the Grace of God*, p. 45.

[56] *A Guide to the Twelve Steps of Alcoholics Anonymous* (Akron, OH: AA of Akron, March, 1989), p. 14.

And another said:

> WE ARE TOLD from the very beginning that AA is a Spiritual
> program, but many of us are perplexed by the meaning of the
> word. There IS NO MYSTERY in the Spiritual side of AA. As
> a matter of fact, the good active member is practicing Christianity
> at all times whether or not he knows it. . . . The Spiritual
> program of AA is a simple and basic thing, as simple as
> attendance at Sunday School of our childhood. In Sunday School
> we were not asked to listen to sermons, and about the only prayer
> we knew was the simplest and best, The Lord's Prayer. We were
> told the stories of David and Goliath, Samson and his amazing
> strength, Adam and Eve in the Garden of Eden, the Prodigal Son,
> the Good Samaritan. As we grew older we learned something of
> the history of religion, something about the more complex parts
> of the Bible. When we outgrew Sunday School we were ready to
> take part in Church with a fair understanding of what it was all
> about. Boiled down to its essence, Christianity, in fact
> Spirituality, is simply LOVE.[57]

Akron's *Spiritual Milestones* was filled with biblical materials:

> When you hear an AA say "I can't understand the spiritual angle
> of the program," note that it is almost invariably said wistfully.
> In other words, he would LIKE TO UNDERSTAND the spiritual
> program. And that in itself is a humble gesture. For humility is
> teachability, the willingness to learn, keeping an open mind. . .
> . Consider the words of St. Paul, whose memory of wrongdoings
> in the past led him to write to the Corinthians (I-15:9) "For I am
> the least of the apostles, that I am not meet to be called an
> apostle, because I persecuted the Church of God." He then goes
> on to say "But by the grace of God I am what I am; and his grace
> which was bestowed upon me was not in vain; but I labored more
> abundantly than they all; yet not I, but the grace of God which
> was with me." These words of deepest humility from the man

---

[57] *Second Reader for Alcoholics Anonymous* (Akron, OH: AA of Akron, March 15,
1989), p. 12.

who, more than any other, kept alive by his perseverance and faith the Christian religion![58]

We cannot pray for something that is apparently out of our reach, then sit back and expect God to dump it in our laps. But if we pray sincerely, then do our part by taking dynamic action, even things we thought beyond attainment will fall like ripe plums. St. Paul put it this way: "I can do all things through Christ which strengtheneth me" (Philippians 4:13).[59]

Practice charity. This is simply another way of saying practice the Twelfth Step. The unselfish helping of others is the practice of love, upon which Christian philosophy is based. Remember at all times our Lord's two commandments: "Thou shalt love the Lord thy God with all thy heart, and with all thy soul and with all thy mind. And . . . thou shalt love thy neighbor as thyself. On these two commandments hang all the Law and the Prophets."[60]

The God of the New Testament is like Dad, kindly and helpful, full of compassion and ever ready to forgive. We should always strive to make God a companion rather than someone from whom we constantly demand gifts.[61]

Ponder the words of St. Paul: "Be not deceived; evil companionships corrupt good morals." (I Corinthians 15:33).[62]

THUS THE STORY of three men who found God in their darkest hours. They are not unusual. History is full of dramatic conversions. Perhaps the story of St. Paul is the most familiar. We read in the ninth chapter of the Acts of the Apostles, how Saul, a persecutor of the Church, was stricken blind near Damascus and heard the voice of Jesus gently chiding him.

---

[58] *Spiritual Milestones in Alcoholics Anonymous* (Akron, OH: AA of Akron, August 1, 1993), pp. 2-3.

[59] *Spiritual Milestones*, p. 3.

[60] *Spritual Milestones*, p. 3.

[61] *Spiritual Milestones*, p. 4.

[62] *Spiritual Milestones*, p. 5.

Changing his name to Paul, he became the most dynamic force the church has ever known. Some three centuries later came another miraculous conversion that made a lasting and vital impression on Christianity. . . . [H]e [St. Augustine] heard a voice say over and over, "Take up and read." Believing it to be a divine command he turned at random to a page in a volume of the Apostles and found himself reading what today we find in Romans 13:13, 14: "Not in revelling and drunkenness, not in chambering and wantonness, not in strife and jealousy. But put ye on the Lord Jesus Christ, and make not provision for the flesh, to fulfill the lusts thereof" (It is strange how many passages in the Bible seem directly aimed at us alcoholics.) And St. Augustine, through reading that passage, found peace, and went on to become one of the greatest theologians.[63]

"Pure religion and undefiled before our God and Father is this, to visit the fatherless and widows in their affliction and to keep oneself unspotted form the world."— The General Epistle of James 1:27. . . . All we need to do in the St. James passage is to substitute the word "Alcoholic" for "Fatherless and Widows" and we have Step Twelve.[64]

What Bill Wilson Said

As we will discuss in more detail later, Bill Wilson characterized himself in the Big Book as having been an agnostic when he first sought spiritual help.[65] But in some of his writings (and in his wife's own words), Bill described himself as an atheist.[66] It is

---

[63] *Spiritual Milestones*, pp. 10-11.

[64] *Spiritual Milestones*, pp. 13-14.

[65] At page 10 of the Big Book, Bill said, "I was not an atheist." At page 46, Bill wrote, "Yes, we of agnostic temperament have had these thoughts and experiences."

[66] In a taped interview which the Reverend T. Willard Hunter conducted with Bill's wife, Lois Wilson (of which tape the author has a copy), Lois informed Hunter that Bill had been an atheist. See also *As Bill See's It*, p. 276; and Dick B., *Turning Point: A History of the Spiritual Roots and Successes of Early A.A.* (San Rafael, CA: Paradise Research Publications, Inc., 1997), p. 96. There the author quotes from Wilson's own
(continued...)

therefore not surprising that Bill made few references to the Bible and that most AAs today seem unaware of Wilson's early references to Bible study at a time before the Big Book was written. Fortunately, however, Wilson's statements about the Bible have survived.

Bill pointed to the daily, morning devotions at the home of Dr. Bob and Anne Smith, in A.A.'s earliest days. He said:

> Each morning there was devotion. After the long silence Anne would read out of the Good Book. James was our favorite.[67]

> I sort of always felt that something was lost from A.A. when we stopped emphasizing the morning meditation.[68]

He also said:

> We much favored the Apostle James. The definition of love in Corinthians also played a great part in our discussions.[69]

When interviewing T. Henry and Clarace Williams (in whose Akron home the earliest A.A. meetings were held), Bill said:

> I learned a great deal from you people, from the Smiths themselves, and from Henrietta [Seiberling]. I hadn't looked in the Bible, up to this time, at all.[70]

---

[66] (...continued)

W. G. Wilson Reflections, pp. 123-24, where Wilson wrote: "Perhaps I wouldn't need an emotional conversion. After all, *a conservative atheist like me* ought to be able to get on without anything like that" (italics added).

[67] *RHS* (New York: The A.A. Grapevine, Inc., 1951), p. 5.

[68] *DR. BOB*, p. 178.

[69] Ernest Kurtz, *Not-God: A History of Alcoholics Anonymous*, exp. ed. (Minnesota: Hazelden, 1991), p. 320, n. 11.

[70] See excerpt from Wilson's December 12, 1954, interview of Mr. and Mrs. T. Henry Williams in Dick B., *The Akron Genesis*, p. 64.

In his Yale lecture in 1945, Bill said:

> For *a great many of us* have taken to reading the Bible. It could not have been presented at first, but sooner or later in his second, third, or fourth year, the A.A. will be found reading the Bible quite as often—or more—as he will a standard psychological work.[71]

In this same lecture, Bill illustrated his point, in part, by telling his distinguished audience the story of how A.A.'s former avowed atheist, Jim B., had been unable to get sober for a long period, had finally almost died from a seizure, and had turned to God after having read a Gideon Bible in a second-rate hotel room.[72]

Anne Ripley Smith (Dr. Bob's wife)

Dr. Bob's wife, Anne Ripley Smith, was an avid Bible student. Anne kept a spiritual journal from the time of her earliest exposures to the Oxford Group with Dr. Bob in Akron in 1933 through some date in 1939.[73] The material was assembled from Oxford Group meetings, early A.A. meetings, and from Anne's studies of the Bible, the Oxford Group, and Christian literature of the day. And it was recorded over the six year period before A.A.'s Big Book was finally published.

Anne's journal was filled with Bible verses and concepts.[74] And she frequently shared from her journal with Dr. Bob, Bill W., and the many alcoholics and their families who came to the Smith

---

[71] W. W., Lecture 29. *The Fellowship of Alcoholics Anonymous* (Yale Summer School of Alcohol Studies: Quarterly Journal of Studies on Alcohol, 1945), p. 467 (italics added).

[72] Dick B., *Dr. Bob's Library: Books for Twelve Step Growth* (San Rafael, CA: Paradise Research Publications, 1994), p. 11, n. 29.

[73] Dick B., *Anne Smith's Journal, 1933-1939: A.A.'s Principles of Success* (San Rafael, CA: Paradise Research Publications, 1994).

[74] Dick B., *Anne Smith's Journal*, pp. 60, 80, 112, 130-33.

home at 855 Ardmore Avenue, in Akron, Ohio, for help.[75]
Speaking about the reading she felt early AAs and their families
should do, Anne wrote (as we have already said): "Of course the
Bible ought to be the main Source Book of all. No day ought to
pass without reading it."[76]   Bill Wilson described Dr. Bob's wife,
Anne, as the "mother of A.A." and "one of the founders."[77] And
Florence B., one of Anne's close friends of the early A.A. days,
summed up as to Anne and the Good Book, "She [Anne] never
sought to rewrite the Bible nor to explain it. She just accepted
it."[78]

Henrietta Seiberling, T. Henry and Clarace Williams, and Clarence Snyder

There were others among A.A.'s "founders" who frequently used
the Bible to help AAs and their families.

Henrietta Seiberling introduced Bill Wilson to Dr. Bob at her
Akron, Ohio, home on Mother's Day, 1935.[79] She and Dr. Bob's
wife (as Bill put it) "infused much needed spirituality" into the two
founders in A.A.'s early days.[80] Henrietta "called the shots" at
the early A.A. meetings in Akron.[81] And she thoroughly studied
and frequently quoted from the Bible in her work with AAs
personally and also at their early meetings.[82]

The home of T. Henry and Clarace Williams on Palisades
Drive in Akron was the site of the early meetings of "the alcoholic
squad of the Oxford Group," as AAs called themselves.[83] T.
Henry had studied the Bible, taught Bible, and been active in both

---

[75] Dick B., *The Akron Genesis*, pp. 109-10.

[76] Dick B., *Anne Smith's Journal*, p. 80.

[77] Dick B., *Anne Smith's Journal*, pp. 10-12.

[78] Dick B., *Anne Smith's Journal*, p. 17.

[79] *DR. BOB*, pp. 63-67.

[80] *The Language of the Heart*, p. 357.

[81] *DR. BOB*, p. 157.

[82] Dick B., *The Akron Genesis*, pp. 90-105.

[83] *DR. BOB*, pp. 100, 137, 156-57.

Baptist and Methodist church communities.[84] T. Henry's second wife Clarace (who, along with T. Henry, worked with the early AAs) was a dedicated church woman, had studied at a Baptist missionary school in Chicago, and later worked with a church helping its young people. Clarace was also a devoted Bible student.[85]

Cleveland A.A. leader Clarence Snyder many times told others:

> A.A.'s basic ideas [came]. . . from Matthew chapters 5–7 (Jesus's Sermon on the Mount), Corinthians 13 [the so-called "love" chapter], and the Book of James.[86]

Evidence from AAs Themselves

Several early AAs commented on the fact that early A.A. meetings in Akron opened with the reading of Scripture.[87] Dr. Bob often had the Bible open in front of him at A.A. meetings and read aloud from it; and it was always on the podium.[88] Bill Wilson's long-time friend and secretary, Nell Wing, commented:

> Members gathered there [at the home of Dr. Bob and Anne in the early days] as well as attending the Oxford Group meetings at the home of T. Henry and Clarace Williams. Early members described how, at their meeting, Bob liked to sit with an open Bible on his lap, out of which a passage would be selected at

---

[84] Dick B., *The Akron Genesis*, pp. 65-66.

[85] As to the Williams's contribution to A.A., see Dick B., *The Akron Genesis*, pp. 65-78.

[86] Dick B., *That Amazing Grace*, p. 34.

[87] Dick B., *The Akron Genesis*, pp. 189-90, 192, 197-98. Cp. the recollections of Duke P., an Akron oldtimer, who got sober in August of 1940. Wally P. reports Duke's stating, "Once in a while, the Chairperson would read something from a Bible if the passage related directly to his story." Wally also said, "Duke remembers one Chairperson reading from the Book of James and Dr. Bob reading Corinthians 1:13 [*sic*]." Apparently, Duke had just celebrated his 90th natal birthday at the time he shared his recollections with Wally. See Wally P., *But, For the Grace of God*, pp. 31-32.

[88] Dick B., *The Akron Genesis*, p. 189.

random and read. A discussion would then follow on its relevance to the personal problems of those present. The emphasis was on day-to-day living, how to cope with personal problems, and self-examination.[89]

Dick S., an early AA, opened meetings with prayer and a passage from the Bible.[90] And so did A.A. No. 3, Bill D. of Akron.[91] As a symbol of the Bible's importance in early Akron A.A., Dr. Bob's own Bible is brought to the lectern to this day at the beginning of every meeting of A.A.'s first group, Akron Number One—a tradition the author has personally witnessed.[92] The prevalence of Scripture reading in early A.A. was underlined by the report of Frank Amos to John D. Rockefeller, Jr., in 1938—a fact we have already covered.

A.A.'s "Conference Approved" literature *often* commented on the importance of Bible study in early A.A., stating, for example:

This [from 1935 forward] was the beginning of A.A.'s "flying blind period." They had the Bible, and they had the precepts of the Oxford Group. They also had their own instincts. They were working, or working out, the A.A. program—the Twelve Steps—without quite knowing how they were doing it.[93]

We had much prayer together in those days and began quietly to read Scripture and discuss a practical approach to its application in our lives.[94]

Hospitalization was another must in the early days. . . . The advantage of having the alcoholic alone in a room as a captive audience also had something to do with it. These patients were

---

[89] Nell Wing, *Grateful to Have Been There*, p. 81.

[90] Dick B., *The Akron Genesis*, p. 189.

[91] Dick B., *The Akron Genesis*, p. 190.

[92] Dick B., *Design for Living*, p. 13; and see *DR. BOB*, p. 228.

[93] *DR. BOB*, p. 96.

[94] *DR. BOB*, p. 111.

allowed only a Bible as reading material. Generally, their only visitors were recovered alcoholics.[95]

According to one A.A. historian, "Many A.A. Pioneers fondly referred to the Holy Bible as the 'Big, Big Book.'"[96]

The Oxford Group-Shoemaker Impact

AAs were not pioneering Bible study on their own.

The early AAs were, both in New York and in Akron, a part of the Oxford Group during A.A.'s developmental years.[97] Official A.A. literature specifically acknowledges that AAs borrowed freely from the Oxford Group in their writings.[98] And the Oxford Group were dedicated to Bible study.[99] An Oxford Group pamphlet, *The Principles of the Oxford Group*, stated, "The principles of 'The Oxford Group' are the principles of the Bible."[100] Oxford Group founder, Dr. Frank N. D. Buchman, was described as "soaked in the Bible."[101] His recipe for Bible-reading was, "Read accurately, interpret honestly, apply drastically."[102] Buchman hired a Bible teacher, Miss Mary Angevine, to teach Bible to the Oxford Group businessmen's team in New York, of which Bill Wilson was a member during A.A.'s earliest days in the Group.[103] And Oxford Group meetings and houseparties, which were attended by Bill and Lois Wilson on the

---

[95] *DR. BOB*, p. 102.

[96] Wally P., *But, For the Grace of God*, p. 225.

[97] *DR. BOB*, pp. 100, 128, 137; *Pass It On*, pp. 167-71, 196-97; *The Language of the Heart*, p. 198.

[98] Dick B., *Design for Living*, pp. 28-29; *Pass It On*, pp. 169, 174, 197.

[99] Dick B., *Design for Living*, pp. 249-53.

[100] Dick B., *Design for Living*, p. 9; Sherwood Sunderland Day, *The Principles of the Group* (Oxford: University Press, n.d.), p. 1.

[101] Lean, *On the Tail of a Comet*, p. 157.

[102] Dick B., *Design for Living*, p. 103; Harry J. Almond, *Foundations for Faith* (London: Grosvenor, 1980), pp 30-31.

[103] Dick B., *The Akron Genesis*, pp. 28-29, 175-76.

East Coast, involved a great amount of Bible study and teaching.[104]

Bill Wilson preferred to ascribe to Oxford Group leader, the Reverend Samuel M. Shoemaker, Jr., of New York, the principles which A.A. took from the Oxford Group.[105] And Shoemaker *was* a devoted Bible student and teacher.[106] He was often called a "Bible Christian."[107] Shoemaker stressed the importance of the Bible, in his church, in his own meditations, and in each individual's daily life.[108]

Bible Devotionals and Other Early A.A. Literature

The books which early AAs studied for spiritual growth were centered on the Bible.[109] Whether one looks at early A.A.'s daily meditation materials such as *The Upper Room, My Utmost for His Highest, The Runner's Bible, Daily Strength for Daily Needs, Victorious Living,* and *The Meaning of Prayer*; or the popular Christian books of the day by Glenn Clark, E. Stanley Jones, and Toyohiko Kagawa; or even the "new thought" books of Emmet Fox and others, the focus of almost every book was the Bible.[110] And early AAs read these books with great frequency.[111]

---

[104] Dick B., *Design for Living*, pp. 87-95.

[105] *Alcoholics Anonymous Comes of Age*, p. 39; *Pass It On*, p. 174.

[106] Dick B., *New Light on Alcoholism: The A.A. Legacy from Sam Shoemaker* (Corte Madera, CA: Good Book Publishing Company, 1994), pp. 32, 40, 42, 67 n. 48.

[107] W. Irving Harris, *The Breeze of the Spirit* (New York: The Seabury Press, 1978), pp. 18, 25.

[108] Dick B., *Design for Living*, pp. 250-52; Harris, *The Breeze of the Spirit*, supra.

[109] See Dick B., *The Books Early AAs Read for Spiritual Growth*, 5th ed. (San Rafael, CA: Paradise Research Publications, 1997).

[110] See Dick B., *Dr. Bob's Library; Anne Smith's Journal; The Books Early AAs Read for Spiritual Growth.*

[111] *DR. BOB*, pp. 151, 310; Bill Pittman, *AA the Way it Began* (Seattle: Glen Abbey Books, 1988), pp. 170-79, 181-83, 192, 197; Mel B., *New Wine: The Spiritual Roots of the Twelve Step Miracle* (Minnesota: Hazelden, 1991), pp. 24, 39-40, 69-70, 77-78, 92-93, 104-06, 111-14, 132-34, 138-40, 145-47; Dick B., *Dr. Bob's Library*, Foreword.

Of corroborative importance also is the frequency with which the Bible was mentioned, quoted, or paraphrased in the story portion of A.A.'s First Edition of the Big Book before some of the earlier stories were replaced in the second and third editions of later years.[112] The author of the story titled **"The Unbeliever"** wrote of God and the Bible (pp. 201-05). **"Our Southern Friend"** spoke of finding God and "a greater love for Our Father in heaven" (pp. 236-41). **"Traveler, Editor, Scholar"** said, "I began to read the Bible daily and to go over a simple devotional exercise as a way to begin each day. Gradually I began to understand" (pp. 263-64). **"My Wife and I"** spoke of "the sincere attempt to follow the cardinal teachings of Jesus Christ" (p. 295). **"The Salesman"** said, "Every morning I read a part of the Bible and ask God to carry me through the day safely" (p. 323). **"Smile with Me, at Me"** said, "I went to my room alone—took my Bible in hand and asked Him, the One Power, that I might open to a good place to read—and I read. 'For I delight in the law of God after the inward man . . .'" (p. 347).[113] Many stories in the First Edition spoke of Almighty God; our Father; the ever-present, all-wise, all-loving, all-forgiving God; "Thy will be done;" and so on.

The Bible Was the Foundation

The Bible was the foundation upon which early AAs built to determine the will of God, their manner of prayer, and the nature of the "Power" in which they had been compelled by circumstances to believe and place their trust.

Perhaps the most revealing statement about the Biblical emphasis in early A.A. was made by Wally G., in whose home in the Ohio area so many early AAs recovered and where there was

---

[112] *Alcoholics Anonymous* (New Jersey: Works Publishing, 1939) is the First Edition of the Big Book.

[113] See Romans 7:22.

always a morning hour of meditation.[114] When Bill Wilson interviewed Wally and his wife, Wally said:

> On the business of surrender which I think was probably the most important part of this whole thing, Dr. Smith took my surrender the morning of the day that I left the hospital. At that time it was the only way you became a member—you became a member by a definite act or prayer and surrender, just as they did in the Group [the Oxford Group]. I'm sorry it has fallen by the wayside. Getting back to the business of how the thing operated: We took the "Upper Room" seriously. We took the meetings seriously, and we very seldom missed a set-up meeting.[115]

> You would be surprised at how little talk there was of drinking experiences. That was usually kept for interviews in the hospital at that time, or interviews with a prospect who wasn't too sure. We were more interested in our everyday life than we were with reminiscing about drinking experiences and that type of thing. Anyway we followed this "Upper Room" which was a quarterly publication of the Methodist Church South, I believe, although it was non-sectarian in character and consisted of a verse and a story in support of the verse from the Bible for each day, and a thought for the day, together with a suggestion as to our reading. Incidentally, we all had either Good [reference not clear—probably "Goodspeed"] or Moffatt's [Bible] because it was much easier to understand than some of the King James translation.[116]

Dr. Bob's daughter, Sue Smith Windows, added these observations about the importance of the Bible in early A.A. In her autobiography, Sue said: "Then they'd have their quiet time, which is a holdover from the Oxford Group, where they read the

---

[114] *DR. BOB*, p. 178.

[115] Dick B., *The Akron Genesis*, p. 188.

[116] Dick B., *The Akron Genesis*, pp. 191-92.

Bible, prayed and listened and got guidance."[117] When the author
was with Sue Smith Windows during the introduction of his title,
The Akron Genesis of Alcoholics Anonymous, in Akron, Ohio, in
January of 1993, a reporter from a Cleveland, Ohio, newspaper,
The Plain Dealer, interviewed Mrs. Windows, who gave several
statements about early A.A. The reporter quoted Sue as saying: "A
God-centered AA program was the most effective. It [A.A.] was
founded on the Bible," she said. "Those who stick with the
program usually believe this."[118]

The Question of Sources

Dr. Ernest Kurtz observed of the early A.A. days and A.A.
meetings:

> It would appear in hindsight that most of their waking lives was
> a continuous A.A. meeting.[119]

To which we would add that Akron AAs *lived* in the homes of Dr.
Bob and Anne Smith, Wally and Annabelle G., Tom L., and
others.[120] Early AAs had quiet times together.[121] They heard
and studied Scripture together at the home of Dr. Bob and Anne

---

[117] Bob Smith and Sue Smith Windows, *Children of the Healer: The Story of Dr. Bob's Kids* (Illinois: Parkside Publishing Corporation, 1992), p. 43. Just how Bill and Lois Wilson continued Oxford Group practices in their own home and meditations is not too clear; but Bill's long-time secretary, Nell Wing, wrote this: "Life at Stepping Stones [the Wilson home] always followed a comfortable domestic pattern. They [Bill and Lois] shared an early morning "quiet time," a custom retained from their Oxford Group experience. Lois . . . enjoyed reading aloud to Bill during their quiet time and he enjoyed listening. They also included a prayer and a short period of silent meditation" (Nell Wing, *Grateful to Have Been There*, pp. 31-32).

[118] *The Plain Dealer*, Cleveland, Ohio, Sunday, January 17, 1993. The article bore the headline, "New Book on AA adds to debate on God's place."

[119] Kurtz, *Not-God*, p. 56.

[120] Dick B., *The Akron Genesis*, pp. 181-215; Wing, *Grateful to Have Been There*, p. 81; *Alcoholics Anonymous Comes of Age*, pp. 10-11, 19, 22, 24; *DR. BOB*, pp. 111-15.

[121] Dick B., *The Akron Genesis*, pp. 184-86; 204-08.

Smith where they went for what some jokingly called "spiritual pablum."[122] They utilized the same or similar Bible devotionals and literature in their meditations.[123] They visited newly hospitalized drunks by going to the hospital together as a team.[124] They characterized themselves as "the alcoholic squad of the Oxford Group."[125] They regularly attended the Wednesday meetings at the home of T. Henry and Clarace Williams on Palisades Drive in Akron; and they also met there for set-up meetings and for socials, particularly on Saturday evenings.[126] They appear to have begun their fellowships with early morning quiet times, to have met and chatted and studied throughout the day, to have kept in touch by phone, and then to have had their formal meetings in the evenings. It is quite accurate to say that most fellowshipped and broke bread together *daily*.

While hardly as intense, as "spiritual," as great in size, or as "house" oriented, the situation with Bill Wilson's work in New York certainly had fellowship parallels. Bill and Lois and their Oxford Group friends (Ebby Thacher, Shep Cornell, and "Fitz") had quiet times together, "constantly" attended Oxford Group meetings, and gathered together at Oxford Group houseparties.[127] Bill was joined by Oxford Group people as he worked with drunks at Shoemaker's Calvary Rescue Mission, Towns Hospital, and even at Oxford Group meetings.[128] The Wilsons kept batches of drunks at their home, much as the Smiths and others did in Akron.[129] Sam Shoemaker's personal journals and correspondence (and the letters from Wilson to Shoemaker)

---

[122] Dick B., *The Akron Genesis*, pp. xv, 110, 133.

[123] Dick B., *The Akron Genesis*, pp. 190-92, 198, 204-08, 211-12.

[124] Dick B., *The Akron Genesis*, pp. 200-01.

[125] Dick B., *Design for Living*, pp. 24-25, 91, 98; *The Akron Genesis*, pp. 188, 200-01; *DR. BOB*, pp. 117, 137, 156, 100.

[126] Dick B., *The Akron Genesis*, pp. 72-76, 197-99.

[127] Dick B., *The Akron Genesis*, pp. 3-4, 144-45, 153-55, 172-76; *New Light on Alcoholism*, pp. 250-51, 337-41.

[128] Dick B., *The Akron Genesis*, pp. 141-50; *New Light on Alcoholism*, pp. 56-57.

[129] *Alcoholics Anonymous Comes of Age*, pp. 10-11.

disclose how much he and Bill Wilson worked closely together and shared together from 1934 on.[130] Bill and Sam frequently discussed the relation between early A.A. ideas and the principles of the New Testament.[131] And Bill Wilson was much involved for a time on a very personal level in the meetings and work of the Oxford Group businessmen's team of which such friends as Shoemaker, Irving Harris, Hanford Twitchell, Shep Cornell, Victor Kitchen, Charles Clapp, Jr., Rowland Hazard, and many other Oxford Group men were a part.[132]

A.A.'s resemblance to the First Century Christian Church, at least in the Akron fellowship and homes, was the subject of comment by many including Dr. Bob.[133] And here we therefore mention a word or two about "houses," "households," and "fellowship" in the First Century Christian Church.[134] In the church of the First Century, each household was a church in itself; and the Apostle Paul often spoke of "the church that is in their house."[135] Churches were named as the "households" of particular individuals such as Priscilla and Aquila, Chloe, Nymphas, and Archippus.[136] The homes in which the churches met were called the houses of God.[137] The believers broke bread together daily.[138] They taught and preached daily from house to house.[139] The "more noble" ones searched the Scriptures daily.[140] And, to use the descriptions in the Book of Acts: "the

---

[130] Dick B., *New Light on Alcoholism*, pp. 241-64.

[131] Dick B., *Design for Living*, pp. 120-23.

[132] Dick B., *New Light on Alcoholism*, pp. 253-57, 333-41, 347-51.

[133] *DR. BOB*, pp. 128-35; Dick B., *The Akron Genesis*, pp. 217-22; *Pass It On*, p. 184; *Robert Thomsen*, Bill W. (New York: Harper & Row, 1975), p. 282.

[134] See also *New Bible Dictionary*, 2d ed. (Wheaton, Illinois, Tyndale House Publishers, 1982), pp. 370-72, 497-98.

[135] Romans 16:5; 1 Corinthians 16:19; compare Colossians 4:15; Philemon 2.

[136] Romans 16:3; 16:5; 1 Corinthians 1:11; 16:19; Colossians 4:15; Philemon 2.

[137] 1 Timothy 3:15.

[138] Acts 2:46.

[139] Acts 5:42; 20:20.

[140] Acts 17:11.

Lord added to the church daily such as should be saved" and "so were the churches established in the faith, and increased in number daily."[141] "And some believed the things which were spoken, and some believed not."[142]

Throughout this book, you will find detailed references to Bible books, segments, and verses. You will also find detailed footnotes on A.A.'s source literature which not only cites the Biblical materials but often discusses them at length. We believe the Bible verses and the Biblical materials were very much a part of the *daily* study and living of the early AAs when they were an integral part of "A First Century Christian Fellowship" (the Oxford Group). But to make our footnotes pertinent and meaningful, it is vital to establish that the books which discussed the Biblical materials were owned, read, studied, and discussed in detail by the early AAs. And not merely on a sporadic, catch-as-catch-can basis. To verify that this was the case, we will look at the historical documentation for each category of literature.

The Bible Devotionals

1. *The Upper Room*. We begin with the Methodist quarterly known as *The Upper Room*. Its first issue was published in April, 1935, just before A.A. was founded. And there are endless references in A.A. writings, tapes, and interviews to the frequent and daily use and study of *The Upper Room* in early Akron A.A.[143] Dr. Bob and Anne used it; and so did Bill Wilson.[144] Henrietta Seiberling used it as she worked with the AAs and did her meditations.[145] The mother of one of the earliest AAs (Ernie

---

[141] Acts 2:47; 16:5.

[142] Acts 28:24.

[143] Dick B., *The Akron Genesis*, pp. 72, 87, 128, 129, 183, 190, 191, 197, 198, 207, 212, 213, 249, 252, 271, 344, 349, 385.

[144] Dick B., *The Books Early AAs Read*, 5th ed., pp. 4-6, 14; *The Akron Genesis*, pp. 204-13.

[145] Dick B., *The Books Early AAs Read*, 5th ed, p. 17; *The Akron Genesis*, pp. 86-87.

G., who was married to Dr. Bob's daughter) either brought copies
of *The Upper Room* to meetings or gave them to her son, Ernie,
to be delivered to the meetings.[146] When hospitalized, early AAs
were given only a Bible to read in the hospital; but it appears that
The Upper Room was usually the first piece of literature handed to
them at meetings.[147] An Akron A.A. pamphlet instructed the
A.A. newcomer as follows as that newcomer came out of the
hospital:

> First off, your day will have a new pattern. You will open the day
> with a quiet time (Oxford Group description of prayer and
> meditation). This will be explained by your sponsor. You will
> read the "Upper Room" or whatever you think best for yourself.
> You will say a little prayer asking for help during the day.[148]

And some AAs said that every early member had a copy of the
little quarterly in his pocket and in his home.[149]

2. *My Utmost for His Highest.* Oswald Chambers' *My Utmost
for His Highest* seemed to be second in widespread use.[150] Bill
and Lois Wilson used it for years.[151] Dr. Bob and Anne used it;
and so did Henrietta Seiberling.[152] Oxford Group people with
whom the author has discussed the matter are also conversant with
the frequent use of the Chambers devotional.[153] Many A.A.

---

[146] Dick B., *Dr. Bob's Library*, p. 31; *The Akron Genesis*, pp. 190-91, 197-98; *The Books Early AAs Read*, 5th ed., p. 14.

[147] See footnote 20 in our next chapter, and the comments by Clancy U. about being handed a copy at one of his first meetings.

[148] *A Manual for Alcoholics Anonymous*, pp. 8-9.

[149] Dick B., *The Akron Genesis*, pp. 197-98, 213; *Dr. Bob's Library*, pp. 29-31.

[150] Dick B., *The Akron Genesis*, p. 212.

[151] Dick B., *The Akron Genesis*, pp. 212, 351; *Dr. Bob's Library*, p. 30; *The Books Early AAs Read*, 5th ed., pp. 25-26.

[152] Dick B., *The Books Early AAs Read*, 5th ed. pp. vii, 17; *Dr. Bob's Library*, p. 30.

[153] And see Dick B., *Dr. Bob's Library*, p. 30.

tapes, interviews, and books mention this devotional's use and the AAs' emphasis on it.[154]

3. *The Runner's Bible.* Often mentioned was *The Runner's Bible.*[155] While not strictly a daily devotional, it contained indexed references to, and brief discussions of, most of the Bible verses referred to in early A.A. Dr. Bob's son informed the author that both of his parents utilized this book and that Dr. Bob gave it great store.[156] Apparently one valuable use was as a quick reference to a desired verse for prayer, meditation, or further study.

4. *The Meaning of Prayer, The Meaning of Faith,* and *The Meaning of Service.* Dr. Harry Emerson Fosdick, well-known minister of the Riverside Church in New York, was a special friend of Bill Wilson's.[157] Fosdick did a book review in 1939 of Wilson's First Edition of *Alcoholics Anonymous.* Among other things, Fosdick said:

> The core of their whole procedure is religious. . . . Let it be said at once that there is nothing partisan or sectarian about this religious experience. Agnostics and atheists, along with Catholics, Jews, and Protestants, tell their story of discovering the Power greater than themselves. . . . They are not partisans of any particular form of organized religion, although they strongly recommend that some religious fellowship be found by their participants. . . . They agree that each man must have his own way of conceiving God, but of God Himself they are utterly sure . . .[158]

---

[154] Dick B., *The Akron Genesis*, pp. 190-91.

[155] Dick B., *Dr. Bob's Library*, pp. 30-31.

[156] The author received this confirmation from Bob S. in two different telephone conversations with Bob S. at his home in Nocona, Texas, and also at A.A.'s International Convention in San Diego, California—the latest conversation being in 1995.

[157] Nell Wing, *Grateful to Have Been There*, p. 73. See also Big Book, p. 574, containing Fosdick's remarks at a dinner given by John D. Rockefeller, Jr., to introduce A.A. to some of his friends.

[158] *Alcoholics Anonymous Comes of Age*, p. 323.

In his autobiography, Fosdick later added:

> These testimonies [in the A.A. *Grapevine*] bear witness to reli-
> gion's reality, for Alcoholics Anonymous is deeply religious. . . .
> I have listened to many learned arguments about God, but for
> honest-to-goodness experiential evidence of God, His power per-
> sonally appropriated and His reality indubitably assured, give me
> a good meeting of A.A.![159]

One can gain from these statements by Fosdick an idea of the
mutual respect between Fosdick and A.A. And Fosdick's books
were owned, studied, and loaned out by Dr. Bob.[160] Some were
recommended by Dr. Bob's wife, Anne Smith.[161] And at least
one Fosdick book was read and mentioned by Henrietta
Seiberling.[162] There was a series of "devotionals" written by the
Reverend Fosdick a number of years before A.A. was founded.
And these—*The Meaning of Prayer*, *The Meaning of Faith*, and
The Meaning of Service—were read and used by AAs.[163]

5. *Victorious Living*. The families of A.A. founders frequently
mentioned the importance of the E. Stanley Jones books. Dr. Bob
owned and read them.[164] Anne Smith commented that "all . . .
are very good."[165] And Henrietta Seiberling read several of
them.[166] Jones' devotional, *Victorious Living*, was mentioned in

---

[159] *Alcoholics Anonymous Comes of Age*, p. 324.

[160] Dick B., *Dr. Bob's Library*, pp. 60-63.

[161] Dick B., *Anne Smith's Journal*, p. 82.

[162] Dick B., *The Books Early AAs Read*, 5th ed., p. 15.

[163] Dick B., *The Books Early AAs Read*, 5th ed., pp. 5-6, 8, 12, 14-15, 17, 29. And
Fosdick's titles such as *The Meaning of Faith* were the subject of citation and comment
in Oxford Group literature, including *Soul Surgery*—which was probably the earliest
Oxford Group book and was owned, read, and circulated by Dr. Bob. See Howard A.
Walter, *Soul Surgery: Some Thoughts on Incisive Personal Work*, 6th ed (London:
Blandford Press, n.d.), p. 68.

[164] Dick B., *Dr. Bob's Library*, pp. 64-66.

[165] Dick B., *Anne Smith's Journal*, p. 82.

[166] Dick B., *The Akron Genesis*, p. 85.

the Big Book's First Edition and was undoubtedly one of the many Jones books early AAs read and circulated.[167]

6. *Daily Strength for Daily Needs*. Another popular Bible devotional of many years standing was *Daily Strength for Daily Needs* by Mary W. Tileston; and this daily Bible study and guide was used by Dr. Bob.[168]

7. *I Will Lift Up Mine Eyes*. The books of Glenn Clark were very popular in early A.A. Many were owned by Dr. Bob; and most were read by the Smiths, Henrietta Seiberling, and early A.A.'s.[169] Clark's *I Will Lift Up Mine Eyes* probably qualified as a devotional because of the way it arranged study of Bible ideas and verses; and we therefore have occasionally cited it as one of the sources for verses which frequently popped up in A.A.

The Sam Shoemaker Writings

Shoemaker was a veritable publication house. By the time the Big Book was published, Shoemaker had written 14 major titles and a number of widely read pamphlets.[170] His books were owned and recommended by Dr. Bob and Anne.[171] Shoemaker's teachings were lauded by Bill Wilson.[172] Henrietta Seiberling read a great many of them.[173] His articles regularly appeared in *The Calvary Evangel* in the 1920's and 1930's. And the author even found a Shoemaker book and some pamphlets stuffed in a copy of Anne Smith's Journal at Bill Wilson's Stepping Stones home at Bedford Hills, New York. Shoemaker's books were among those Oxford Group materials regularly recommended for reading by *The*

---

[167] First Edition ("A Feminine Victory"), p. 223.

[168] Dick B., *Dr. Bob's Library*, pp. 29-30.

[169] Dick B., *Dr. Bob's Library*, pp. 33-34, 42, 55-59; *The Akron Genesis*, pp. 84-89; *The Books Early AAs Read for Spiritual Growth*, 5th ed., pp. 5-8, 14, 17, 27, 29, 30.

[170] See Bibliography at the end of this title; and Dick B., *New Light on Alcoholism*, pp. 16, 42, 48, 81-216, 248, 258-64, 319-21, 348-49, 353-55.

[171] Dick B., *Dr. Bob's Library*, pp. 46-50, 75-79; *Anne Smith's Journal*, pp. 81-85.

[172] Dick B., *New Light on Alcoholism*, pp. 2-4, 9-10, 34-35.

[173] Dick B., *The Books Early AAs Read for Spiritual Growth*, 5th ed., p. 15.

Calvary Evangel; and publication of the Shoemaker books was often announced there as new titles were released.[174] Hence AAs in New York and in Akron, as well as other Oxford Group people all over America, were kept familiar with what Sam Shoemaker was writing. As the years went by and A.A. continued to grow, Shoemaker often spoke on, and wrote about the Twelve Steps.[175]

The Other Oxford Group Literature

There is ample evidence that Oxford Group literature was not only available but widely read by early AAs. Dr. Bob apparently devoured it.[176] Anne Smith read and recommended it.[177] Henrietta Seiberling was reported to have read *all* the Oxford Group literature of the 1930's.[178] T. Henry and Clarace Williams were avid Oxford Group supporters for a lifetime; and Oxford Group literature was often available for the taking at all of the early A.A. meetings held in the Williams home.[179] Where not available for purchase, the Oxford Group books were frequently "swapped" for reading among the Oxford Group people.[180]

---

[174] Dick B., *New Light on Alcoholism*, pp. 258-62, 319-21; 347-51; *The Akron Genesis*, pp. 56-58.

[175] S. M. Shoemaker, Jr., *The Twelve Steps of A.A.* (New York: The Evangel, n.d.), pp. 5-6; *12 Steps to Power* (Faith at Work News, December, 1983). The author found and was allowed to copy these pamphlets from the Episcopal Church Archives in Austin, Texas. Shoemaker also wrote for A.A. itself: *Those Twelve Steps as I Understand Them*, Volume II The Best of the Grapevine, pp. 125-34. See Dick B., *New Light on Alcoholism*, pp. 217-37.

[176] Dick B., *Dr. Bob's Library*, pp. 2, 6, 9, 10, 12, 42-50, 54, 75-79.

[177] Dick B., *Anne Smith's Journal*, pp. 79-85; *Dr. Bob's Library*, pp. 6-7.

[178] Dick B., *The Akron Genesis*, pp. 79-90, 97-102, 104-05.

[179] Dick B., *The Akron Genesis*, pp. 65-74.

[180] Dick B., *The Akron Genesis*, pp. 56-58, 67.

Other Popular Christian Literature of the Day

Dr. Bob stressed the importance of Henry Drummond's *The Greatest Thing in the World*.[181] Dr. Bob seemed to study everything about Jesus Christ's Sermon on the Mount that he could get his hands on. For Dr. Bob's library contained copies of books on the Sermon by Oswald Chambers, Glenn Clark, Emmet Fox, and E. Stanley Jones.[182] Classics such as Brother Lawrence's *The Practice of the Presence of God* and Augustine's *Confessions*, as well as later writings such as James Allen's *As a Man Thinketh* and Charles Sheldon's *In His Steps* were in use.[183] Anne Smith placed much emphasis on Toyohiko Kagawa's *Love: The Law of Life*; and the book was also read by Dr. Bob and by Henrietta Seiberling.[184] The books of Carl Jung and Williams James were also much read.[185] Titles on the life of Jesus Christ were recommended by Anne Smith and read to or by many early AAs.[186] And the writings of Leslie D. Weatherhead not only surfaced in connection with Bill Wilson and Henrietta Seiberling, but also appear to have provided some very simple and structured explanations of Oxford Group ideas.[187] Because of the paucity of Oxford Group publications in the earlier years, Oxford Group people themselves frequently read and recommended the same

---

[181] Dick B., *Dr. Bob's Library*, pp. 14, 41-42.

[182] Dick B., *Dr. Bob's Library*, pp. 38-40.

[183] Dick B., *The Books Early AAs Read*, 5th ed., pp. 5, 8-9, 13, 17, 27, 29, 30; *Dr. Bob's Library*, p. 67.

[184] Dick B., *Anne Smith's Journal*, pp. 83-85; *Dr. Bob's Library*, pp. 40, 66; *The Akron Genesis*, p. 88.

[185] Dick B., *Dr. Bob's Library*, pp. 51-53; *Anne Smith's Journal*, pp. 27-28, 64-65, 68, 101; *The Akron Genesis*, pp. 5, 10, 23, 28, 48, 56, 88, 131, 138, 141-43, 165, 168, 185, 214, 231, 235, 252-53, 265, 315, 318, 327, 328, 346-47, 369, 384; *Design for Living*, pp. 35-36, 58-64, 126, 129, 130, 276-78, 314, 323-24, 335; *The Books Early AAs Read*, 5th ed., pp. 8, 9, 17, 26, 27, 29, 30.

[186] Dick B., *Anne Smith's Journal*, pp. 8-9, 82-83.

[187] Dick B., *The Books Early AAs Read*, 5th ed., pp. 17, 25, 29.

Christian materials that were studied by early AAs, whether AAs were studying them by reason of Group association, or not.[188]

The question here is whether one can validly assume that the Biblical materials which were discussed so extensively in the foregoing books were not only read or heard by early AAs but were actually influential on their thinking and language. And we believe the answer is yes.

AAs did not have their own literature prior to the Big Book. They were in constant touch, often living together, breaking bread together, meeting together, having quiet times together, and working with other drunks together.[189] Their families were a part of the process. They were taught by Dr. Bob, Anne, Henrietta, and the Williams family in Akron and certainly by Sam Shoemaker and his circle of clergy and Oxford Group team members in New York. And the subject of the teachings was consistently the Bible. The Oxford Group called itself "A First Century Christian Fellowship" because its methods of almost daily meeting, praying, studying, and fellowshipping together could be said to follow the First Century Church pattern of house meetings. As we've shown, they called their larger gatherings "houseparties." They were called by some newspapers the "houseparty religion."[190] And both Dr. Bob and early AAs called themselves a Christian Fellowship. Observers of early A.A. such as John D. Rockefeller, Jr., cohorts Frank Amos, the Reverend Willard Richardson, and Albert Scott in New York specifically commented on A.A.'s resemblance to First Century Christianity.[191] And we believe it fair to conclude that most early AAs were or became Bible

---

[188] This point was made to the author in several interviews between the author and long-time Oxford Group activists, James Draper and Eleanor Forde Newton, and also in phone conversations with Mrs. W. Irving Harris, widow of Shoemaker's assistant minister at Calvary Church during A.A.'s formative years.

[189] See Wally P., *But, For the Grace of God*, p. 41.

[190] The author found such an article at the Hartford Seminary Archives in Connecticut among the Frank N. D. Buchman papers there.

[191] *DR. BOB*, pp. 129, 131, 135-36; Robert Thomsen, *Bill W.* (New York: Harper & Row, 1975), pp. 275, 282; *Pass It On*, p. 184.

students who read, studied, and attempted to practice the principles of the Good Book daily; and they used their other literature to learn *more* about the Bible they were studying.

Thus when one finds the Biblical language and Biblical literature of early A.A. used and discussed with so much frequency, and when one finds the literature centered on words and ideas which became a part of A.A. language and literature, we believe that literature is a very reliable source for determining what early AAs took from the Bible for the spiritual program of recovery they were fashioning.

The Purpose of Our Book

Our major purpose, then, in writing this book is to examine from an evidentiary standpoint just exactly what the early AAs studied in the Bible. To learn the chapters and verses that were most quoted in their literature, talks, and meetings. To learn the specific ideas that must have commanded their continuing attention. To determine what books of, and teachings from, the Bible they probably used for information, inspiration, and their recovery ideas. To see where the Biblical ideas can be found in today's A.A., *if at all.* And to learn how all this information about A.A.'s Biblical roots can be of help to those of us actively participating in Twelve Step programs. Also to those who refer people to, and utilize, Twelve Step programs for recovery. To the churches, clergy, and lay religious who are really searching for an informed link between present-day A.A. and its rich, successful, Biblical-Christian beginnings. And to provide facts for those historians and scholars who want or need further information as to how and why early A.A. achieved its impressive, high success rate at a time when the Bible was its principal resource book.

Sad indeed today is the fact that A.A. and other Twelve Step programs are almost universally characterized as "self-help" programs instead of the "divine help" recovery program the Steps were able to provide in the 1930's. *Alcohol Health & Research World* recently stated: "The best-known and most frequently used self-help program is AA."[192] The Fifth Edition of "The Self-Help Sourcebook" *lists a host of Twelve Step programs as "Self-Help" programs.* The list includes Al-Anon Family Groups; Alcoholics Anonymous World Services, Inc.; Co-Dependents Anonymous; Debtors Anonymous, Cocaine Anonymous, Narcotics Anonymous, Gamblers Anonymous, Overeaters Anonymous, Sex Addicts Anonymous, and so on.[193] Sad also is the fact that perhaps the best-known comprehensive history of Alcoholics Anonymous is titled *Not-God.*[194] So an important purpose of this title is to fix clearly in the minds of Twelve Step people and others that the evidence proves beyond the shadow of a doubt that *Alcoholics Anonymous was about God—the Creator, Maker, Father, Almighty God* that was, in the beginning, so frequently mentioned. God as He was and is described in the Good Book.

But this is not intended to be a mere historical tome. Those who understand the *precise sources* of A.A.'s biblical concepts will *better understand the A.A. concepts* themselves. Those who know what *A.A.'s biblical words and phrases meant* when they were written and used by early AAs *will better understand the spiritual message* those words and phrases were intended to convey. Perhaps most important of all, *some of us wish to tread the same spiritual path that early AAs (who read and believed their biblical sources) were able to mark out for us.* And it is therefore essential to have an *accurate* historical record of *exactly what path they took.* That, in fact, is the very premise underlying the Big Book's recovery approach.[195] Unfortunately, however, almost

---

[192] Alcoholism Treatment in the United States, *Alcohol Health & Research World* (a publication of the United States Department of Health and Human Services), Volume 18, Number 4, 1994, p. 255.

[193] *The Self-Help Source Book: The Comprehensive Reference of Self-Help Group Resources*, 5th ed. (Denville, NJ: American Self-Help Clearinghouse, Northwest Covenant Medical Center, 1995), pp. 31-40.

[194] Kurtz, *Not-God.*

[195] Big Book (3rd ed.): "To show other alcoholics *precisely how we have recovered* is the main purpose of this book" (p. xiii). "If you are an alcoholic who wants to get

(continued...)

every detail concerning the daily prayers, the daily listening for guidance, the daily Bible study, the daily reading, and the daily Quiet Time discussions are missing from the account in the Big Book of what the pioneers did. And we shall endeavor to fill some of the vacuum in this work about the Good Book's role. We particularly want to suggest to others how they may, as the author himself did, (and did also with the many AAs he sponsored) successfully combine A.A.'s Big Book principles and practices with the promises of power, guidance, healing, forgiveness, deliverance, and love in the Bible to prove that recovery can and should be far more than abstinence from drinking or using. It should enable a more than abundant life.[196]

---

[195] (...continued)
over it, you may be asking—'What do I have to do?' It is the purpose of this book to answer such questions specifically. We shall tell you exactly what we have done" (p. 20). "Further on, clear-cut directions are given showing how we recovered" (p. 29).

[196] See John 10:10; Ephesians 3:20.

2

God!

In its pioneer days, A.A. offered specific ideas about, and descriptions of, God and His characteristics. Most of these were embodied in A.A.'s basic textbook. And our first question is whether the ideas and descriptions came from the Good Book? Let's answer the question by comparing present-day language in A.A.'s Big Book with some language in the Bible.

The Frequency of Biblical Names for God

"God" is mentioned 277 times by name, *with* a capital "G," in the third edition of A.A.'s Big Book.[1] The Big Book also contains 107 specific pronouns—he, him, his, and himself—which are

---

[1] *Alcoholics Anonymous* (New York: Alcoholics Anonymous World Services, 1976). Except where otherwise noted, we shall refer to this basic text by the affectionate name AAs use—the Big Book. *Big Book* is a registered trademark of Alcoholics Anonymous World Services, Inc.; used here with permission of A.A.W.S. Several writers have counted the usage of "God" in the Big Book's Third Edition. We have accepted the count by A.A. historian George T. of Illinois, who informed us by phone on April 25, 1995, that he had counted the use of the word "God" and compared and confirmed his count with the number of appearances of the word "God" listed in Stephen E. and Frances E. Poe's *A Concordance to Alcoholics Anonymous* (Nevada: Purple Salamander Press, 1990)—a reference work we have found to be definitive and very helpful on such points.

capitalized and clearly refer to "God."[2] Counting the Big Book's use of Biblical names for God (such as "Creator," "Maker" and as specified below), the God of the Bible is mentioned over 400 times.[3]

The Bible, of course, *begins* with "God."[4]

Genesis 1:1 speaks of God in relation to *creation*. And the Bible frequently calls God the *Creator*. For example, Isaiah 40:28 says: "Hast thou not known? hast thou not heard, *that* the everlasting God, the Lord, the Creator of the ends of the earth, fainteth not, neither is weary?"[5] A.A.'s Big Book refers to God as "Creator" twelve times.[6] And in one of those references, it addresses a prayer to "My Creator," in what AAs call their "Seventh Step Prayer."[7]

Other Biblical names for God are often used in the Big Book and other A.A. literature. The Big Book uses the Biblical expressions "Maker,"[8] "Father,"[9] "Father of Light,"[10] and "Spirit."[11] Bill Wilson and Dr. Bob both described God as their "Heavenly Father," just as Jesus Christ did in his Sermon on the Mount.[12] In an early draft of the Big Book, Bill Wilson spoke of "the way in which he happened to find the *living God*" (italics

---

[2] Count by George T., *supra*.

[3] The total count is 277 references to "God;" 107 references to God by pronouns used as substitutes for the name "God;" at least 17 references to Biblical names for God; which add up to more than 400 references to the God of the Bible.

[4] Genesis 1:1 states: "In the beginning God created the heaven and the earth."

[5] See also Ecclesiastes 12:1 ("Remember now thy Creator in the days of thy youth . . ."). Also Isaiah 43:15; Romans 1:25; 1 Peter 4:19.

[6] Big Book, pp. 13, 25, 28, 56, 68, 72, 75, 76, 80, 83, 158, 161.

[7] Big Book, p. 76.

[8] Psalm 95:6; Big Book, pp. 57, 63.

[9] Matthew 5:45; Big Book, p. 62.

[10] James 1:17 (rendered "Father of lights" in James); Big Book, p. 14.

[11] John 4:24; Big Book, p. 84.

[12] Matthew 6:32; *Alcoholics Anonymous Comes of Age* (New York: Alcoholics Anonymous World Services, 1979), p. 234; Big Book, p. 181 (Dr. Bob's personal story).

added).[13] And the Bible often referred to God as "the living God."[14] Wilson had also remarked that alcoholics had "a form of lunacy which only *God Almighty* could cure" (italics added).[15] And he wrote of "*God, our Father*, who very simply says, 'I am waiting for you to do my will'" (italics added).[16]

There are two other important ideas *about* God which A.A. took directly from the Bible.

God is

The first has to do with the belief that "God is." Hebrews 11:6 states: "But without faith *it is* impossible to please *him*: for he that cometh to God must believe that he is, and *that* he is a rewarder of them that diligently seek him." Oxford Group writers, including Dr. Sam Shoemaker, frequently cited Hebrews 11:6 for the proposition that one must start his or her experiment of faith by believing that God is.[17] Sam Shoemaker wrote, "Security lies in a faith in God which includes an experiment. It lies in believing that God is . . . ."[18] Earlier, Shoemaker had written, in a title owned and circulated by Dr. Bob among early AAs: "God is, or

---

[13] Dick B., *Design for Living: The Oxford Group's Contribution to Early A.A.* (San Rafael, CA: Paradise Research Publications, 1995), p. 155, n. 18.

[14] Matthew 16:16; Acts 14:15; Romans 9:26; 2 Corinthians 3:3, 6:16; 1 Timothy 3:15, 4:10; Hebrews 9:14; 10:31; and Revelation 7:2.

[15] Dick B., *The Akron Genesis of Alcoholics Anonymous* (Corte Madera, CA: Good Book Publishing Company, 1994), pp. 12-13. For "Almighty God" in the Bible, see Genesis 17:1; 35:11; Exodus 6:3; Ezekiel 10:5; Revelation 15:3.

[16] *A.A. Comes of Age*, p. 105. For "God our Father" in the Bible, see Romans 1:7; 1 Corinthians 1:3; 2 Corinthians 1:2; Ephesians 1:2; Philippians 1:2; Colossians 1:2; 1 Thessalonians 1:1; 2 Thessalonians 1:1.

[17] Dick B., *Design for Living*, p. 165. See also Leslie D. Weatherhead, *How Can I Find God?* (London: Hodder & Stoughton, 1933), p. 72. Weatherhead was a distinguished British clergyman who frequently wrote about the Oxford Group. Two of his titles were owned by A.A. co-founder, Bill Wilson.

[18] Samuel M. Shoemaker, Jr., *National Awakening* (New York: Harper & Brothers, 1936), pp. 40-41.

He isn't. You leap one way or the other."[19] Dr. Bob frequently insisted that a newcomer profess his belief in God.[20] And Bill Wilson pursued the same path when he used the following language in A.A.'s Big Book (which language closely parallels the foregoing quote of Shoemaker's language): "Either God is everything or else He is nothing. God either is, or He isn't. What was our choice to be?" (Big Book, p. 53).

A Loving God

The second important A.A. concept from the Bible describes "God" as a loving God. The idea almost certainly has origins in 1 John 4:8 and 4:16 where the Bible twice declares, "God is love." Dr. Bob's wife, Anne Smith, frequently used the verse "God is love" to help downhearted, confused, and frustrated alcoholics with whom she worked.[21] Dr. Bob emphasized God as

---

[19] Samuel M. Shoemaker, Jr., *Confident Faith* (New York: Fleming H. Revell, 1932), p. 187. As to the importance of this Shoemaker book to Dr. Bob, see Dick B., *Dr. Bob's Library: Books for Twelve Step* Growth (San Rafael, CA: Paradise Research Publications, 1994), pp. 47-48.

[20] *DR. BOB and the Good Oldtimers* (New York: Alcoholics Anonymous World Services, 1980), p. 144. This title will hereinafter be called *DR. BOB*.

[21] Dick B., *Anne Smith's Journal: 1933-1939* (San Rafael, CA: Paradise Research Publications, 1994), pp. 4, 15; *The Akron Genesis*, p. 121; Ernest Kurtz, *Not-God: A History of Alcoholics Anonymous*. Exp. ed (Minnesota: Hazelden, 1991), p. 55. See also *The Upper Room: Daily Devotions for Family and Individual Use* for 5/24/36; 5/4/37; 8/27/37. Note that *The Upper Room* is a quarterly daily Bible devotional, which commenced publication in April, 1935, and was published by the General Committee on Evangelism through the Department of Home Missions, Evangelism, Hospitals Board of Missions, Methodist Episcopal Church, South, Nashville, Tennessee. The little pamphlet contained for each day the date, a Bible verse, a comment on the subject of the verse, a prayer, and a Thought for the Day. The pamphlets were furnished to early AAs in Akron mostly by "Mother G.," the mother-in-law of Dr. Bob's daughter (Sue), and the mother of Sue's first husband, Ernie G., an early A.A. The pamphlets were brought to early meetings by Mother G. or delivered to Ernie G. who distributed them among early AAs. Many early AAs commented that almost every member had a copy with him and also that there seemed to be a copy in almost every A.A. home in Akron. Clancy U., an early AA who had been sponsored by Dr. Bob and by the venerable Clarence S., wrote

(continued...)

a God of love who was interested in individual lives.[22] Bill
Wilson embodied the idea of a loving God in A.A.'s Tradition
Two, which states, "For our group purpose there is but one
ultimate authority—a loving God as He may express Himself in
our group conscience."[23]

A Special "god" for A.A.?

What about the "god" in A.A.'s *later* years? What of the
elaborations on a "power greater than yourself" that one hears in
today's recovery center talk, hears in A.A. meetings, and even
reads in A.A.'s own *later* literature? About some "god" who has
been called a "lightbulb," a "chair," a "bulldozer," a "stone," a
"tree," "Santa Claus," "the Big Dipper," "Good," "Good Orderly
Direction," the "group," "Group Of Drunks," the "man upstairs,"
and "Ralph!" Are we exaggerating? The answer is that the author
has personally heard in hundreds of A.A. meetings, and read in
A.A. literature, almost every one of these appellations; and many
others actively involved in, or who are observers of today's A.A.,
have heard one or more of the expressions.[24] A.A. pioneer

---

[21] (...continued)
to the manager of Dr. Bob's Home on April 4, 1988, and recalled, "I was handed 'The
Upper Room' at one of my first meetings" (The author was given a copy of this letter
by the manager at Dr. Bob's Home). The author was able to obtain copies of the
quarterly for almost the entire formative period of early A.A. from 1935 to 1939. In
some cases, we were unable to determine whether the issue was for 1936 or 1939 and
have listed both as possible dates.

[22] *DR. BOB*, p. 110.

[23] Big Book, pp. 564-65.

[24] See Dick B., *Design for Living*, p. 158, n. 35. Refer also to *Daily Reflections*
(New York: Alcoholics Anonymous World Services, 1990): pp. 79 ("Good Orderly
Direction"), 175 ("a table, a tree, then my A.A. group"), 334 ("Him, or Her, or It").
Furthermore, in a tape provided to the author by a student of A.A.'s old-timer, Clarence
S., Clarence refers to the frequency and absurdity of the use by some AAs of the phrase
"lightbulb" to describe "God." And Clarence traveled the country far and wide in a half-
century of sobriety. Others have made similar observations about these unusual names
for some "god" of A.A.'s own understanding. See Barnaby Conrad, *Time Is All We*
(continued...)

Clarence Snyder was so concerned about the absurd names for god, which have their beginnings in the phrase "higher power" that Clarence wrote a pamphlet which has been widely distributed in A.A. Its title is *My Higher Power—The Lightbulb*.[25]

We certainly know that the foregoing names, some just plain ridiculous, did not come from the Bible. And we have not found any in the basic text of A.A.'s Big Book.

But what about A.A.'s *own* "Higher Power?" "A Power greater than ourselves?" And "God *as we understood Him*?" Phrases which AAs frequently use today. Phrases which some present-day commentators and even some A.A. Conference Approved literature seem to have codified into a special A.A. deity which some "choose to call God." Could these concepts, which appear to have given rise to strange ideas about "a" god, possibly have had their origins in the Bible or have come from A.A.'s Biblical roots?

Whence Came "Higher Power?"

First, what about "Higher Power?"

You will not find this expression in the King James Version of the Bible which was in such widespread use in early A.A.[26]

---

[24] (...continued)
Have (New York: Dell Publishing, 1986), p. 21; Nan Robertson, *Getting Better: Inside Alcoholics Anonymous* (New York: Fawcett Crest, 1988), pp. 124, 129; Jan R. Wilson and Judith A. Wilson, *Addictionary: A Primer of Recovery Terms and Concepts from Abstinence to Withdrawal* (New York: Simon and Schuster, 1992), pp. 181-83. For other usages of a similar nature in A.A.'s *own* literature, see *Twelve Steps and Twelve Traditions* (New York: Alcoholics Anonymous World Services, 1953), p. 27; Big Book, p. 248; *Members of the Clergy Ask about Alcoholics Anonymous* (New York: Alcoholics Anonymous World Services, 1961, revised 1992), p. 13.

[25] Clarence S., *My Higher Power—The Lightbulb*, 2d ed. (Altamonte Springs, FL: Stephen Foreman, 1985). The contents are reprinted in full and discussed in Dick B., *That Amazing Grace: The Role of Clarence and Grace S. in Alcoholics Anonymous* (San Rafael, CA: Paradise Research Publications, 1996), pp. 46-50.

[26] See Robert Young, *Young's Analytical Concordance*. Newly Revised and Corrected (Nashville, TN: Thomas Nelson Publishers, 1982), pp. 481-82, 765-66. Compare Romans 13:1 which uses the expression "higher powers" and is speaking of "rulers" and the "powers that be."

In the fourteen Shoemaker books and many pamphlets the Reverend Sam Shoemaker wrote prior to 1939, we have not located any instance of Shoemaker's using the phrase "higher power." There were, however, occurrences in later years after Shoemaker's close friend, Bill Wilson, himself had begun using the phrase with some frequency.[27]

In an interview with the author in the summer of 1991, the Reverend T. Willard Hunter (a long-time Oxford Group activist and writer) informed the author that he (Hunter) had never heard the expression "Higher Power" used in the Oxford Group.[28] And, in reviewing thousands of pages of early Oxford Group writings, the author himself has seen the expression used by an Oxford Group writer only once. Bill Wilson's Oxford Group team cohort and friend, Victor C. Kitchen, wrote, "I concluded that there must be some Higher Power to account for all the things taking place in space much as scientists concluded that there must be an atom to account for all the things taking place in physics."[29] Kitchen's statement is contained in a paragraph in which Kitchen writes of "God" by name, with a capital "G," and is describing the way in which he (Kitchen) came to "know" God. And Kitchen's title is liberally sprinkled with references to the Bible, Jesus Christ, and Christianity, as well as specific references to God, His Power, and His Guidance.

The author has found only one other early reference to "Higher Power" in A.A. root literature. That reference is contained in a title owned and read by Dr. Bob.[30] This was Ralph Waldo

---

[27] Samuel M. Shoemaker, Jr., *How to Become a Christian* (New York: Harper & Brothers, 1953), p. 143. But note Shoemaker's criticism of the idea of "Higher Power" as "God."

[28] Dick B., *Design for Living*, p. 157, n. 33.

[29] Victor C. Kitchen, *I Was a Pagan* (New York: Harper & Brothers, 1934), p. 85.

[30] Dick B., *Dr. Bob's Library*, pp. 18, 67, 68, 82. See also Mel B., *New Wine: The Spiritual Roots of the Twelve Step Miracle* (Minnesota: Hazelden, 1991), pp. 105-06, 111.

Trine's *In Tune with the Infinite*.[31] It could possibly be argued that Trine was referring to "God" as He is described in the Bible, for Trine uses many Biblical references and verses in his book. However, Trine had his own brand of "new thought" and hence cannot be said specifically to have referred to God as He was, in Trine's book, or in later A.A., understood in terms of the Bible's own descriptions of God.

Now let's go to A.A.'s Big Book and "Higher Power." In the Big Book's Third Edition basic text (the first 164 pages), the expression "Higher Power" is used, with capitalized letters, just twice. Does this phrase refer to God as He is described in the Bible? Most AAs today might answer with an emphatic "no." But we believe that is because so few know just where the expression came from. And because the expression has been taken out of context in A.A.'s later years.

The phrase "Higher Power" is used on page 43, where the Big Book states that the alcoholic's defense against the first drink "must come from a Higher Power." Note that the two words are capitalized. Note that they follow a paragraph which states that the "average alcoholic" has a generally hopeless plight and is in fact "100% hopeless, apart from *divine help*" (Big Book, p. 43, italics added). Note also that the "Higher Power" phrase is followed, two *and* three pages later, by statements that the Big Book is "going to talk about God" (p. 45), and that "we commenced to get results, even though it was impossible for any of us to fully define or comprehend that Power, which is God" (p. 46). Therefore, given the frequency with which the Big Book mentions God by name and describes Him as Creator, Maker, and so on, we believe the reference on page 43 is to the same God Almighty of the Bible, to whom more than 400 references were made in the Big Book. This even though the Big Book's chapter to agnostics encourages them to effect their "first conscious relation with God" as they

---

[31] Ralph Waldo Trine, *In Tune with the Infinite*, 1933 ed. (Indianapolis: Bobbs-Merrill, 1897), p. 199.

understood Him by *starting* with their "own conception of God, however limited it was" (p. 47).

A similar case can be made for the only other occurrence of "Higher Power" in the basic text portion of the Big Book. On page 100, the Big Book suggests, "Follow the dictates of a Higher Power and you will presently live in a new and wonderful world, no matter what your present circumstances!" Does this phrase imply Wilson was creating some new kind of universal deity? Not if we consider the preceding sentence which says, "When we look back, we realize that the things which came to us when we put ourselves in God's hands were better than anything we could have planned."[32] There are many instances of Oxford Group Biblical references, and references in the Bible itself, to trust in Almighty God by placing things "in God's hands" and awaiting His direction.[33] And Dr. Norman Vincent Peale, who knew Bill Wilson quite well, personally informed the author in an interview at Pawling, New York, in August of 1992, that he (Peale) had never talked to anyone familiar with the expression "Higher Power" who did not believe that the expression referred to God.

---

[32] The phrase "Higher Power" on page 100 should also be considered in the context of the following specific, unqualified references to God in other portions of the chapter: (1) relying upon human assistance "rather than upon God" (p. 98); (2) placing "dependence upon other people ahead of dependence on God" (p. 98); (3) burning into the consciousness of every man that he must "trust in God and clean house" (p. 98); stressing that "his recovery is not dependent upon people. It is dependent upon his relationship with God" (pp. 99-100); and saying to the reader: "Keep on the firing line of life with these motives and God will keep you unharmed" (p. 102).

[33] See Kitchen, *I Was a Pagan*, p. 108; Geoffrey Allen, *He That Cometh* (New York: The Macmillan Company, 1933), p. 161—"He will come with the promise of new health, if we give ourselves entirely into His Hands;" Samuel M. Shoemaker, Jr., *The Experiment of Faith: A Handbook for Beginners* (New York: Harper & Brothers, 1957), p. 63—"They all prayed together and put themselves in God's hands, and a change began;" *The Church Alive* (New York: E. P. Dutton & Co., 1950), p. 145—"The results of our efforts are not in our hands but His." See also Psalm 31:5: "Into thine hand I commit my spirit;" and comment in Mary W. Tileston, *Daily Strength for Daily Needs* (New York: Grosset & Dunlap, 1928), p. 110.

Peale wrote to the same effect in his book, *The Power of Positive Thinking*.[34]

Bill Wilson's Higher Power

Bill Wilson, however, set a different course in his own, later title, *Twelve Steps and Twelve Traditions*—published after Dr. Bob's death in 1951.[35] Wilson there referred several times to a "Higher Power" (pp. 25, 28, 34, 38, 39, 107). Wilson did refer to "God" in that title with much more frequency than he did to a "higher power." But he said, "You can, if you wish, make A.A. itself your 'higher power'" (p. 27). He added: "You will find many members who have crossed the threshold just this way. . . . Relieved of the alcohol problem, their lives unaccountably transformed, they came to believe in a Higher Power, and most of them began to talk of God" (pp. 27-28). Yet the idea of entreating A.A.'s "to look to a 'Higher Power'—namely their own group"— was an idea that Wilson pursued in his later writings.[36]

Wilson's unique, later suggestion that "the group" could be one's "higher power" seemed to open the door for many to call the A.A. "group" their substitute for God. The God of the Bible whom Wilson had defined as Creator. In fact, Wilson had virtually invited some to "substitute" when he wrote: "Many a man like you has begun to solve the problem by the method of substitution."[37] Yet such reasoning was something Dr. Bob's

---

[34] See discussion of Dr. Peale's interview and Peale's opinion in Dick B., *New Light on Alcoholism: The A.A. Legacy from Sam Shoemaker* (Corte Madera, CA: Good Book Publishing, 1994), p. 87, n. 17. See also Norman Vincent Peale, *The Power of Positive Thinking* (New York: Prentice-Hall, 1952), pp. 268, 272, where Peale was writing about Alcoholics Anonymous and twice indicated that the A.A. expression "Higher Power" referred to God.

[35] *Twelve Steps and Twelve Traditions* (New York: Alcoholics Anonymous World Services, 1953).

[36] *As Bill Sees It: The A.A. Way of Life . . . selected writings of A.A.'s co-founder* (New York: Alcoholics Anonymous World Services, 1967), pp. 276, 310.

[37] *Twelve Steps and Twelve Traditions*, p. 27.

wife, Anne Ripley Smith, had criticized at a much earlier point in time. She called a similar characterization of the group a "funk hole."[38]

Apparently, however, Anne's views got lost in a shuffle to shelve the "God of our fathers," to whom Bill still sometimes referred even in his later writings.[39] Of course, when Bill did use the expression "God of our fathers," he was utilizing solid Biblical terminology for God, both God as He is described in the Old Testament and God as He is described in the New.[40] But a different kind of thinking seems to have been brewing. And if her remarks represented Bill Wilson's views, Bill's wife, Lois, explained this thought process as follows:

> Finally [speaking about the language of the Big Book which was being readied for publication] it was *agreed* that the book should present a universal spiritual program, not a specific religious one, since all drunks were not Christian (italics added).[41]

We are not aware that any such "agreement" occurred *prior* to publication of the Big Book in the Spring of 1939, *or even after that time*. But Lois's *assumption* about universality may have applied to the way Bill Wilson *later* viewed the fellowship's thinking. Wilson wrote his Roman Catholic "spiritual sponsor" Father Ed Dowling in 1952 and stated:

> The problem of the Steps has been to broaden and deepen them, both for newcomers and oldtimers. But the angles are so many, it's hard to shoot them rightly. We have to deal with atheists, agnostics, believers, depressives, paranoids, clergymen,

---

[38] Dick B., *Anne Smith's Journal*, pp. 89-90.

[39] See, for example, *Twelve Steps and Twelve Traditions*, p. 29.

[40] See Exodus 3:13; Deuteronomy 1:11; Joshua 18:3; 1 Chronicles 12:17; Daniel 2:23; Acts 3:13; 5:30; 7:32; 22:14; 24:14.

[41] *Lois Remembers: Memoirs of the Co-founder of Al-Anon and Wife of the Co-founder of Alcoholics Anonymous* (New York: Al-Anon Family Group Headquarters, 1987), p. 113.

psychiatrists, and all and sundry. How to widen the opening so it seems right and reasonable to enter there and at the same time avoid distractions, distortions, and the certain prejudices of all who may read, seems fairly much of an assignment.[42]

The Foreword to the Big Book's *Second* Edition, describing the Fellowship "as it was in 1955," does assert that "By personal religious affiliation, we include Catholics, Protestants, Jews, Hindus, and a sprinkling of Moslems and Buddhists."[43] The Big Books's *Third* Edition, published in 1976, does declare that "the Realm of Spirit is broad, roomy, all inclusive; never exclusive or forbidding to those who earnestly seek. It is open, we believe, to all men."[44]

Yet this "broad, roomy, all inclusive" language can also be found in the Big Book's *First* Edition; and the phrase is used in the context of choosing "your own conception of God."[45] The First Edition context did *not* refer to a "Higher Power," but rather to "a higher Power."[46] And, as we've shown, this First Edition reference to God as a "Power" simply followed Oxford Group descriptions of God. But the First Edition did not refer to the "Group," or to a "Lightbulb" in connection with God. Nor even to some "universal" spiritual idea. For the foregoing "higher Power" usage is found in the First Edition's chapter to agnostics which stated it was "going to talk about God."[47]

That First Edition chapter also stated "we had to stop doubting the power of God."[48] It then related the story of a minister's son who had found and established a relationship with God, "his Creator."[49] As a punch line in the story, the First Edition stated,

---

[42] *Pass It On*, p. 354.

[43] Big Book, p. xx.

[44] Big Book, p. 46.

[45] First Edition, p. 59.

[46] See First Edition, p. 55.

[47] First Edition, p. 57.

[48] First Edition, p. 65.

[49] First Edition, pp. 68-69.

in capital letters, as to the man's "great thought" (the message the man had received): "WHO ARE YOU TO SAY THERE IS NO GOD."[50] And it concluded, as to God, "Even so has God restored us all to our right minds."[51] Interestingly, in his 1939 book review of *Alcoholics Anonymous*, Dr. Harry Emerson Fosdick quoted the foregoing passage—WHO ARE YOU TO SAY THAT THERE IS NO GOD; and Fosdick concluded of AAs and their basic text, "of God Himself they are utterly sure."[52]

The author reviewed the correspondence between Dr. Bob and Bill at the time Bill was sending the Big Book's proposed chapters to Akron for review. And there seemed to be nothing but acceptance on Dr. Bob's part. Very little, if any, discussion of Bill's drafts. No apparent disagreement. And this is not surprising considering Dr. Bob's firm belief in God and the frequency with which Bill had written of God the Creator, God the Maker, and God the Father in the Big Book that was being fashioned. The co-founders may have expressly or tacitly concurred that the Big Book's references to God were sufficient without detailed elaboration of God's characteristics; but in five years of researching this topic, we have found nothing that establishes they agreed on a "universal spiritual program," though that may well be what many AAs believe is representative of the A.A. fellowship as it exists today.

Today, understandably, there are varied opinions as to what A.A., as such, believes about God and A.A.'s own "Higher Power." One thing is certain: present-day A.A. literature is saturated with references to *some* "Higher Power."[53] We think the appropriate view of today's A.A. would be that there probably is not and cannot be any definition acceptable to all AAs, other

---

[50] First Edition, p. 69.

[51] First Edition, p. 69.

[52] *Alcoholics Anonymous Comes of Age*, p. 323.

[53] As examples, see *Twelve Steps and Twelve Traditions*, pp. 24, 25, 28, 34; *As Bill Sees It*, pp. 73, 116, 200, 276; *Came to Believe* (New York: Alcoholics Anonymous World Services, 1973), pp. 5, 30, 81, 95; *Daily Reflections*, pp. 79, 175, 334, 335.

than the definition the Big Book itself suggests. That suggestion is that the newcomer *commence* spiritual growth by choosing his or her own conception of *God*.[54]

Two historians of A.A., Dr. Ernest Kurtz and Katherine Ketcham, concluded, however:

> The use of the phrase *Higher Power*—his, hers, yours, or mine—rather than the word *God*, reminds members of A.A.'s tolerance of individual differences in religious belief and spiritual inclination. The most basic understanding of the concept "Higher Power" within Alcoholics Anonymous is that it is *that which keeps me sober*.[55]

The problem with such a conclusion is that the "lightbulbs," "chairs," "tables," and "trees" (which have become higher powers for many present-day AAs) can hardly be said to keep anyone sober. At least the author has seen no instances of sustained "lightbulb sobriety" among the thousands of people he has met in A.A.

Our own attendance at A.A. meetings, together with our sponsorship of many men in A.A., causes us to doubt the accuracy of the foregoing quote. We do not believe there is any clarity of understanding among the members of Alcoholics Anonymous about the meaning of "higher power." In fact, we have often felt, in hearing the "higher power" expression at meetings in the United States, that the phrase has no meaningful understanding *at all* to most of its users except when they *do* refer to God as they *have* formulated an understanding of Him.

We believe our observation is corroborated by that of Mel B., an A.A. with almost half a century of sobriety, who still actively attends meetings and writes and speaks extensively on A.A. history and ideas. Mel wrote:

---

[54] Big Book, pp. 12, 46-47.

[55] Ernest Kurtz and Katherine Ketcham, *The Spirituality of Imperfection: Modern Wisdom from Classic Stories* (New York: Bantam Books, 1992), p. 208.

But AA went no further than this [referring to the existence of Creative Intelligence, a Spirit of the Universe underlying the totality of things] in defining what it meant by "Spirit," and never insisted that even this was the end of the matter. This open-minded, conciliatory approach headed off arguments before they ever started. AA members have always issued disclaimers when discussing God: Typical is, "Our program is spiritual, not religious." If pressed for what the program's actual definition of *spiritual* is, however, it is doubtful that many AA members could explain.[56]

We definitely agree with Mel B.'s conclusion as to confusion among AAs over the meaning of "spiritual." But we do not believe that AAs "have always issued disclaimers when discussing God." At best, Mel B.'s statement can only apply to A.A. Conference Approved literature of *today*; for neither Dr. Bob nor Bill, nor many of those who wrote stories for A.A.'s First Edition of the Big Book, had any hesitancy about mentioning *God*. And most early AAs spoke frequently of their studies about God in the Bible and in the Bible devotionals in such wide use in early A.A.

At one point before Dr. Bob died, Henrietta Seiberling apparently saw a drift in A.A. away from the God of the Bible about whom she and Bill and Dr. Bob had taught among early AAs. Dr. Bob and Bill had suggested to Henrietta that perhaps they should not talk too much about religion or God. But Henrietta said this to her two co-founder friends:

Well, we're not out to please the alcoholics. They have been pleasing themselves all these years. We are out to please God. And if you don't talk about what God does, and your faith, and your guidance, then you might as well be in the Rotary Club or something like that. Because God is your only source of power.

---

[56] Mel B., *New Wine*, pp. 4-5.

Henrietta said Bill and Dr. Bob agreed with her on that point.[57]

"God As We Understood Him"

What then of A.A.'s use of the phrase "God as we understood Him."[58] Was this "God" some new "god" fabricated by Bill Wilson to suppress controversy and which ignored the "God Almighty" and "Creator" (so named in the Bible) to which Wilson so often referred in his Big Book text and other early statements and writings?

The answer lies with history.

Bill Wilson said his friend and "sponsor" Ebby Thacher had suggested to him (Bill) before Bill got sober, "*Why don't you choose your own conception of God?*" (Big Book, p. 12; italics in original). And it is important to remember the context of Ebby's suggestion. When Ebby first witnessed to Bill, Bill had begun ruminating about his childhood antipathy toward ministers, the world's religions, and God. (And though it is not well known, Bill had characterized himself as an atheist).[59] Hence Ebby suggested that Bill start with the Oxford Group concept from John 7:17 of "willingness to believe."[60] Echoing Ebby's teaching, Bill said,

---

[57] This account can be found in Dick B., *The Akron Genesis*, p. 98, which sets forth some of the specifics Henrietta Seiberling related to her son, Congressman John F. Seiberling, in a taped interview he prepared with his mother in the spring of 1971.

[58] See the specific language of A.A.'s Third Step and Eleventh Step which use the phrase "God *as we understood Him*" (Big Book, pp. 59-60; italics in original).

[59] See Bill's statement in *As Bill Sees It*, p. 276, speaking of "A Higher Power for Atheists," and stating: "I was once that way myself;" also our discussion elsewhere of Lois Wilson's statement to T. Willard Hunter that Bill had been an atheist.

[60] John 7:17: "If any man will do his [God's] will, he shall know of the doctrine, whether it be of God, or *whether* I speak of myself," said Jesus. Sam Shoemaker and the Oxford Group utilized this concept for their so-called "experiment of faith." A person could begin his quest for God, they said, by obeying what he or she had heard from Scripture about God's will. Then, by obeying that known word of God, he or she would quickly see that the doctrine was of God and would therefore confirm the initial belief in God and know more about God. Quoting John 7:17, Shoemaker put it this way in *Religion That Works* (New York: Fleming H. Revell, 1928), p. 36: "If any man will

(continued...)

"Nothing more was required of me to make my beginning" (p. 12, italics in original).

So obeying the known precepts of God *as one conceived of Him* at the *beginning* of surrender was how the unbeliever or doubter could *start*. The famous Bible scholar, theologian, and philosopher B. H. Streeter, of Oxford University, had been teaching the Oxford Group people from the Bible:

> "Straight is the gate, and narrow is the way."[61] Those who have entered in thereby tell us that we may expect another prize—a new conviction that God exists and a new understanding of His will, as well as new strength and happiness in His free service. "If any man willeth to do his will, he shall know of the teaching, whether it be of God (John vii. 17)." The truth of this is a thing which can be tested by experiment; and it can be tested in no other way. It is by getting into water that you prove the practicability of swimming—and its joy.[62]

Unfortunately, Bill left material out of the Big Book which he had used in his earlier pre-Big Book manuscripts and which showed that Ebby had given him specific instructions on commencing an experiment with the "God as you understand Him" idea, when Ebby was showing Bill how to begin Bill's quest for "faith." For, said Bill, in two early accounts of his first visit with Ebby Thacher—accounts not included in A.A.'s Big Book—Ebby had suggested to him in 1934 that he (Bill) should surrender himself to God *as Bill understood God.*[63] Ebby's suggestion

---

[60] (...continued)
begin by living up to as much as he understands of the moral requisites of God, he will later, in the light of his experience, come to see straight intellectually. . . . A moral experiment is worth ten times an intellectual investigation in apprehending spiritual truth. Obedience is as much the organ of spiritual understanding as reason."

[61] See Matthew 7:14.

[62] B. H. Streeter, *The God Who Speaks* (London: Macmillan & Co., 1943), p. 126.

[63] See Bill Wilson, *Original Story*, a thirty-four page document located at the archives at Bill's Home at Stepping Stones in New York. Each line of the document is numbered;

(continued...)

certainly did not counter the information that Ebby had been giving
Bill as to "God" from the Oxford Group. In fact, Ebby's
suggestion followed Oxford Group practice rather well. For
Oxford Group people had long suggested that one begin his or her
experiment of faith through "surrender as much of himself as he
understands to as much of God as he understands" or that he or
she "surrender as much of himself as he knows to as much of God
as he knows."

And let's look at this history.

The American Oxford Group leader Sam Shoemaker had
frequently taught of surrender to God *as you understand Him.*[64]
Shoemaker wrote, for example: "So they prayed together, opening
their minds to as much of God as he understood . . ."[65] Other
Oxford Group people *and* Dr. Bob's wife, Anne Smith, spoke of
"a surrender of all that I know of self, to all that I knew of

---

[63] (...continued)
and the author was permitted to copy and retain a copy of the document. On page 30,
Bill stated: "This is what my friend [Ebby Thacher] suggested I do: Turn my face to God
as I understand Him and say to Him with earnestness—complete honesty and
abandon—that I henceforth place my life at His disposal and direction forever" (lines
989-92). See also W.W., "The Fellowship of Alcoholics Anonymous," *Quarterly Journal
of Studies on Alcohol* (Yale University, 1945), pp. 461-73, in which Bill is quoted on
page 463 as saying that Ebby Thacher had told him, "So, call on God as you understand
God. Try prayer."

[64] See Dick B., *Design for Living*, p. 306.

[65] Samuel M. Shoemaker, Jr., *Children of the Second Birth* (New York: Fleming H.
Revell, 1927), p. 47. See also page 25, where Shoemaker wrote: "So he said that he
would "surrender as much of himself as he could, to as much of Christ as he
understood." Later, Shoemaker also wrote: (1) "We begin the actual Christian experience
when we surrender as much of ourselves as we can to as much of Christ as we
understand. . . . Commit yourself to Him in an act of dedication." *How to Become a
Christian* (New York: Harper & Brothers, 1953), p. 72. (2) "Begin honestly where you
are. Horace Bushnell once said, 'Pray to the dim God, confessing the dimness for
honesty's sake.'" *How to Find God*, p. 6 (New York: Reprint from Faith at Work
Magazine, n.d.). For other examples of such Shoemaker language, see Dick B., *Design
for Living*, p. 306, n. 21.

God."[66] In no sense were these writers speaking about any deity but God—the God of the Bible. Anne Smith and the Oxford Group people were, for the most part, devoted and daily Bible students who had a firm belief in God as He is described *in* the Bible.[67]

We believe the understanding of God held by Ebby Thacher, Bill Wilson, Dr. Bob, and Anne Smith during A.A.'s development years is *not* the "God as we understood Him" which sometimes sweeps through the meetings of A.A. today. For we have observed that phrases such as "Higher Power," "God as we understood Him," and a "Power greater than ourselves" have often become vehicles for expressing a belief in just about anything a speaker may wish to call "god," whatever the Big Book said or meant and whatever the founders of A.A. understood by that expression in the 1930's. But the fact remains that Sam Shoemaker, Oxford Group writers such as Stephen Foot, and Anne Smith all were writing about the God of the Bible and suggesting surrender to as much of *God* as one understands or knows. And they made those suggestions before Bill Wilson ever discussed the matter with Ebby Thacher and well before Wilson wrote the Twelve Steps.

When Ebby suggested to Bill in 1934 that Bill surrender to God as Bill then understood God, Bill reported in the First and Third Editions of the Big Book that he (Bill) did just that. Bill said that, at Towns Hospital:

> I humbly offered myself to God, as I *then* understood Him, to do with me as He would. I placed myself unreservedly under His care and direction.[68]

---

[66] See Stephen Foot, *Life Began Yesterday* (New York: Harper & Brothers, 1935), pp. 12-13, 175; James D. Newton, *Uncommon Friends: Life with Thomas Edison, Henry Ford, Harvey Firestone, Alexis Carrel, & Charles Lindbergh* (New York: Harcourt Brace, 1987), p. 154; Dick B., *Anne Smith's Journal*, pp. 25, 95.

[67] See Dick B., *Design for Living*, pp. 152-58, 163-66, 249-53, 302-04; *New Light on Alcoholism: The A.A. Legacy from Sam Shoemaker* (Corte Madera, CA: Good Book Publishing Company, 1994), pp. 63-64, 67, 311-12, 316.

[68] Big Book, First Edition, p. 22; Third Edition, p. 13 (italics added).

Bill's reference to God as Bill *then* understood God should be considered in light of Bill's own starting point as either an atheist or an agnostic—someone who does not believe in or is still in doubt about God.[69] Bill's reference to God as Bill *then* understood Him should be taken in light of his statement to T. Henry and Clarace Williams in 1954 that he (Bill) really knew little (in 1935) about the Bible *until* he came to Akron and learned from the Smiths, Mr. and Mrs. Williams, and Henrietta Seiberling.[70]

In contrast to Dr. Bob, who believed in God and insisted upon such belief as a condition to beginning recovery, Bill had started his recovery six months earlier in New York without such belief. And Bill was therefore advised, in accordance with John 7:17, to surrender to God as Bill then understood God and to follow the moral precepts of God which would produce an experience of God and convince Bill of God's existence and the validity of God's moral doctrine. Which surrender must, with those very ideas, have been made by Bill!

For, when Bill took the Oxford Group "steps" at Towns Hospital, and underwent his "hot flash" experience, he announced almost triumphantly:

This . . . must be the great reality. The God of the preachers.[71]

---

[69] As we've said, Bill stated on one occasion that he was an atheist. His wife, Lois, informed T. Willard Hunter in an interview that Bill had been an atheist (Tape of the Hunter/Lois Wilson interview in the author's possession). In the Big Book itself, Bill made two statements on the subject: (1) "I was not an atheist" (p. 10), though it is not clear from the statement that Bill had not *previously* been an atheist. (2) "But cheer up, something like half of *us* thought we were atheists or agnostics" (p. 44, italics added).

[70] See Dick B., *The Akron Genesis*, p. 64; and page 69 contains the following remarks by T. Henry Williams (which probably represent what Williams taught Bill Wilson): "Our conception of God makes all the difference in the world as to our attitude toward others. Either we accept the fact that there is a God and put Him on the throne in our lives and community or we deny His existence and climb up and usurp the throne for ourself . . ."

[71] *Pass It On*, pp. 120-21; Big Book, pp. 13-14.

Note that Bill had begun an experiment of faith as an atheist *or* an agnostic. He had admitted   alcohol had become his master.[72] After some self-wrangling, Bill surrendered and found himself "in the sunlight at last;" he had become *willing to believe* and concluded, "Nothing more was required for me *to make my beginning.*"[73] Then, he humbly surrendered, took an inventory, and sought to change his life.[74] When he had done that, he had his famous conversion experience and claimed knowledge of the "great reality"—the "God of the preachers."[75] These latter expressions seem very likely to have been expressions Bill had been hearing from Ebby Thacher and Oxford Group people.

Thus Oxford Group theologian B. H. Streeter had been saying (about God) to Oxford Group people: "He [God] is the *all-pervading Reality.*"[76] And Sam Shoemaker's teachings to his Oxford Group circle, including Ebby, about the experiment to find faith in God seem exemplified by this quote:

> Every so often in human history, the Spirit of God comes into the world in fresh manifestation of power. We notice a kind of cycle in the spiritual life of mankind: somewhere a *great Reality is born,* which brings a new discovery of God and new tides of life . . ."[77]

Atheists and agnostics in the Oxford Group had, despite their doubts or denials, *begun* their experiment of faith with a belief that God is.[78] From there, they had acted on the declaration in John

---

[72] From Bill's Story, Big Book, p. 8: "I had met my match. I had been overwhelmed. Alcohol was my master."

[73] Big Book, p. 12 (italics in original).

[74] Big Book, pp. 13-14.

[75] *Pass It On*, pp. 120-21.

[76] Streeter, *The God Who Speaks*, p. 12 (italics in quote were added). See also, p. 1: "a great Unseen Reality to which could be given the name of God."

[77] Samuel M. Shoemaker, Jr., *National Awakening* (New York: Harper & Brothers, 1936), p. 23. For other significant references to the "Great Reality" among A.A.'s sources, see Clark, *The Soul's Sincere Desire*, p. 30.

[78] See Hebrews 11:6; Dick B., *Design for Living*, pp. 163-66.

7:17 and experimented by following God's known moral precepts as set forth in the Bible. They believed this action would leave them with faith *in*, a "conscious contact" *with*, and substantial knowledge *about* God. In other words, they began with such understanding of God as they had, and then learned about God and the truth of His doctrine from the action they took in obedience to God's known will.[79]

A.A. legend has it that the expression "as we understood Him" was the product of a suggestion by former atheist, Jim B. And Jim B. told it that way in his Big Book story "The Vicious Cycle" and also in a history of early A.A. which Jim compiled.[80] However, Jim B.'s recollection never produced an acknowledgement by Bill Wilson that the "God as we understood Him" language *originated* with Jim B., rather than having arisen out of Bill's own earlier Oxford Group exposure.

In fact, in a letter from Wilson to Tom B., dated March 25, 1968, Bill wrote of Jim B.'s history of A.A. and commented that he felt "in some respects his [Jim's] recollections are rather mistaken."[81] Bill also said that "Jim, along with Hank Parkhurst and others, brought a strenuous objection to my use of the word God throughout the Steps. [and Bill added] It was out of this discussion, in which Jim participated, that we came on the idea of toning the thing down by the use of "God as we understand Him." Then Bill referred Tom B. to Bill's own history of early A.A. And there Bill had said, "Who first suggested the actual compromise words I do not know."[82]

---

[79] Dick B., *Design for Living*, pp. 50, 54-56, 160-63, 272-75.

[80] See Big Book, p. 248: "so my only contribution to their literary efforts was my firm conviction, being still a theological rebel, that the word God should be qualified with the phrase 'as we understand Him'—for that was the only way I could accept spirituality." In his *Evolution of Alcoholics Anonymous*, Jim B. wrote: "Another thing changed in this last rewriting was qualifying the word 'God' with the phrase 'as we understand him' (This was one of the writer's few contributions to the book)."

[81] Letter furnished to the author by Maryland archivist, Bill R.

[82] *Alcoholics Anonymous Comes of Age*, p. 167. See also p. 17.

In another account concerning the issue, Bill said at Fort Worth, Texas, in 1954, "The idea of 'God as you understand Him' came out of that perfectly ferocious argument and we put that in."[83] Unfortunately, Bill did not refer to the earlier "God-as-you-understand-Him" expressions in the Oxford Group and in the teachings of Anne Smith. But Bill indicated that, while Hank Parkhurst was *quoting* Jim B. to support Parkhurst's arguments against using "God" in the Big Book text, Jim B. was probably not even present when the compromise language was finalized.[84]

The fact is that "God as we understood Him" seemed to shock no one when that expression was adopted in the office of Bill Wilson's first secretary, Ruth Hock, at the time the Big Book was being put together. Ruth Hock said that adding the phrase "God as we understood Him" to A.A.'s Big Book and Twelve Step language at the formative stage never "had much of a negative reaction anywhere."[85] Her comment seems to hold water as of the date it was made.

As we've shown, Oxford Group adherents and people in Akron's Alcoholic Squad of the Oxford Group such as Anne Smith had been using such an expression or similar phrases for many years prior to the Big Book's writing in 1938.[86] And Bill had told a very revealing story about Jim B. when Bill addressed the Yale Summer School of Alcohol Studies in 1945.

Bill devoted much of his talk to "Jimmy" [Jim B.] "an alcoholic . . . [of] the type that some of us now call the blockbuster variety." Bill pointed to the number of times "Jimmy" objected to "this God business." Jim was staying drunk, and

[83] Tape, titled, "How the Big Book Was Put Together, Bill Wilson, 1954, Fort Worth, Texas" (copy supplied to author by A.A. General Services in New York).

[84] Speaking of the battle in Henry Parkhurst's office, Bill said: "Present were Fitz, Henry, our grand little secretary Ruth, and myself. . . . Praying to God on one's knees was still a big affront to Henry. He argued, he begged, he threatened. He quoted Jimmy to back him up. . . . Little by little both Fitz and Ruth came to see the merit in his contentions." *Alcoholics Anonymous Comes of Age*, pp. 166-67.

[85] *Pass It On*, p. 199.

[86] See discussion in Dick B., *Anne Smith's Journal*, pp. 24-29.

"louder and louder did he get with his anti-God talk." Finally, as Bill said Jim had told the story, Jim thought to himself, "Maybe these fellows have got something with their God-business." For Jim had reached out for a Gideon Bible when he was very sick. He picked it up and read from it; and Bill recounted that "Jimmy has not had a drink to this day, and that was about 5 years ago."[87]

The point is that when Bill was completing the Big Book in late 1938 and early 1939, there was nothing new about "the God-business" or "God as you understand Him." History is clear that a couple of former atheists objected to Bill's *incessant use* of the word "God" in the Big Book. There *was* a dispute in the New York area. There *was* a "compromise" in that Bill inserted "God as we understood Him" in two of the Twelve Steps. But the Big Book *retained* over 400 references to God, *without qualification*. And the phrase "as we understood Him" was something Bill had heard from his friend and Oxford Group sponsor, Ebby. Bill specifically so stated. The phrase is something Bill also probably heard from the Oxford Group circles in which he traveled in New York. And the phrase is something he well could have heard from Anne Smith when Bill lived with Dr. Bob and Anne in Akron and heard Anne teaching daily from the Scriptures, from Oxford Group literature, and from her spiritual notes about surrendering to God *as you know Him.*[88]

Further, such firm believers in God as A.A. co-founder, Dr. Bob, and his Akron AAs, had had the opportunity to review, prior to publication, every page of Wilson's Big Book manuscript—a manuscript containing hundreds of references to God as He *is* described in the Bible. There is no evidence that the Akron people had agreed with Bill or among themselves to a deletion of God from the Big Book; for they saw or had the opportunity to see the

---

[87] See W. W., Lecture 29, "The Fellowship of Alcoholics Anonymous" (New Haven: Quarterly Journal of Studies on Alcohol, 1945), pp. 461-473, particularly p. 468.

[88] Dick B., *Anne Smith's Journal*, p. 25. Anne wrote: "Try to bring a person to a *decision* to surrender as much of himself as he knows to as much of God as he knows" (italics added).

Bible's God named and described hundreds of times in the Big Book drafts and stories as they were proposed. And these Akron people gave the basic text of Bill's Big Book their "warmest support."[89] Warmest support even with the Big Book's very few and very limited references to "Higher Power" and "God as we understood Him" which apparently had produced no negative reaction.[90]

"A Power Greater Than Ourselves"

We've shown that the Oxford Group commonly spoke about opening one's heart, and surrendering, to one's own conception of God, to as much of God as one knows (in other words, to as much of God as one understands *at the time of surrender*). Also, at least one of their writers did call God a "Higher Power." And Oxford Group-Shoemaker writings are filled with the mention of *God* as a "Power" to be sought and a "Power" to bring about life-change.

Thus Stephen Foot's popular Oxford Group title of the 1930's, *Life Began Yesterday*, contains good examples of the Oxford Group's synonymous references to God and Power—the God of the Bible.[91] Foot spoke extensively of the "Power that can change human nature" and "this Power by which human nature can be changed."[92] In the next breath, Foot was writing, in language prophetic of that in A.A.'s Third Step, about "a decision to surrender to God."[93] As we stated, a companion Oxford Group title of the same period, *I Was a Pagan*, spoke *once* of a "Higher

---

[89] Dick B., *The Akron Genesis*, pp. 223-33; *A.A. Comes of Age*, p. 159.

[90] Even in the Third Edition, "Higher Power" was mentioned only twice in the basic text (pp. 43, 100). "God as we understood Him" phraseology was used only seven times in the basic text (pp. 13, 47, 59, 60, 63, 164). But, as we have shown, the *unqualified* language about "God," the use of pronouns specifically referring to Him, and the inclusion of Biblical names for Him occurred over 400 times in the Third Edition.

[91] Foot, *Life Began Yesterday*, pp. 4-5, 13, 15, 22-23, 30, 35, 47, 87, 112.

[92] Foot, *Life Began Yesterday*, p. 22.

[93] Foot, *Life Began Yesterday*, p. 44.

Power" and *then* asked "just what this secret or this power was."[94] Kitchen's next sentence referred to "God-consciousness"—an expression that seems to have found its way to A.A.'s Big Book.[95] Kitchen also wrote of "A power within yet coming from outside myself—a power far stronger than I was."[96] Again, Kitchen was talking about "God."[97]

Dr. Bob's wife, Anne, wrote in her journal about the Apostle Paul's lack of power and said:

> A stronger power than his [Paul's] was needed. God provided the power through Christ.[98]

Clearly, Anne was speaking of the power of God. And Bill Wilson's spiritual teacher Sam Shoemaker spoke of God in terms of "A vast Power outside themselves."[99] And "A Force outside himself, greater than himself."[100]

Bill Wilson followed suit in the Big Book when he spoke of the need in recovery for a willingness to believe in a Power greater

---

[94] Kitchen, *I Was a Pagan*, p. 28.

[95] Kitchen, *I Was a Pagan*, p. 28. See also Dick B., *Design for Living*, pp. 277, n. 458 and 339-40, for other Oxford Group references to "God-consciousness." Also, see Big Book, pp. 13, 51, 85, 569-70.

[96] Kitchen, *I Was a Pagan*, 63; compare p. 78.

[97] Kitchen, *I Was a Pagan*: (1) "that was what gave them the power to *apply* beliefs and *carry out* the plan of God—a power that I did not have" (p. 56, italics in original); (2) "they said I would have to surrender my will and make it subject to the will of God" (p. 56); (3) "Forming a clean contact with God, however, does no good unless God then chooses to release His power. And God, as I have said before, will not do so unless He knows that He can *trust* you with that power" (pp. 66-67, italics in original); (4) "With my new experience, however, the Holy Ghost or Spirit became a definite force flowing from God to me as electricity flows from a power house" (p. 78).

[98] Dick B., *Anne Smith's Journal*, p. 22; Big Book, p. 45: "Lack of power, that was our dilemma. We had to find a power by which we could live, and it had to be a *Power greater than ourselves*" (italics in original).

[99] Samuel M. Shoemaker, Jr., *A Young Man's View of the Ministry* (New York: Association Press, 1923), p. 42.

[100] Samuel M. Shoemaker, Jr., *If I Be Lifted Up* (New York: Fleming H. Revell, 1931), p. 176.

than ourselves and then made it clear that the Power "is God."[101] Bill underlined this "God" point many times by pointing out that the aim of the recovery program of Alcoholics Anonymous, at the time of the writing of the Big Book, was the establishment of a "relationship with God."[102]

Again, one can hardly claim that the "power greater than ourselves" in today's A.A. is inevitably God Almighty as He is described in the Bible. But we think a strong case can be made that there was *no other understanding* of that phrase when Oxford Group writers, as well as Bill Wilson and Dr. Bob's wife, Anne Smith, first began using it. There can be little doubt that when Sam Shoemaker spoke of a "Power," Shoemaker was speaking of God; for his sermons and writings are filled with references to God and Power.[103] So too the Oxford Group writers mentioned above.[104] So too Anne Smith, in the sentences quoted above, when she spoke of God's providing the power through Christ. As we've shown, Dr. Bob frequently spoke of God and his (Dr. Bob's) Heavenly Father. And so did Bill Wilson.

Based on all our research, we therefore believe that from the time of A.A.'s founding in 1935: (1) Bill Wilson and Dr. Bob believed in, and relied upon, God as He is described in the Bible.[105] (2) They used Bible terminology to describe God in

---

[101] Big Book, p. 46.

[102] See Big Book, pp. 29, 13, 28, 100, 164. For the historical roots of this "relationship with God" idea, see Dick B., *Design for Living*, pp. 36, 78, 155, 168, 180, 223, 274, 302, 323, 325, 332-33 (and note particularly the citations on p. 332, n. 105).

[103] See, for example, one of Shoemaker's earliest titles, *A Young Man's View of the Ministry*, p. 42, where Shoemaker commented that changed people seemed "propelled by a vast Power outside themselves."

[104] For an example, see Streeter, *The God Who Speaks*, p. 110 (quoting 1 Corinthians 2:4-5, and stating): "Not argument, but fact, says Paul; not persuasion but power from God. It is clear that things happened to people as a result of this experience." Compare also Acts 1:8: "But ye shall receive power . . ." and Streeter, *The God Who Speaks*, p. 111.

[105] Thus, by 1937, when he was speaking of how he and Dr. Bob realized they had developed a successful recovery program out of their period of "flying blind" with the

(continued...)

their work with others. (3) And—however roomy and inclusive they wished to make early A.A. and later A.A.—they did not endeavor *in their early days* to establish some new theology, religion, or sectarian doctrine about a "god" of their own creation or perception.[106] They were, at most, proposing for those of little or no faith an experiment of faith that would enable them to *begin* their path to a relationship with God and then, for the great majority, to *believe* in God.[107]

Consider, for example, these statements by Bill Wilson even as the years rolled on:

[Speaking in July, 1953, about what Ebby had first told him:] I had to pray to God for guidance and strength, even though I wasn't sure there was any God;[108]

[July, 1953:] Those expressions ["a Higher Power" or "God as we understand Him"] . . . have enabled thousands of us *to make a beginning* . . . (italics added).[109]

---

[105] (...continued)
Bible and the Oxford Group precepts, Bill said: "A beacon had been lighted. God had shown alcoholics how it might be passed from hand to hand." *RHS* (New York: AA Grapevine, Inc., 1951), p. 8. *DR. BOB* stated at p. 96: "This [the period from 1935 on, when there were no Twelve Steps] was the beginning of A.A.'s 'flying-blind' period. They had the Bible, and they had the precepts of the Oxford Group. They also had their own instincts. They were working, or working out, the A.A. program—the Twelve Steps—without quite knowing how they were doing it." And, as Oxford Group spokesman Sherwood Sunderland Day had written in the first page of his Oxford Group pamphlet, *The Principles of the Group* (Oxford: Oxford University, n.d.): "The principles of 'The Oxford Group' *are* the principles of the Bible" (italics added).

[106] In *A.A. Comes of Age*, Bill said at page 232: "Speaking for Dr. Bob and myself I would like to say that there never has been the slightest intent, on his part or mine, of trying to found a new religious denomination. Dr. Bob held certain religious convictions, and so do I. This is, of course, the personal privilege of every A.A. member."

[107] See, for example, Bill's comment in *A.A. Comes of Age*, p. 81: "Alcoholics may be led to believe in God, but none can be forced."

[108] *The Language of the Heart*, p. 196.

[109] *The Language of the Heart*, p. 201.

[1957:] In Step Two we decided to describe God as a "Power greater than ourselves." In Steps Three and Eleven we inserted the words "God *as we understood Him . . .*" Such were the final concessions to those of little or no faith; this was the great contribution of our atheists and agnostics. They had widened our gateway so that all who suffer might pass through, regardless of their belief or *lack of belief.* God was certainly there in our Steps, but He was now expressed in terms that anybody—*anybody at all*—could accept and try (italics in original).[110]

[January, 1958:] Like any good scientist in his laboratory, our friend can assume a theory and pray to a "higher power" that *may* exist and *may* be willing to help and guide him. He keeps on experimenting—in this case, praying—for a long time. . . . As he goes along with his process of prayer, he begins to add up the results. . . . Even if few of these things happen [serenity, tolerance, less fear, less anger], he will still find himself in possession of great gifts. . . . He can now accept himself and the world around him. He can do this because he now accepts a God who is All—and who loves all. When he now says, "Our Father who art in Heaven, hallowed be thy name," our friend deeply and humbly means it.[111] When in good meditation and thus freed from the clamors of the world, he knows that he is in God's hand . . . (italics in original).[112]

[January, 1958:] Mine was exactly the kind of deep-seated block we so often see today in new people who say they are atheistic or agnostic. Their will to disbelieve is so powerful that apparently they prefer a date with the undertaker to an open-minded and experimental *quest* for God (italics added).[113]

---

[110] *Alcoholics Anonymous Comes of Age*, p. 167 (published in 1957).

[111] Bill here virtually quotes verbatim a portion of the Lord's Prayer in Jesus's Sermon on the Mount (Matthew 6:9).

[112] *The Language of the Heart*, pp. 241-42.

[113] *The Language of the Heart*, pp. 245-46.

[June, 1961:] Perfect humility would be a full willingness, in all times and places, to find and do the will of God. . . . I see that my journey toward God has scarce begun.[114]

[June, 1966, speaking about his sponsor, Ebby:] he was proposing the attitudes and principles that I used later in developing AA's Twelve Steps to recovery. . . . He had pushed ajar that great gate through which all in AA have since passed to find their freedom under God.[115]

Were these the words of a co-founder who believed that "god" could be a light-bulb, a chair, or the group? We think not. Bill sometimes said he was an atheist and sometimes said he was an agnostic *before* he had his conversion experiences at Calvary Rescue Mission and at Towns Hospital. But, at *those* places, he was surrendering to God—"the God of the preachers"—as Ebby had explained Him to Bill from Oxford Group precepts and as Bill had heard Him preached at the Calvary Mission and later at Shoemaker's Oxford Group meetings at Calvary House.

The Oxford Group often spoke of the *experiment of faith* which began with obeying as much of the will of God as one knew.[116] And that seemed to be the gateway to God which Bill was suggesting with his use of the word "Power" and the phrase "as we understood Him." But the gateway in those early days led most assuredly to the God of the Bible which Bill had mentioned so many times in his drafts of the Big Book.

We cannot say Bill's approach appeals to us. Nor do we believe it was the approach Dr. Bob used when he asked a newcomer if

---

[114] *The Language of the Heart*, p. 259.

[115] *The Language of the Heart*, p. 368.

[116] John 7:17. See Streeter, *The God Who Speaks*, p. 126: "The truth of this [John 7:17] is a thing which can be tested by experiment; and it can be tested in no other way;" Shoemaker, *National Awakening*, p. 40: "It [true security] lies in a faith in God which includes an experiment. It lies in believing that God is, that He has a plan, and that He will reveal that plan to us. It lies in fitting in with that plan ourselves, and finding that God will take care of us when we dare to make that experiment."

the newcomer *believed* in God—the God of the Bible.[117] This God of love Who was the subject of Dr. Bob's daily Bible study. Nor do we believe Bill's approach is easy for the Christian to take as he or she ponders the words of Jesus, Peter, and Paul in the books of John, Acts, and Romans.[118]

Whatever today's AAs might wish to believe or come to believe, we conclude that Bill Wilson's *own* early access to "faith" occurred through his believing basic ideas *from the Good Book* which: (1) He heard from Ebby Thacher when Ebby visited Bill and flatly declared that God had done for him (Ebby) what he could not do for himself.[119] (2) He utilized when he "gave his life to God" at Sam Shoemaker's Calvary Rescue Mission where there had been hymns, Bible reading, and an altar call (All of which, according to Mrs. Samuel Shoemaker, Jr., who said she was present, resulted in Bill's making his "decision for Christ").[120] (3) He further pursued when he checked in at Towns Hospital, followed Ebby Thacher's instructions, and humbly entrusted his life to God's care.[121] Recall again, Dr. Bob's

---

[117] *DR. BOB and the Good Oldtimers* recorded this typical colloquy between Dr. Bob and a newcomer about belief in God: [Dr. Bob]: "Do you believe in God, young fella ?" [Clarence]: "I guess I do." [Dr. Bob]: "Guess, nothing! Either you do or you don't." [Clarence]: "I do." [Dr. Bob]: "That's fine. . . . Now we're getting someplace. All right, get out of bed on your knees. We're going to pray" (p. 144). See Also, Dick B., *Design for Living*, p. 166.

[118] John 14:6: "Jesus saith unto him, I am the way, the truth, and the life; no man cometh unto the Father, but by me." Acts 4:7-12: "By what power, or by what name, have ye done this? Then Peter, filled with the Holy Ghost, said unto them. . . . Be it known unto you all, and to all the people of Israel, that by the name of Jesus Christ of Nazareth, whom ye crucified, whom God raised from the dead, *even* by him doth this man stand here before you whole. . . . Neither is there salvation in any other: for there is none other name under heaven given among men, whereby we must be saved." Romans 10:8-9: ". . . that is, the word of faith, which we preach; That if thou shalt confess with thy mouth the Lord Jesus, and shalt believe in thine heart that God hath raised him from the dead, thou shalt be saved."

[119] Big Book, p. 11.

[120] Dick B., *New Light on Alcoholism*, p. 242.

[121] See, for example, Proverbs 3:5-6; Dick B., *Design for Living*, pp. 158-63; Big Book, p. 13.

statement, about Bill and himself, that "We got them [the basic ideas] . . . as a result of our study of the Good Book."[122]

Bill's own learning experiences from his visit with Ebby, his surrender at Calvary Rescue Mission, and his "hot flash" conversion at Towns Hospital caused Bill, we believe, to declare that he had given his life to God as Bill *then* understood God.[123] We believe those experiences caused Bill to declare, *at least twice*, "For sure I had been born again."[124] And Bill's understanding at that time (of the God of the Bible) permeated and remained in the language of the Big Book he wrote some four years later.

Furthermore, the persistence of *Bill's* Biblical understanding of God, whether Bill called Him a "Higher Power" or "God as we understood Him" or "A Power greater than ourselves," is exemplified by the following statement by Bill on A.A.'s Twentieth Anniversary:

> Many people wonder how A.A. can function under such a seeming anarchy. . . . Happily for us, we found we need no human authority whatever. We have two authorities which are far more effective. One is benign, the other malign. There is God, our Father, who very simply says, "I am waiting for you to do my will." The other authority is named John Barleycorn, and he says, "You had better do God's will or I will kill you." . . . So, when all the chips are down, we conform to God's will or perish.[125]

---

[122] *DR. BOB*, p. 97.

[123] Big Book First Edition, p. 22: "There I humbly offered myself to God, as I then understood Him, to do with me as He would."

[124] See documentation in Dick B., *The Akron Genesis*, pp. 328-31.

[125] *Alcoholics Anonymous Comes of Age*, p. 105. See also Nell Wing, *Grateful to Have Been There*, p. 22.

3

Biblical Impact on Big Book Language

Now to some of the Bible's direct impact on A.A. language—in the Big Book and elsewhere. To some in today's A.A.—who are pelted with references to a "higher power," "a god of someone's understanding," and fatalistic references to the God "with a sense of humor"—there are words in A.A.'s Big Book which must seem very strange. Many newcomers simply must be familiar with words like Creator, Father, and Maker. They must also have heard "Love thy neighbor as thyself" and "Thy will be done." And it must be difficult to sort out the meaning of such words in the Big Book midst proclamations that A.A. left the Bible behind in Akron, that it is "spiritual and not religious," and that the word "God" scares away the newcomer. For any newcomer who has gone to Sunday School or to any Judeo or Christian denominational church must quickly recognize that the foregoing words are from the Bible. And that recognition must begin once the early confusion of withdrawal begins to pale. To be sure, the words are from the Bible; and A.A. should be the first the say so! But it has not done so.

Direct Quotes from the Bible

Even today's Third Edition of the Big Book contains a number of direct quotes from the King James Version of the Bible early AAs used. The following direct quotes can be found in the basic text portion of the Big Book:

1. Thy will be done.[1]
2. Thy will (not mine) be done.[2]
3. Love thy neighbor as thyself.[3]
4. Faith without works is dead.[4]
5. Father of Light.[5]

Recognizable Biblical Words and Concepts

The following words and ideas, though not necessarily verbatim quotes from the Bible, are firmly embedded in A.A. and have specific sources in the Bible and in the books Dr. Bob studied and recommended. In the footnotes, we list a reference to the

---

[1] Big Book, pp. 67, 88; compare p. 443; From a portion of the Lord's Prayer in the Sermon on the Mount—Matthew 6:10. See The Layman with a Notebook, *What is the Oxford Group?* (London: Oxford University Press, 1933), p. 48; Samuel M. Shoemaker, Jr., *Children of the Second Birth* (New York: Fleming H. Revell, 1927), pp. 175-87. *Big Book*° is a registered trademark of Alcoholics Anonymous World Services, Inc.; used here with permission of A.A.W.S.

[2] Big Book, p. 85; and compare "Thy will be done, not mine," pp. 229, 381. As rendered in the King James Version, Luke 22:42: "nevertheless not my will, but thine, be done." See *What is the Oxford Group?* p. 48; Shoemaker, *Children of the Second Birth*, pp. 58, 182; Glenn Clark, *The Soul's Sincere Desire* (Boston: Little Brown, 1925), p. 40.

[3] Big Book, p. 153; compare p. 236; Leviticus 19:18; Matthew 19:19; 22:39; Mark 12:31; Romans 13:9; Galatians 5:14; James 2:8. (and compare Luke 10:27; and Matthew 5:43). See Glenn Clark, *I Will Lift up Mine Eyes* (New York: Harper & Brothers, 1937), p. 63; Nora Smith Holm, *The Runner's Bible* (New York: Houghton Mifflin Company, 1915), pp. 27, 66; Mary W. Tileston, *Daily Strength for Daily Needs*, 1977 printing (Boston: Roberts Brothers, 1884), p. 138; B. H. Streeter, *The God Who Speaks* (London: Macmillan & Co., Ltd., 1936), p. 151.

[4] Big Book, pp. 76, 88; compare pp. 14, 473; James 2:20, 26 (compare James 2:14, 17); *What is the Oxford Group?*, p. 36.

[5] Big Book, p. 14 [sic]; the Biblical text reads: "Father of lights". See James 1:17; Holm, *The Runner's Bible*, p. 9.

expression in A.A. literature, then to the Biblical source(s), and finally to books in Dr. Bob's library where they are discussed.

1. God.[6]
2. God is.[7]
3. God is love.[8]
4. God-sufficiency.[9]
5. Creator.[10]
6. Maker.[11]
7. Father.[12]
8. Spirit.[13]
9. Honesty ("Absolute Honesty").[14]

---

[6] Big Book (Over 200 specific, unqualified references to God); Genesis 1:1; Harold Begbie, *Life Changers* (London: Mills and Boon, Ltd., 1923), pp. 47-48.

[7] Big Book, p. 53; Hebrews 11:6; Samuel M. Shoemaker, Jr., *The Gospel According To You* (New York: Fleming H. Revell, 1934), p. 47; *Confident Faith* (New York: Fleming H. Revell, 1932), p. 187.

[8] Dick B., *The Akron Genesis of Alcoholics Anonymous* (Corte Madera, CA: Good Book Publishing, 1994), p. 121; Ernest Kurtz, *Not-God: A History of Alcoholics Anonymous*. Exp. ed (Minnesota: Hazelden, 1991), p. 55; 1 John 4:8; 4:16; Holm, *The Runner's Bible*, p. 6; Streeter, *The God Who Speaks*, p. 104; Clark, *I Will Lift Up Mine Eyes*, pp. 79, 89, 93, 132; Tileston, *Daily Strength for Daily Needs*, p. 139; *The Upper Room* for 5/24/36, 5/4/37, 8/27/37.

[9] Big Book, pp. 52-53; 2 Corinthians 3:5; 9:8; Samuel M. Shoemaker, Jr., *If I Be Lifted Up* (New York: Fleming H. Revell, 1931), p. 107; Holm, *The Runner's Bible*, p. 138.

[10] Big Book, pp. 13, 25, 28, 56, 68, 72, 75, 76, 80, 83, 158, 161; Isaiah 40:28; (compare Genesis 1:1); Begbie, *Life Changers*, p. 20.

[11] Big Book, pp. 57, 63; compare p. 525; Psalm 95:6. We found no correlative Oxford Group source; so Bill and Dr. Bob may have taken this directly from the Bible.

[12] Big Book, p. 62; Matthew 5:45; Philip Marshall Brown, *The Venture of Belief* (New York: Fleming H. Revell, 1935), p. 25; Clark, *The Soul's Sincere Desire*, p. 8.

[13] Big Book, p. 46 ("the Realm of Spirit"); p. 66 ("the sunlight of the Spirit"); p. 84 ("the world of the Spirit"); p. 85 ("the flow of His Spirit into us"); p. 164 ("the Fellowship of the Spirit"); John 4:24; Holm, *The Runner's Bible*, pp. 16-19; Streeter, *The God Who Speaks*, pp. 109-10.

[14] Big Book, pp. 13, 28, 32, 57-58, 63-65, 67, 70, 73, 83, 145; Matthew 5:33-37; Ephesians 4:25; Philippians 4:8; *Pass It On* (New York: Alcoholics Anonymous World Services, 1984), p. 114; *The Language of the Heart: Bill W.'s Grapevine Writings* (New

(continued...)

10. Unselfishness ("Absolute Unselfishness").[15]
11. Love ("Absolute Love").[16]
12. Patience.[17]
13. Tolerance.[18]
14. Kindness.[19]
15. Forgiveness.[20]
16. Restitution (Amends).[21]

---

[14] (...continued)
York: The AA Grapevine, Inc., 1988), p. 200; *The Co-Founders of Alcoholics Anonymous: Biographical sketches Their last major talks* (New York: Alcoholics Anonymous World Services, Inc., 1972, 1975), p. 13; Robert E. Speer, *The Principles of Jesus* (New York: Association Press, 1902), p. 35; Henry B. Wright, *The Will of God and a Man's Lifework* (New York: The Young Men's Christian Association Press, 1909), p. 187; *What Is The Oxford Group?*, pp. 73-83; A. J. Russell, *For Sinners Only* (London: Hodder & Stoughton, 1932), pp. 320-21;Samuel M. Shoemaker, Jr., *Twice-Born Ministers* (New York: Fleming H. Revell, 1929), p. 150; Clark, *I Will Lift Up Mine Eyes*, pp. 54-60.

[15] Big Book, pp. xxv, 93, 127; Matthew 5:41-42; 16:24-26; Philippians 2:4-8; *Co-Founders*, p. 13; Stephen Foot, *Life Began Yesterday* (New York: Harper & Brothers, 1935), pp. 47, 57, 80; Speer, *The Principles of Jesus*, p. 35; Wright, *The Will of God*, p. 197; Russell, *For Sinners Only*, pp. 324-29.

[16] Big Book, pp. 83-84, 86, 153, 118; Matthew 5:43-46; 1 Corinthians 13; *What is the Oxford Group?*, pp. 107-08; Henry Drummond, *Addresses* (Philadelphia: Henry Altemus, 1892), pp. 11-20, 31-33; Helen Smith Shoemaker, *I Stand By The Door: The Life of Sam Shoemaker* (Texas: Word Books, 1967), p. 24; *Co-Founders*, p. 13; *The Upper Room* for 5/22/35, 9/13/38.

[17] Big Book, pp. 67, 70, 83, 111, 163; 1 Corinthians 13:4; James 1:3-4; Hebrews 10:36; Drummond, *The Greatest Thing in the World*, pp. 28-30; Tileston, *Daily Strength for Daily Needs*, p. 32; *The Upper Room* for 4/24/36 or 4/24/39.

[18] Big Book, pp. 19, 67, 70, 83-84, 118, 125; *Co-Founders*, pp. 4-5; 1 Corinthians 13:5; Drummond, *The Greatest Thing in the World*, pp. 28, 39-46.

[19] Big Book, pp. 67, 82, 83, 86; Ephesians 4:32; 1 Corinthians 13:4; Holm, *The Runner's Bible*, p. 66; Drummond, *The Greatest Thing in the World*, pp. 28, 30-33; *The Upper Room* for 12/26/35.

[20] Big Book, pp. 77, 79, 86; Matthew 6:14-15; Luke 17:3-4; Colossians 3:13; Emmet Fox, *The Sermon on the Mount* (New York: Harper & Row, 1934), pp. 183-91; Holm, *The Runner's Bible*, pp. 82-83, 88.

[21] Big Book, p. xvi; compare p. 292; see also pp. 76-83; Numbers 5:6-7; Russell, *For Sinners Only*, pp. 119-35; *What is The Oxford Group?* pp. 55-65.

17. Grudges.[22]
18. Self-examination (Step Four).[23]
19. Admission of shortcomings or wrongs (Step Five).[24]
20. Setting things right with your brother (Steps Eight and Nine).[25]
21. Guidance of God (Step Eleven—"prayer and meditation").[26]
22. Witnessing (Step Twelve—"passing it on").[27]

---

[22] Big Book, p. 65; James 5:9; Shoemaker, *Twice-Born Ministers*, p. 182; Begbie, *Life Changers*, p. 38; Ebenezer Macmillan, *Seeking and Finding* (New York: Harper & Brothers, 1933), pp. 96-98.

[23] Big Book, pp. 64-71, 76, 84, 86, 98; Matthew 7:3-5; Oswald Chambers, *My Utmost for His Highest* (New Jersey: Barber and Co., 1963), pp. 169, 174; Victor C. Kitchen, *I Was a Pagan* (New York: Harper & Brothers, 1934), pp. 110-11; Russell, *For Sinners Only*, pp. 309-16; Geoffrey Allen, *He That Cometh* (New York: The Macmillan Company, 1933), p. 140; Samuel M. Shoemaker, Jr., *The Church Can Save the World* 2d ed (New York: Harper & Brothers, 1938), pp. 81-121; Dick B., *Anne Smith's Journal, 1933-1939: A.A.'s Principles of Success* (San Rafael, CA: Paradise Research Publications, 1994), pp. 30-31.

[24] Big Book, pp. 72-75; James 5:16; *What Is The Oxford Group?*, p. 29; Samuel M. Shoemaker, Jr., *The Conversion of the Church* (New York: Fleming H. Revell, 1932), pp. 35-39; *The Upper Room* for 12/4/35; Dick B., *Anne Smith's Journal*, pp. 36-41.

[25] Big Book Steps Eight and Nine; Matthew 5:23-26; *DR. BOB and the Good Oldtimers* (New York: Alcoholics Anonymous World Services, 1980), p. 308—this title will hereinafter be called *DR. BOB*; Russell, *For Sinners Only*, p. 120; Leslie D. Weatherhead, *Discipleship* (London: Student Christian Movement, 1934), p. 113; Macmillan, *Seeking and Finding*, p. 176; Shoemaker, *The Conversion of the Church*, pp. 47-48; Holm, *The Runner's Bible*, p. 67; Chambers, *My Utmost for His Highest*, pp. 182-83; *The Upper Room* for 1/12/36 or 1/12/39; E. Stanley Jones, *The Christ of the Mount: A Working Philosophy of Life* (New York: The Abingdon Press, 1930), p. 140.

[26] There are a host of Bible verses connected with this principle. For a discussion of the Big Book materials, the Bible verses, and the roots sources, see Dick B., *New Light on Alcoholism: The A.A. Legacy from Sam Shoemaker* (Corte Madera, CA: Good Book Publishing Company, 1994), pp. 66-67; *Design for Living: The Oxford Group's Contribution to Alcoholics Anonymous* (San Rafael, CA: Paradise Research Publications, 1995), pp. 221-36, 246-69; *The Akron Genesis*, pp. 274-75; *Anne Smith's Journal*, pp. 53-64, 107-16.

[27] Again, there are a host of Bible verses connected with the idea of witnessing. Such verses as (1) Matthew 4:19, containing Jesus's suggestion that his disciples become "fishers of men" (See Shoemaker, *Realizing Religion*, New York: Association Press,

(continued...)

23.   Trust in God.[28]
24.   Draw near to God, and He will draw near to you.[29]
25.   Humble yourself.[30]
26.   Seek ye first the Kingdom of God.[31]
27.   Good Samaritan.[32]

---

[27] (...continued)
1923, p. 82); (2) 2 Corinthians 5:20, containing Paul's writings about being "ambassadors for Christ" (See *The Upper Room* for 8/28/38; *What Is The Oxford Group?*, p. 35); (3) Acts 1:8: "and ye shall be witnesses unto me both in Jerusalem, and in all Judaea, and in Samaria, and unto the uttermost part of the earth" (See Dick B., *Design for Living*, pp. 293-297; *New Light on Alcoholism*, p. 68, for references to A.A. root sources; also *The Upper Room* for 4/11/35). The A.A. expression "pass it on" could well have originated in the following witnessing challenge by Oxford Group founder, Dr. Frank N. D. Buchman, who said: "The best way to keep an experience of Christ is to pass it on" (Frank N. D. Buchman, *Remaking the World: The Speeches of Frank N. D. Buchman*. London: Blandford Press, 1961, p. x).

[28] Big Book, pp. 68, 98; Proverbs 3:5; Jeremiah 17:5-8; Dick B., *Dr. Bob's Library* (San Rafael, CA: Paradise Research Publications, 1994), pp. 96-97; Holm, *The Runner's Bible*, pp. 41-45, 126; *The Upper Room* for 5/15/35; 10/17/35; Tileston, *Daily Strength for Daily Needs*, p. 31. Shoemaker wrote: "People [who] have 'got something' . . . believe in and trust God. They generally trust God as they have come to know Him in Christ." See Samuel M. Shoemaker, Jr., *Religion That Works* (New York: Fleming H. Revell, 1928), pp. 24-25.

[29] Big Book, p. 57; James 4:8; *What Is The Oxford Group?*, p. 17; Chambers, *My Utmost for His Highest*, p. 309.

[30] Big Book, pp. 13, 57, 68; James 4:7, 10; 1 Peter 5:5, 6; Holm, *The Runner's Bible*, pp. 59, 81, 94. Speaking of humility, Dr. Bob said: "I'm talking about the attitude of each and every one of us toward our Heavenly Father. Christ said, 'Of Myself, I am nothing—My strength cometh from My Father in heaven.' If He had to say that, how about you and me?" *Co-founders*, pp. 14-15. Cp. John 5:19, 30; 8:28—which seem to contain the ideas to which Dr. Bob referred.

[31] Big Book, p. 60; compare p. 135; Matthew 6:33; *DR. BOB*, p. 144; Samuel M. Shoemaker, Jr., *National Awakening* (New York: Harper & Brothers, 1936), p. 42; *The Upper Room* for 9/4/35; 11/19/35; 5/20/37; 12/2/38; Oswald Chambers, *Studies in the Sermon on the Mount* 4th ed (London: Simpkin Marshall, n.d.), pp. 60-61; Dick B., *Anne Smith's Journal*, p. 132.

[32] Big Book, p. 97; Luke 10:33-37.

A.A. Slogans and Watchwords with Biblical Roots

Either from Dr. Bob's own explanations, from specific religious literature read by early AAs, or from the nature of the language itself, one can readily identify Biblical concepts in some well-known A.A. slogans and watchwords. They are as follows:

1.   First Things First.[33]
2.   One day at a time.[34]
3.   But for the grace of God.[35]

---

[33] Big Book, p. 135; Matthew 6:33. Dr. Bob stated specifically that "First Things First" came from "Seek ye first the Kingdom of God" in the Sermon on the Mount. See *DR. BOB*, pp. 144, 192. The phrase "First Things First" can also be found in Oxford Group writings such as Howard A. Walter, *Soul Surgery: Some Thoughts on Incisive Personal Work*, 6th ed (London: Blandford Press, n. d.), p. 25; Macmillan, *Seeking and Finding*, p. 17.

[34] Matthew 6:34: "Take therefore no thought [be not anxious] for the morrow: for the morrow shall take thought for the things of itself. Sufficient unto the day is the evil thereof." The popular A.A. idea ("one day at a time") was specifically taught by Dr. Bob's wife, Anne Smith, in her journal. See Dick B., *Anne Smith's Journal*, pp. 50, 53-54, 59, 62 63, 134. Dr. Bob stated that the A.A. expression "Easy Does It" means "you take it a day at a time;" *DR. BOB*, p. 282. And Dr. Bob informed his sponsee, Clarence Snyder, that the concept of "one day at a time" came from Matthew 6:34 in the Sermon on the Mount. Mitch K., Clarence's A.A. sponsee, provided the information about Matthew 6:34 to the author in a personal interview in Charleston, West Virginia, in August, 1992. See also *The Upper Room* for 11/25/35; 8/17/37; 9/26/38; 6/19/36 or 6/19/39.

[35] Big Book, p. 25; Luke 2:40; Acts 11:23; Romans 5:15; 2 Corinthians 1:12. AAs are very familiar with the Biblical expression—the Grace of God—which connotes that their recovery appears neither to have been deserved nor earned, but rather came to them as a gift because of the love of a gracious God. Anne Smith wrote, for example: "Takes whole power of Christ to help us do the smallest thing. Step that puts man in position to receive Grace of God who alone commands;" Dick B., *Anne Smith's Journal*, p. 24. Bill Wilson wrote: "We knew that ours was a fellowship of the Spirit and that the grace of God was there;" *Alcoholics Anonymous Comes of Age* (New York: Alcoholics Anonymous World Services, 1957), p. 44. Dr. Bob said: "I don't believe I have any right to get cocky about getting sober. It's only through God's grace that I did it." *Co-founders*, p. 15.

4.   Easy Does It.[36]
5.   Let go and let God.[37]

Two Other Biblical Concepts

There are two other important concepts found in A.A. history and traditions that also seem to have Biblical roots.

The Erring Tongue

The first concerns the idea of "guarding that erring member, the tongue." James 3:1-13 discusses at some length the trouble that the tongue can cause. In a major A.A. address, Dr. Bob cautioned AAs about the hurtful use of the tongue.[38] Dr. Bob's wife, Anne, was also concerned about the hurtfulness of the loose tongue; for she spoke of the problem several times in her spiritual journal.[39] And the admonitions in the Book of James were noticed by other A.A. roots sources.[40]

---

[36] Big Book, p. 135; Matthew 6:34. As discussed above in connection with "one day at a time," Dr. Bob explained to his sponsee, Clarence Snyder, that "Easy Does It" and "One day at a time" were synonymous in their meaning; and that Matthew 6:34 was the source of the expression; see also Dick B., *The Akron Genesis*, p. 118.

[37] That "let go and let God" is an expression commonly heard in A.A. is beyond doubt. The author has personally heard it many times in A.A. meetings. See also Bill Wilson's use of the expression in *Alcoholics Anonymous Comes of Age*, p. 48. But the Biblical origins, if any, are less clear. The expression was common among A.A.'s religious sources. See, for example, Clarence I. Benson, *The Eight Points of the Oxford Group* (London: Oxford University Press, 1936), p. 68; Clark, *The Soul's Sincere Desire*, p. 60. The expression's closest Biblical relative can perhaps be found in Shoemaker's *National Awakening* where Shoemaker utilized the Moffatt translation of Psalm 46:10. Shoemaker said we need to "give in," and admit that God is God, and self is not God (pp. 45-51).

[38] *Co-Founders*, p. 5; *DR. BOB*, p. 338.

[39] Dick B., *Anne Smith's Journal*, pp. 28, 44, 76, 77.

[40] Tileston, *Daily Strength for Daily Needs*, p. 324; Walter, *Soul Surgery*, p. 62.

The Principle of Anonymity

We have located no A.A. writings which credit the all important anonymity principle of Alcoholics Anonymous to the Bible. Yet Dr. Bob certainly felt A.A.'s philosophy came from the Sermon on the Mount; and Bill Wilson certainly stressed anonymity as a spiritual principle.

A.A.'s Eleventh and Twelfth Traditions in the "long form" state in part:

> Our relations with the general public should be characterized by personal anonymity. We think A.A. ought to avoid sensational advertising. . . . There is never need to praise ourselves. We feel it better to let our friends recommend us. And finally, we of Alcoholics Anonymous believe that the principle of anonymity has an immense spiritual significance.[41]

In his Sermon on the Mount, Jesus repeatedly proclaimed a principle of anonymity and in several ways. In Matthew 6:1, Jesus said:

> Take heed that ye do not your alms before men, to be seen of them; otherwise ye have no reward of your Father which is in heaven.

Jesus then denounced as hypocrites those who did their alms in public and who "sound a trumpet before thee . . . that they may have the glory of men." He said alms should be given in secret and that God, who sees in secret, will reward openly.[42] Jesus took the same position as to prayer, denouncing those who "love to pray standing in the synagogues and in the corners of the streets, that they may be seen of men." He told his followers to enter into a closet and pray to the Father in secret.[43]

---

[41] Big Book, pp. 567-68.

[42] Matthew 6:1-4.

[43] Matthew 6:5-6.

He also cautioned against "vain repetitions" [as to prayers], saying "your Father knoweth what things ye have need of, before ye ask him."[44] Then Jesus taught his followers the Lord's Prayer (Matthew 6:9-13).

Jesus concluded his anonymity teaching by declaring that "fasting" should also be done in secret to avoid hypocrisy.[45] In other words, Jesus devoted a large segment of his Sermon on the Mount to the proposition that people should not be showing off before men in their almsgiving, prayers, and fasting, but rather should address themselves to God for such reward as God gives for such actions. And many of A.A.'s root sources discuss these Biblical principles at some length.[46]

Bill Wilson said of the anonymity principles in A.A.'s Traditions Eleven and Twelve:

> So the Eleventh Tradition stands sentinel over the lifelines, announcing that there is no need for self-praise . . . no press agents, no promotional devices, no big names. . . . One may say that anonymity is the spiritual base, the sure key to all the rest of our Traditions. It has come to stand for prudence and, most importantly, for self-effacement. . . . In it we see the cornerstone of our security as a movement; at a deeper spiritual level it points us to still greater self-renunciation.[47]

While Bill did not, in these phrases, tie self-effacement and self-renunciation to worship of God, he did speak of the end of serving God; and Bill's Twelve Steps and Twelve Traditions certainly do rest on the idea of surrender of self to God. We believe, therefore,

---

[44] Matthew 6:7-8. See Dick B., *Anne Smith's Journal*, p. 57 [the verse is erroneously cited as Matthew 6:33 in that title].

[45] Matthew 6:16-18.

[46] *The Upper Room* for 5/11/35; 8/22/35; 10/21/35; 7/25/37; 6/26/38; Holm, *The Runner's Bible*, pp. 61-62; E. Stanley Jones, *The Christ of the Mount*, pp. 200, 203, 206; Harry Emerson Fosdick, *The Meaning of Prayer* (New York: Association Press, 1915), p. 57; Clark, *The Soul's Sincere Desire*, pp. 38-39, 54-54.

[47] *The Language of the Heart*, pp. 91-94.

that the principles of anonymity Jesus taught were probably a cornerstone of the self-effacement ideas in A.A.'s Traditions considering A.A.'s own emphasis on the Sermon on the Mount as embodying its spiritual philosophy.

4

The Parts Dr. Bob Found "Essential"

Dr. Bob had said in his last major address to AAs in Detroit that he and the older members of A.A. considered the thirteenth chapter of First Corinthians, the Book of James, and the Sermon on the Mount to be "absolutely essential" to their successful recovery program. And we believe you will want to know what the early AAs took from those Bible sources. We also believe you have seen, and will see throughout this book, how the various segments of those particular Biblical materials seem quite clearly to have influenced or found their way into the Big Book and the Twelve Steps. We think those materials so important that they justify a separate item-by-item review at this point.

The Thirteenth Chapter of First Corinthians

1 Corinthians 13 is often called the Bible's "love" chapter because it focuses on the importance of love in the Christian's life. In the King James Version, the word "charity" is used, but the underlying Greek word is *agapē*, which is more properly translated "love." And the most significant characteristics of love are found in the following verses:

> Charity [love] suffereth long, *and* is kind; charity envieth not; charity vaunteth not itself, is not puffed up, Doth not behave itself

unseemly, seeketh not her own, is not easily provoked, thinketh no evil, Rejoiceth not in iniquity, but rejoiceth in the truth (1 Corinthians 13:4-6).

One of the most popular books in early A.A. was Professor Henry Drummond's study of 1 Corinthians 13.[1] The title of the book, *The Greatest Thing in the World*, was taken from the last verse of the Corinthians chapter, which read:

And now abideth faith, hope, charity, these three; but the greatest of these *is* charity (1 Corinthians 13:13).[2]

Drummond's book was part of Dr. Bob's library, and a copy is still owned by Dr. Bob's family.[3] A.A. oldtimer Bob E. sent a memo to Bill Wilson's wife, Lois, in which Bob E. listed *The Greatest Thing in the World* as one of three books Dr. Bob regularly provided to alcoholics with whom he worked.[4] In fact, Dr. Bob's enthusiasm for Drummond's book is dramatized by the following remarks of Dorothy S. M.:

---

[1] Henry Drummond, *Addresses* (Philadelphia: Henry Altemus, 1892). Drummond's study of 1 Corinthians 13 has been reprinted many times; and we shall use here for our citations the following popular edition: Henry Drummond, *The Greatest Thing in the World and other addresses* with introduction by J. Y. Simpson (World Bible Publishers, Inc., n.d.). The wide use of Drummond's book in early A.A. is discussed in *DR. BOB and the Good Oldtimers* (New York: Alcoholics Anonymous World Services, Inc., 1980), pp. 151, 310. See also Dick B., *Anne Smith's Journal, 1933-1939: A.A.'s Principles of Success* (San Rafael, CA: Paradise Research Publications, 1994), p. 131; *The Books Early AAs Read for Spiritual Growth*, 2d ed (San Rafael, CA: Paradise Research Publications, 1994), pp. 1, 7, 9, 29; *Dr. Bob's Library: Books for Twelve Step Growth* (San Rafael, CA: Paradise Research Publications, 1994), pp. xi, 12-14, 18, 21, 41, 43, 53, 60, 64, 82, 92.

[2] See Drummond, *The Greatest Thing in the World*, pp.18-19. See also references in *The Upper Room* for 10/8/35; 9/11/38.

[3] Dick B., *Dr. Bob's Library*, pp. 41-42.

[4] Dick B., *Dr. Bob's Library*, pp. 21. The other two books that were mentioned by Bob E. and regularly provided to alcoholics by Dr. Bob were James Allen's *As a Man Thinketh* and Emmet Fox's *The Sermon on the Mount*.

Once, when I was working on a woman in Cleveland, I called and asked him [Dr. Bob], "What do I do for somebody who is going into D.T.'s?" He told me to give her the medication, and he said, "When she comes out of it and she decides she wants to be a different woman, get her Drummond's 'The Greatest Thing in the World.' Tell her to read it through every day for 30 days, and she'll be a different woman."[5]

Interestingly, Henry Drummond himself had made a similar suggestion at the close of the lecture in which he delivered his "greatest thing in the world" address, which later became incorporated in his best-selling book. Drummond said:

Now I have all but finished. How many of you will join me in reading this chapter [1 Corinthians 13] once a week for the next three months? A man did that once and it changed his whole life. Will you do it? It is for the greatest thing in the world. You might begin by reading it every day, especially the verses which describe the perfect character. "Love suffereth long, and is kind; loveth envieth not; love vaunteth not itself." Get these ingredients into your life.[6]

The important Drummond influence on A.A. from 1 Corinthians 13 can be seen from Drummond's own simplified description of love's *ingredients*. Drummond listed nine.[7] And we here set them forth with footnote references to correlative A.A. ideas:

---

[5] *DR. BOB and the Good Oldtimers* (New York: Alcoholics Anonymous World Services, Inc., 1980), p. 310. Hereinafter this title is called *DR. BOB.*

[6] Drummond, *The Greatest Thing in the World*, p. 53.

[7] Drummond, *The Greatest Thing in the World*, pp. 26-27.

Drummond's Version of Meaning	Authorized (King James) Version
1. Patience	"Love suffereth long."[8]
2. Kindness	"And is kind."[9]
3. Generosity	"Love envieth not."[10]
4. Humility	"Love vaunteth not itself, is not puffed up."[11]
5. Courtesy	"Doth not behave itself unseemly."[12]
6. Unselfishness	"Seeketh not her own."[13]
7. Good Temper	"Is not easily provoked."[14]
8. Guilelessness	"Thinketh no evil."[15]
9. Sincerity	"Rejoiceth not in iniquity, but rejoiceth in truth."[16]

---

[8] See our discussion of "patience" in connection with the Book of James where we cite the frequent occurrences of the *patience* principle in the Big Book. **Big Book** is a registered trademark of Alcoholics Anonymous World Services, Inc.; used here with permission of A.A.W.S.

[9] Big Book, pp. 67, 82, 83, 86.

[10] See our discussion of "envy" and "jealousy" in connection with the Book of James, with citations as to the occurrence of these words and ideas in the Big Book.

[11] See our discussion of "humility" in connection with the Book of James, with citations of the occurrences of this principle in the Big Book.

[12] Drummond said, at page 31: "Courtesy is said to be love in little things." He equated it with being "considerate." And the Big Book stresses this latter principle (p. 69).

[13] "Absolute Unselfishness" was one of the four standards embodied in the Oxford Group's Four Absolutes. And the Big Book specifically decries "selfishness" many times (pp. 62, 69, 84, 86).

[14] Drummond wrote at length on the vice of "ill temper," pointing out that it involved want of patience, want of kindness, want of generosity, want of courtesy, and want of unselfishness. Drummond said all are instantly symbolized in one flash of Temper. Certainly one aspect of such Temper is *lack of tolerance*, And the Big Book stressed the principle of tolerance and used the slogan, "Live and let live," to symbolize the importance of tolerance (Big Book, pp. 19, 67, 70, 83-84, 125, 118, 135).

[15] Drummond essentially equates this principle with looking on the bright side, looking for the best in others. Perhaps his analysis equates with A.A. stress on unselfishness, tolerance, and certainly on love.

[16] Here Drummond covered a cardinal A.A. spiritual principle—*honesty*. Honesty was one of the Oxford Group's Four Absolutes; and the principle appears throughout the Big Book as a vital spiritual concept (Big Book, pp. xiv, xxvii, 13, 26, 28, 32, 44, 47, 55, 57-58, 63-65, 67, 70, 73, 117, 140, 145).

Dr. Bob stressed that A.A.'s steps could be simmered down to love and service.[17] He presented God as a God of love.[18] Dr. Bob's wife, Anne, frequently quoted the "God is love" verses in 1 John 4:8; 4:16.[19] Dr. Bob and Anne both studied Kagawa's book on love.[20] Kagawa devoted an entire chapter of his book not only to 1 Corinthians 13, but also to Drummond's analysis of chapter Thirteen of 1 Corinthians in Drummond's *The Greatest Thing in the World*.[21] And the Big Book itself talks repeatedly of the principle of love.[22]

Jesus Christ's greatest message, as stated in Mark 12:30-31, concerned the two great commandments on love:

And thou shalt love the Lord thy God with all thy heart, and with all thy soul, and with all thy mind, and with all thy strength; this is the first commandment. And the second is like, namely this, Thou shalt love thy neighbor as thyself. There is none other commandment greater than these.[23]

The foregoing verses from Mark were cited for the standard of "Absolute Love," as it was discussed in Akron's *A Manual for*

---

[17] *DR. BOB*, p. 338.

[18] *DR. BOB*, p. 110.

[19] *DR. BOB*, pp. 116, 117. See also *The Upper Room* for 5/24/36, 5/4/37, 8/22/37; Nora Smith Holm, *The Runner's Bible* (New York: Houghton Mifflin Company, 1915), pp. 6, 27, 29, 31-32. In a telephone conversation held May 23, 1995, Dr. Bob's son, Robert R. Smith, confirmed to the author that *both* Dr. Bob and Anne frequently used *The Runner's Bible* for prayer and meditation; and the pages just cited from *The Runner's Bible* quote 1 John 4:16 and the entirety of 1 Corinthians 13.

[20] Toyohiko Kagawa, *Love The Law of Life* (Philadelphia: The John C. Winston Company, 1929). Dick B., *Dr. Bob's Library*, pp. 40-41; *Anne Smith's Journal*, pp. 83-85.

[21] Kagawa, *Love the Law of Life*, pp. 137-44.

[22] Big Book, pp. 83-84, 86, 118, 122, 153.

[23] See also Luke 10:27 and Holm, *The Runner's Bible*, p. 27; Harry Emerson Fosdick, *The Meaning of Faith* (New York: The Abingdon Press, 1917), p. 104; Mary W. Tileston, *Daily Strength for Daily Needs* 1977 printing (New York: Grosset and Dunlap, 1884), p. 205; *The Upper Room* for 5/19/37; T. R. Glover, *The Jesus of History* (New York: Association Press, 1919), p. 60.

Alcoholics Anonymous, from which we have previously quoted. The Old Testament contained the same commandments.[24]

We believe—from examining 1 Corinthians 13; from the frequent mention of "love" in the Big Book; from studying the reading and remarks of Dr. Bob and Anne; from Bill Wilson's mention of Corinthians, and from the repeated mention of 1 Corinthians 13 in A.A.'s religious sources—that the love ingredients summarized by Henry Drummond probably had a direct impact on Twelve Step principles and Big Book language.[25]

The Book of James

Of probably even greater importance in early A.A. was the Book of James. It was much studied by A.A.'s co-founders.[26] Quotes and ideas from the Apostle James can be found throughout the Big Book and in A.A. literature. The book was considered so important that many favored calling the A.A. fellowship the "James Club."[27] And even the most fundamental phrases in A.A. such as "It Works" and Bill Wilson's own "Works Publishing Company," which published the First Edition of the Big Book,

---

[24] Deuteronomy 6:5; Leviticus 19:18. See also B. H. Streeter, *The God Who Speaks* (London: Macmillan & Co., 1943), pp. 48-49.

[25] See also the discussions in Glenn Clark's books which were read by A.A.'s founders and much used by some of the early AAs. Glenn Clark, *The Soul's Sincere Desire* (Boston: Little, Brown, and Company, 1927), pp. 69-70; *I Will Lift Up Mine Eyes* (New York: Harper & Brothers, 1937), pp. 65-66; also, Clarence I. Benson, *The Eight Points of the Oxford Group: An Exposition for Christians and Pagans* (London: Oxford University Press, 1936), p. 47.

[26] *DR. BOB*, pp. 71, 213; Dick B., *Design for Living: The Oxford Group's Contribution to Early A.A.* (San Rafael, CA: Paradise Research Publications, 1995), pp. 10-12; *The Akron Genesis of Alcoholics Anonymous* (Corte Madera, CA: Good Book Publishing Company, 1994), pp. 272-73; *Dr. Bob's Library*, pp. 9, 12, 38, 82, 89, 90; *Anne Smith's Journal*, pp. 36, 38, 40, 76, 99, 122, 129, 131, 138, 144.

[27] *DR. BOB*, p. 71; *Pass It On: The Story of Bill Wilson and how the A.A. Message Reached the World* (New York: Alcoholics Anonymous World Services, 1984), p. 147.

may have had their origin in the "Faith without works is dead" ideas in James.[28]

We will therefore review the Book of James, chapter by chapter. As we do so, we will point to traces of that book which we believe can be found in, or probably influenced the text of the Big Book. At the outset, we would report that as our research into the Biblical roots of A.A. has progressed, so has our understanding of some root sources that previously went unnoticed.

For example, some time back, Dr. Bob's son, Bob Smith, told the author by phone that his father had placed great stake in *The Runner's Bible*.[29] We had encountered difficulty locating a copy. And we were still looking for some commentary on the Book of James similar to the many on the Sermon on the Mount (by Oswald Chambers, Glenn Clark, Emmet Fox, and E. Stanley Jones) and on 1 Corinthians 13 (by Henry Drummond, for example) which Dr. Bob had studied.[30] We believed such commentaries probably impacted upon the thinking of Dr. Bob, Anne, Henrietta, and the early AAs as have the actual Bible verses in Matthew 5, 6, and 7, and 1 Corinthians 13 . But we could find no similar commentary on the Book of James despite A.A.'s emphasis on James. Finally, as we were preparing this current title on the Good Book, we noticed in *The Runner's Bible* the frequency with which all Dr. Bob's "essential" books and chapters of the Bible (Matthew 5, 6, 7; 1 Corinthians 13; and James) were there mentioned. And we particularly noticed the frequency with which *The Runner's Bible* mentioned and discussed verses from the Book of James.

---

[28] See, for example, Big Book, p. 88: "It works—it really does. . . . Faith without works is dead;" Nell Wing, *Grateful to Have Been There* (Illinois: Parkside Publishing, 1992), pp. 70-71.

[29] This book is mentioned in A.A's memorial issue on Dr. Bob's death—*RHS* (New York: AA Grapevine, Inc., 1951), p. 34. Dr. Bob owned, loaned out, and on one occasion actually sent this and another spiritual book to a friend who was having trouble with anger. See also Dick B., *Dr. Bob's Library*, pp. 30-31.

[30] Dick B., *Dr. Bob's Library*, pp. 38-42.

Hence our reader will find many references to *The Runner's Bible* in our footnotes on James; for we believe that this little devotional book may have provided Dr. Bob, Anne Smith, and perhaps even Bill Wilson, with much of the fodder that caused them to focus on James and conclude that James was their "favorite" book of the Bible. In a phone conversation with the author in 1995, from his home in Texas, Dr. Bob's son stated he felt it would be almost impossible to confirm that *The Runner's Bible* was the source of either A.A.'s or its founders' emphasis on James and other Biblical sources. But he pointed out that this little Biblical reference was used by those who wanted a quick and easy source for Biblical ideas in which they were interested. Perhaps, then, that book became a reference source for Dr. Bob, Anne, and even Bill Wilson when they were studying the pertinent Biblical ideas they extracted from 1 Corinthians 13, the Sermon on the Mount, and James.

James Chapter 1

1. *Patience*. Chapter One is not the only chapter in the Book of James which mentions patience.[31] Nor is it the only portion of the Bible that stresses patience.[32] But James was a favored Biblical source in early A.A., and James 1:3-4 states:

> Knowing *this*, that the trying of your faith worketh patience. But let patience have *her* perfect work, that ye may be perfect and entire, wanting nothing.[33]

---

[31] See also James 5:7-11: "Be *patient*, therefore, brethren, unto the coming of the Lord. . . . Be ye also *patient*; stablish your hearts; for the coming of the Lord draweth nigh . . . ; Take, my brethren, the prophets, who have spoken in the name of the Lord, for example of suffering affliction, and of *patience*. Behold, we count them happy which endure. Ye have heard of the *patience* of Job, and have seen the end of the Lord; that the Lord is very pitiful, and of tender mercy" (italics added).

[32] See, for example, Hebrews 10:36: "For ye have need of *patience*, that, after ye have done the will of God, ye might receive the promise" (italics added). See Tileston, *Daily Strength for Daily Needs*, p. 325.

[33] See Tileston, *Daily Strength for Daily Needs*, pp. 32, 48; *The Upper Room* for 4/24/36 or 4/24/39.

Patience certainly wound up as one of the most frequently mentioned spiritual principles in the Big Book.[34]

2. *Asking wisdom of God with unwavering believing.* James 1:5-8 states:

> If any of you lack wisdom, let him ask of God, that giveth to all
> *men* liberally, and upbraideth not; and it shall be given him.
> But let him ask in faith, nothing wavering. For he that wavereth
> is like a wave of the sea driven with the wind and tossed.
> For let not that man think that he shall receive anything of the
> Lord.
> A double minded man *is* unstable in all his ways.[35]

Asking for God's direction and strength and receiving "Guidance" from Him, are major themes in both the Old and New Testaments, and were important Oxford Group ideas as well. We discussed them at length in our titles on the Oxford Group and on Anne Smith's spiritual journal.[36] And the Big Book, including the Eleventh Step itself, is filled with such Guidance concepts.[37]

3. *Every good and perfect gift comes from God, the Father of lights.* James 1:17 states:

---

[34] Big Book, pp. 67, 70, 83, 111, 118, 163.

[35] These verses were discussed in Holm, *The Runner's Bible*, pp. 51, 60, 62; and in other favorites of Dr. Bob and Henrietta Seiberling such as Glenn Clark, *The Soul's Sincere Desire* (Boston: Little, Brown, 1927), p. 59; *I Will Lift Up Mine Eyes*, pp. 136-37; Harry Emerson Fosdick, *The Meaning of Prayer* (New York: Association Press, 1915), p. 118.

[36] Dick B., *Design for Living*, pp. 246-69, 319-22, 337-38; *New Light on Alcoholism: The A.A. Legacy from Sam Shoemaker* (Corte Madera, CA: Good Book Publishing, 1994), pp. 66-67; *Anne Smith's Journal*, pp. 53-64, 107-116. See also Holm, *The Runner's Bible*, pp. 126-30; Oswald Chambers, *My Utmost for His Highest* (New Jersey: Barbour and Company, 1963), pp. 155, 319.

[37] Big Book, pp. 13, 46, 49, 62-63, 69-70, 76, 79-80, 83, 84-88, 100, 117, 120, 124, 158, 164.

Every good gift and every perfect gift is from above, and cometh down from the Father of lights, with whom is no variableness, neither shadow of turning.

Bill seemed to be referring to this verse when he wrote on page 14 of the Big Book:

I must turn in all things to the Father of Light [*sic*] who presides over us all.[38]

The Big Book often describes God as a loving and providing God.[39]

4. *Let every man be slow to speak, slow to wrath.* James 1:19-20 states:

Wherefore, my beloved brethren, let every man be swift to hear, slow to speak, slow to wrath: For the wrath of man worketh not the righteousness of God.

The verse is quoted in *The Runner's Bible* and seems quite relevant to the Big Book's injunction, "If we were to live, we had to be free of anger. . . . God save me from being angry."[40]

---

[38] Note that at the conclusion of the "Long Form" Twelve Traditions in Appendix One of the Big Book, Bill wrote: "To the end that our great blessings may never spoil us; that we shall forever live in thankful contemplation of Him who presides over us all" (Big Book, p. 568). See Holm, *The Runner's Bible*, p. 9, quoting: "The Father of lights, with whom is no variableness, neither shadow of turning." Dr. Bob perhaps mentioned this concept of God as a good and loving provider in his last major address in 1948, stating: "Christ said, 'Of Myself, I am nothing—My strength cometh from My Father in heaven.' If He had to say that, how about you and me?" See *The Co-Founders of Alcoholics Anonymous* (New York: A.A. World Services, Inc., 1972, 1975), p. 15. Compare 1 John 1:5: "This then is the message which we have heard of Him, and declare unto you, that God is light, and in Him is no darkness at all."

[39] Big Book, pp. 10-11, 13, 25, 28, 49, 52, 56-57, 59, 63, 68, 76, 83, 85, 100, 117, 120, 124, 130, 133, 158, 161, 164. See also Holm, *The Runner's Bible*, pp. 65, 140.

[40] Holm, *The Runner's Bible*, pp. 31, 49; Big Book, pp. 66-67.

5. *Be ye doers of the word, and not hearers only.* James 1:21-22 states:

> Wherefore lay apart all filthiness and superfluity of naughtiness, and receive with meekness the engrafted word, which is able to save your souls.
> But be ye doers of the word, and not hearers only, deceiving your own selves.

Shoemaker devoted an entire chapter in one of his titles to this verse, stating:

> I think St. James' meaning is made much clearer in Dr. Moffatt's translation, "Act on the Word, instead of merely listening to it." Try it out in experiment, and prove it by its results—otherwise you only fool yourself into believing that you have the heart of religion when you haven't.[41]

In the same chapter, Shoemaker also pointed out that prayer is often more a struggle to find God than the enjoyment of Him and cooperation with His will. He added that "God is and is a Rewarder of them that seek Him."[42]

We cannot find a specific reference to James 1:21-22 in the Big Book; but A.A. stresses over and over that A.A. is a program of *action*,[43] that probably no human power can relieve a person of alcoholism, and "That God could and would if He were *sought*" (p. 60). A.A.'s program emphasizes action in the experiment of faith it adopted from John 7:17—*seeking* God by *following* the path that leads to a relationship with God.[44] James 1:22 stresses *doing*

---

[41] Samuel M. Shoemaker, *The Gospel According to You* (New York: Fleming H. Revell, 1934), pp. 45-55; Holm, *The Runner's Bible*, pp. 47, 135, 148; Tileston, *Daily Strength for Daily Needs*, p. 272. For the full text, see James 1:21-25.

[42] Hebrews 11:6; Shoemaker, *The Gospel According to You*, p. 47.

[43] Big Book, pp. 14-15, 19, 25, 57, 59-60, 63-64, 72, 75-77, 85, 87-88, 89-103.

[44] As to relationship with God, see Big Book, pp. 13, 28-29, 72, 100, 164; compare p. 452. As to the path, see Big Book, pp. xxii, 15, 58, 72, 100, 116; compare p. 349.

God's will as expressed in His Word—not merely listening to it. James was an Akron favorite. Shoemaker was a Wilson favorite. "Faith without works" was a Big Book favorite; and it therefore seems possible that A.A.'s stress on *action* might have derived from in part from James 1:21-22.

6. *Pure religion and undefiled before God . . . to visit the fatherless and widows in their affliction.* James 1:27 states:

> Pure religion and undefiled before God and the Father is this, To visit the fatherless and widows in their affliction, *and* to keep oneself unspotted from the world.

At the very least, this verse bespeaks unselfishness and helpfulness to others which were cardinal A.A. principles.[45]

James Chapter 2

Chapter Two of the Book of James may have made two direct and major contributions to the language of the Big Book and also to A.A.'s philosophy. The concepts were "Love thy neighbor as thyself" and "Faith without works is dead."

1. *Love thy neighbor as thyself.* James 2:8 states:

> If ye fulfill the royal law according to the scripture, Thou shalt love thy neighbor as thyself, ye do well.

This commandment, "Love thy neighbor," exists in other parts of both the Old and New Testaments. Thus, when the Big Book uses this phrase, we cannot say for sure whether the quote is from

---

[45] See Holm, *The Runner's Bible*, p. 78; Tileston, *Daily Strength for Daily Needs*, p. 251; Big Book, pp. 14, 20, 89, 159.

James or from one of the other Bible verses to the same effect.[46] But the Big Book certainly does state:

> Then you will know what it means to give of yourself that others may survive and rediscover life. You will learn the full meaning of "Love thy neighbor as thyself" (p. 153).[47]

James seems a very probable source for this Biblical quote since Dr. Bob favored both the "love" concept *and* the Book of James.[48]

2. *Faith without works is dead*. Said to be the favorite verse of Anne Smith and perhaps the origin of many expressions in A.A. concerning "works," this expression, or variations of it, appear several times in Chapter Two of the Book of James.[49] For example, James 2:20 states:

> But wilt thou know, O vain man, that faith without works is dead?

The "faith without works" phrase and its action concept are quoted or referred to many times in the Big Book.[50] Oxford Group people also put emphasis on these James verses, using them in connection with the importance of witnessing.[51]

---

[46] See Matthew 5:43; 19:19; 22:39; Mark 12:31; 12:33; Luke 10:27; Romans 13:9; Galatians 5:14; Leviticus 19:18.

[47] See also Big Book, p. 236. And review James 2:14-17, which specifically discusses helping a brother or sister who is naked and in lack of daily food. See also Holm, *The Runner's Bible*, pp. 77-78.

[48] *DR. BOB*, pp. 338, 110; and see Holm, *The Runner's Bible*, p. 28; Tileston, *Daily Strength for Daily Needs*, p. 46.

[49] James 2:14, 17-18, 20, 22, 26. See Wing, *Grateful to Have Been There*, pp. 70-71.

[50] Big Book, pp. 14-15, 76, 88, 93, 97.

[51] See The Layman with a Notebook, *What Is The Oxford Group?* (London: Oxford University Press, 1933), pp. 35-38.

James Chapter 3

1. *Taming the tongue.* In his Farewell Address to A.A., Dr. Bob said:

> Let us also remember to guard that erring member the tongue, and if we must use it, let's use it with kindness and consideration and tolerance.[52]

A major portion of James, Chapter Three, is devoted to the trouble that can be caused by an untamed tongue.[53] These are a few of the verses:

> Even so the tongue is a little member and boasteth great things. Behold, how great a matter a little fire kindleth! And the tongue *is* a fire, a world of iniquity; so is the tongue among our members that it defileth the whole body, and setteth on fire the course of nature; and *it is* set on fire of hell. . . . But the tongue can no man tame; it is an unruly evil, full of deadly poison.
> . . . Out of the same mouth proceedeth blessing and cursing. My brethren, these things ought not to be.

These verses do not appear in the Big Book. But Anne Smith referred to them frequently in her journal, as did other A.A. roots sources.[54] But, in paraphrasing the verses, Dr. Bob seemed to be speaking of tolerance, courtesy, consideration, and kindness. James said that good *conversation* should be a focus—conversation, we believe, laced with consideration, kindness, and tolerance.[55] And these latter principles *are* very much stressed in the Big Book.[56]

---

[52] *DR. BOB*, p. 338.

[53] James 3:1-13.

[54] Dick B., *Anne Smith's Journal*, pp. 28, 44, 76, 77; Holm, *The Runner's Bible*, p. 68; Tileston, *Daily Strength for Daily Needs*, p. 324; *The Upper Room* for 9/22/38; Walter, *Soul Surgery*, p. 62. See also James 1:26.

[55] See James 3:13.

[56] Big Book, pp. 67, 69-70, 83-84, 97, 118, 125, 135.

2. *Avoidance of envy, strife, and lying.* James 3:14-16 makes clear that a heart filled with envy, strife, and lies is not receiving wisdom from God, but rather from devilish sources. The verses state:

> But if ye have bitter envying and strife in your hearts; glory not, and lie not against the truth.
> This wisdom descendeth not from above, but is earthly, sensual, devilish.
> For where envying and strife is, there is confusion and every evil work.

We do not find "envy" as much decried in the Big Book as jealousy; but a more modern translation of these King James verses equates "envy" *with* "jealousy."[57] And the Big Book most assuredly condemns jealously.[58] In fact, it states as to jealousy *and* envy:

> Keep it always in sight that we are dealing with that most terrible human emotion—jealousy (p. 82).

> The greatest enemies of us alcoholics are resentment, jealousy, envy, frustration, and fear (p. 145).

As to strife, the Big Book states:

> After all, our problems were of our own making. Bottles were only a symbol. Besides, we have stopped fighting anybody or anything. We have to (p. 103)![59]

---

[57] *The Revised English Bible* (London: Oxford University Press, 1989), New Testament, p. 208.

[58] Big Book, pp. 37, 69, 82, 100, 119, 145, 161.

[59] See James 3:17-18: "But the wisdom that is from above is first pure, then peaceable, gentle, *and* easy to be intreated, full of mercy and good fruits, without partiality, and without hypocrisy. And the fruit of righteousness is sown in peace of them that make peace." And see Holm, *The Runner's Bible*, pp. 46, 54.

On the lying and dishonesty counts, we point to the Four Absolutes, and suggest the frequency with which the Big Book emphasizes A.A.'s requirement of grasping and developing a manner of living which "demands rigorous honesty" (p. 58).[60] In the case of James 3:14-16, however, we move farther from the level of certainty that these particular verses were an exclusive or even major source for the traits of envy, jealousy, strife, and dishonesty, decried also in many other parts of the Bible.[61]

James Chapter 4

1. *Asking amiss for selfish ends.* We shall have much more to say about selfishness and self-centeredness. But we do point to the following in James 4:3:

> Ye ask, and receive not, because ye ask amiss, that ye may consume it upon your lusts.

Some Christian sources that were favorites of Dr. Bob's discuss this verse at length.[62] And the Big Book authors may have obtained from James 4:3 their inspiration for the following:

> We ask especially for freedom from self-will, and are careful to make no request for ourselves only. We may ask for ourselves, however, if others will be helped. We are careful never to pray for our own selfish ends. Many of us have wasted a lot of time doing that and it doesn't work (p. 87).

---

[60] See also Big Book: (1) p. 58: "Those who do not recover are people who cannot or will not completely give themselves to this simple program, usually men and women who are constitutionally incapable of being honest with themselves." (2) p. 58: "many of them do recover if they have the capacity to be honest." (3) p. 64: "We took stock honestly." (4) p. 65: "Nothing counted but thoroughness and honesty."

[61] See, however, Holm, *The Runner's Bible*, p. 54.

[62] See Clark, *The Soul's Sincere Desire*, p. 35; Holm, *The Runner's Bible*, p. 60; *The Upper Room* for 6/17/36.

2. *Humility*. The Book of James has no corner on the Biblical injunction to be humble.[63] But the importance of James, and the remarks of Shoemaker under Item 3 immediately below, suggest that the following verses from James may have been a source of the Big Book ideas quoted below. James 4:7, 10 state:

> Submit yourselves therefore to God. Resist the devil, and he will flee from you.
> Humble yourselves in the sight of the Lord, and he shall lift you up.[64]

The Big Book is filled with discussions of humility, of humbling one's own self before God, and of humbly asking for His help. Examples include:

> There I humbly offered myself to God, as I understood Him, to do with me as He would (p. 13).

> He humbly offered himself to his Maker—then he knew (p. 57).

> Just to the extent that we do as we think He would have us, and humbly rely on Him, does He enable us to match calamity with serenity (p. 68).

> We constantly remind ourselves we are no longer running the show, humbly saying to ourselves many times each day "Thy will be done" (pp. 87-88).[65]

3. *Trusting God and cleaning house*. James 4:8 states:

> Draw nigh to God, and he will draw nigh to you. Cleanse your hands, ye sinners; and purify your hearts, ye double minded.[66]

---

[63] See Matthew 18:4; 23:12; 1 Peter 5:6; Micah 6:8; 2 Kings 22:19; 2 Chronicles 33:23.

[64] See also, Holm, *The Runner's Bible*, pp. 59, 94, 112.

[65] See also Big Book, pp. 59, 63, 73, 76, 85, 164.

[66] See for discussion, Chambers, *My Utmost for His Highest*, p. 309.

The Big Book says on page 98:

> Burn the idea into the consciousness of every man that he can get
> well regardless of anyone. The only condition is that he trust in
> God and clean house.

Pointing out that one can establish conscious companionship with
God by simply, honestly, and humbly seeking Him, the Big Book
says at page 57:

> He has come to all who have honestly sought Him. When we
> drew near to Him He disclosed Himself to us!

In Step Seven, the Big Book relates "cleaning house" of
character defects to "humbly asking" God to remove them. The
verses in James, which speak of drawing near to God, cleansing
our hearts, humbling ourselves in His sight, and then being
"lifted" up by God, seem directly involved in the Big Book's
Seventh Step language. In fact, many years after the Big Book was
written, Sam Shoemaker wrote about his understanding of the
Seventh Step and said in A.A.'s *Grapevine* in 1964:

> Sins get entangled deep within us, as some roots of a tree, and do
> not easily come loose. We need help, grace, the lift of a kind of
> divine derrick.[67]

4. *Taking your own inventory*. James 4:11-12 states:

> Speak not evil one of another, brethren. He that speaketh evil of *his*
> brother, and judgeth his brother, speaketh evil of the law, and
> judgeth the law: but if thou judge the law, thou art not a doer of the
> law, but a judge. There is one lawgiver, who is able to save and to
> destroy: who art thou that judgest another?[68]

---

[67] Samuel M. Shoemaker, *Those Twelve Steps as I Understand Them*; Volume II,
Best of the Grapevine (New York: The A.A. Grapevine, Inc., 1986), p. 130.

[68] Holm, *The Runner's Bible*, p. 68; Tileston, *Daily Strength for Daily Needs*, p. 13.

We will be discussing the Fourth Step idea of taking your own inventory in connection with relevant verses in the Sermon on the Mount which were often quoted by Oxford Group people and by Anne Smith. Yet the Big Book makes much of looking "for our own mistakes," asking "Where were we to blame," and realizing that "The inventory was ours, not the other man's."[69] Since AAs favored the Book of James and its insights, we believe the foregoing James verses also had an impact on the A.A. idea of avoiding judgment of another in favor of examining one's own conduct for wrongdoing.[70]

James Chapter 5

1. *Patience*. In our discussion of James, Chapter One, we have already covered the verses on patience in James 5:7, 8, 10, 11.

2. *Grudge not one against another*. James 5:9 reads:

Grudge not one against another, brethren, lest ye be condemned; behold, the judge standeth before the door.

A major portion of the Big Book's Fourth Step discussion is devoted to resentment, about which page 64 says:

Resentment is the "number one" offender. It destroys more alcoholics than anything else. From it stem all forms of spiritual disease.

The Big Book then suggests putting resentments on paper—making a "*grudge list*" (pp. 64-65). Oxford Group spokesman Ebenezer Macmillan wrote at length on the importance of eliminating resentments, hatred, or the "*grudge*" that "blocks God out

---

[69] Big Book, p. 67.
[70] See also Big Book, p. 66.

effectively."[71] Shoemaker specified "grudges" as one of the "sins" to be examined in an inventory of self.[72] Since the Big Book lists resentments or "grudges" as one of the four major "character defects" which *block us from God*,[73] we think it quite possible that the "grudge" language in the Big Book was influenced by Akron's interest in James, and perhaps specifically in James 5:9.

3. *Asking God's forgiveness for sins*. We repeat James 5:15, partially quoted above. The entire verse says:

> And the prayer of faith shall save the sick, and the Lord shall raise him up; and if he have committed sins, they shall be forgiven him.[74]

The Big Book says this of asking God's forgiveness when we fall short:

> If we are sorry for what we have done, and have the honest desire to let God take us to better things, we believe we will be forgiven and will have learned our lesson (p. 70).

> When we retire at night, we constructively review our day. . . . After making our review, we ask God's forgiveness and inquire what corrective measures should be taken (p. 86).

The foregoing Big Book quotes show that its authors believed they could, after surrender, still gain forgiveness from God for the

---

[71] Ebenezer Macmillan, *Seeking and Finding* (New York: Harper & Brothers, 1933), pp. 96-98. There is a copy of Macmillan's book in the library of Bill's home at Stepping Stones; and it is one of the very few Oxford Group books to be found anywhere at Stepping Stones.

[72] Samuel M. Shoemaker, *Twice-Born Ministers* (New York: Fleming H. Revell, 1929), p. 182; *How to Become a Christian* (New York: Harper & Brothers, 1953), pp. 56-67.

[73] See Big Book discussions at pages 71-72, 64-65, 84, 86.

[74] Holm, *The Runner's Bible*, p. 114; Fosdick, *The Meaning of Prayer*, pp. 157-58.

shortcomings in which they indulged after their initial surrender. Here again, James has no corner on the statement that God makes it possible, through forgiveness, for a believer to regain fellowship with Him. 1 John 1:9 may also have been a source of these Big Book ideas:

> If we confess our sins, he is faithful and just to forgive us *our* sins, and to cleanse us from all unrighteousness.

See also our discussion of forgiveness in connection with the Sermon on the Mount. The Books of James, 1 John, or Matthew could each or all have been the basis for the Big Book forgiveness concept.

4. *Confess your sins one to another*. It has often been noted that *both* the Oxford Group concept of sharing by confession *and* Step Five in the Big Book were derived from James 5:16:

> Confess your faults one to another, and pray for one another, that ye may be healed.[75]

5. *Effectual, fervent prayer works*. James 5:16 states:

> The effectual fervent prayer of a righteous man availeth much.

The Big Book abounds with prayers.[76] And it states:

> Step Eleven suggests prayer and meditation. We shouldn't be shy on this matter of prayer. Better men than we are using it constantly. It works, if we have the proper attitude and work at it.

---

[75] See Dick B., *Design for Living*, pp. 72, 189-92, 311-12; *New Light on Alcoholism*, pp. 70, 160, 209, 230, 236, 314; *Anne Smith's Journal*, p. 131; *What Is The Oxford Group?*, p. 31; *The Upper Room* for 12/4/35; Fosdick, *The Meaning of Prayer*, pp. 157-58.

[76] See, for example, Big Book, pp. 63, 67, 69, 70, 76, 80, 82-88, 164.

James 5:16 could well have been a major foundation for the Big Book's statements about the effectiveness of prayer.[77]

The Sermon on the Mount

Our discussion here will not deal with this or that commentary on Matthew Chapters 5-7. It will focus on the Sermon on the Mount itself; for this Sermon which Jesus delivered was not the property of some particular writer. The fact that Dr. Bob read the Matthew chapters *themselves* as well as the many interpretations of them seems to verify an A.A. belief that the Sermon itself is one of the principles comprising "the common property of mankind," which Bill Wilson said the AAs had borrowed. And we will now review some major points we believe found their way from the Sermon into the thinking behind the Big Book.

The Lord's Prayer—Matthew 6:9-13

Oxford Group meetings closed with the Lord's Prayer—in New York and in Akron.[78] The author has attended at least two thousand A.A. meetings, and almost every one has closed with the Lord's Prayer. At the 1990 International A.A. Conference in Seattle, which this author attended, some 50,000 members of Alcoholics Anonymous joined in closing their meetings with the Lord's Prayer. The question here concerns what parts, if any, of the Lord's Prayer found their way into the Big Book; and we do point out here that the prayer is *part of the Sermon on the Mount.*

Here are the verses of the Lord's Prayer (King James Version) as found in Matthew 6:9-13. Jesus instructed the Judaeans, "After this manner therefore pray ye":

---

[77] Holm, *The Runner's Bible*, pp. 62, 114; *The Upper Room* for 8/19/35; Macmillan, *Seeking and Finding*, p. 128; Walter, *Soul Surgery*, p. 29; Fosdick, *The Meaning of Prayer*, p. 158.

[78] Telephone interview by the author with Mrs. Julia Harris, October 5, 1991; *DR. BOB*, pp. 137-42.

Our Father which art in heaven, Hallowed be thy name.
Thy kingdom come. Thy will be done in earth, as *it is* in heaven.
Give us this day our daily bread.
And forgive us our debts, as we forgive our debtors.[79]
And lead us not into temptation, but deliver us from evil: For
thine is the kingdom, and the power, and the glory, for ever.
Amen.

Dr. Bob studied commentaries on the Sermon by Oswald
Chambers, Glenn Clark, Emmet Fox, and E. Stanley Jones.[80]
And these writers extracted a good many teachings, prayer guides,
and theological ideas from the Lord's Prayer verses in the Sermon.
But there are a few concepts and phrases in the Lord's Prayer
which either epitomize A.A. thinking or can be found in its
language—whether the A.A. traces came from the Lord's Prayer
itself or from other portions of the Bible.

The Big Book uses the word "Father" when referring to God;
and the context of the usage shows that the name came from the
Bible.[81] The Oxford Group also used the term "Father," among

---

[79] AAs substitute the word "trespasses" for "debts," as do many Christian
denominations.

[80] See Dick B., *Dr. Bob's Library*, pp. 38-40; Oswald Chambers, *Studies in the
Sermon on the Mount* 4th ed (London: Simpkin, Marshall, Ltd., n.d.); Glenn Clark, *The
Soul's Sincere Desire; The Lord's Prayer and Other Talks on Prayer from The Camps
Farthest Out* (Minnesota: Macalester Publishing, 1932); *I Will Lift Up Mine Eyes* (New
York: Harper & Brothers, 1937); Emmet Fox, *The Sermon on the Mount* (New York:
Harper & Row, 1934); E. Stanley Jones, *The Christ of the Mount: A Working Philosophy
of Life* (New York: The Abingdon Press, 1931).

[81] Thus the Big Book, at page 14, speaks of "Father" and "God" in the context of
"Father of Light" from James 1:17 [there rendered "Father of Lights"]; and, at page 62,
of "Father" and "God," stating "He is the Father, and we are His children." See, for
example, 1 John 3:2, "Beloved, now are we the sons of God;" and 1 John 5:2, "By this
we know that we love the children of God, when we love God, and keep his
commandments." In *Alcoholics Anonymous Comes of Age*, Bill Wilson wrote: "There is
God, our Father, who very simply says, 'I am waiting for you to do my will'" (p. 105);
"We knew that ours was a fellowship of the Spirit and that the grace of God was there"
(p. 44); "Clearly my job henceforth was to *let go* and *let God* . . . " (p. 48).

other names, when referring to God.[82] The concept and expression of God as "Father" is not confined to the Sermon on the Mount. It can be found in many other parts of the New Testament.[83] But AAs have given the "Our Father" prayer a special place in their meetings.[84] So the Lord's Prayer seems the likely source of their use of the word "Father."

The phrase "Thy will be done" is directly quoted in the Big Book and underlies A.A.'s contrast between "self-will" and "God's will."[85] The Oxford Group stressed, as do A.A.'s Third and Seventh Step prayers, that there must be a *decision to do God's will and to surrender to His will*. These ideas were often symbolized in the prayer, "Thy will be done."[86]

Finally, "Forgive us our debts" or "trespasses" clearly implies that God can and will "forgive;" and these concepts can be found in the Big Book, whether they came from the Lord's prayer or from other Biblical sources such as the Book of James.[87]

The Sermon on the Mount—Matthew Chapters 5-7

Dr. Bob studied a book by E. Stanley Jones, which outlined the Sermon's contents in this fashion:

---

[82] Dick B., *Design for Living*, pp. 152-55; *New Light on Alcoholism*, pp. 63, 114, 135, 141.

[83] See, for example, Matthew 10:20; 11:25; 12:50; 15:13; 18:35; 26:39; John 10:25; 12:28; 16:27; 17:24; Acts 1:4; 2:33; Romans 1:7; 1 Corinthians 8:6; Ephesians 2:18; Colossians 1:12; 1 Thessalonians 3:13; James 1:27; 1 Peter 1:17; 1 John 2:1.

[84] See comment about this in Mel B., *New Wine: The Spiritual Roots of The Twelve Step Miracle* (Minnesota: Hazelden, 1991), p. 157.

[85] Big Book, pp. 67, 85, 88. See also p. 63: "May I do Thy will always." And pp. 86-87, "we ask God to direct our thinking. . . . We ask especially for freedom from self-will."

[86] Henry Wright, *The Will of God and a Man's Lifework* (New York: The Young Men's Christian Association Press, 1909), pp. 50-51; Macmillan, *Seeking and Finding*, p. 273; *What Is The Oxford Group?*, pp. 47-49; Samuel Moor Shoemaker, *Children of the Second Birth* (New York: Fleming H. Revell, 1927), pp. 58, 175-87; *If I Be Lifted Up* (New York: Fleming H. Revell, 1931), p. 93; *The Upper Room* for 12/3/37.

[87] Big Book, pp. 70, 86.

1. The goal of life: To be perfect or complete as the Father in heaven is perfect or complete (5:48) with twenty-seven marks of this perfect life (5:1-47).

2. A diagnosis of the reason why men do not reach or move on to that goal: Divided personality (6:1-6; 7:1-6).

3. The Divine offer of an adequate moral and spiritual re-enforcement so that men can move on to that goal: The Holy Spirit to them that ask him (7:7-11).

4. After making the Divine offer he gathers up and emphasizes in two sentences our part in reaching that goal. Toward others—we are to do unto others as we would that they should do unto us (7:12); toward ourselves—we are to lose ourselves by entering the straight gate (7:13).

5. The test of whether we are moving on to that goal, or whether this Divine Life is operative within us: By their fruits (7:15-23).

6. The survival value of this new life and the lack of survival value of life lived in any other way: The house founded on rock and the house founded on sand (7:24-27).[88]

We will review Jesus's Sermon chapter by chapter to locate some principal thoughts that Dr. Bob may have had in mind when he said A.A. embodied the philosophy of the Sermon.

Matthew Chapter 5

1. *The Beatitudes*. The *Beatitudes* are found in Matthew 5:3-11. The word "beatitudes" refers to the first word "Blessed" in each of these verses. Merriam Webster's says "blessed" means

---

[88] E. Stanley Jones, *The Christ of the Mount* (New York: The Abingdon Press, 1931), pp. 36-37.

"enjoying the bliss of heaven." "Bliss" is defined as "complete happiness." The word in the Greek New Testament from which "blessed" was translated means, according to Ethelbert Bullinger, a Greek Biblical scholar, "happy."[89] *Vine's Expository Dictionary of Old and New Testament Words* explains the word "blessed" as follows: "In the beatitudes the Lord indicates not only the characters that are blessed, but the nature of that which is the highest good."[90] We have italicized Webster's definitions for the key words in each verse, quoting also the King James Version, which was the version Dr. Bob and early AAs most used.

The Sermon says: "Blessed" are: (v. 3) the poor (*humble*) in spirit: for theirs is the kingdom of heaven; (v. 4) they that mourn (*feel or express grief or sorrow*): for they shall be comforted; (v. 5) the meek (*enduring injury with patience and without resentment*); for they shall inherit the earth; (v. 6) they which do hunger and thirst after righteousness (*acting in accord with divine or moral law*): for they shall be filled; (v. 7) the merciful (*compassionate*): for they shall obtain mercy; (v. 8) the pure (*spotless, stainless*) in heart: for they shall see God; (v. 9) the peacemakers: for they shall be called the children of God; (v. 10) they which are persecuted for righteousness' sake: for theirs is the kingdom of heaven; (v. 11) ye when men shall revile you, and persecute you, and shall say all manner of evil against you falsely, for my sake (*end or purpose*): for great is your reward in heaven: for so persecuted they the prophets which were before you.

Did Dr. Bob, Anne, Bill, or Henrietta Seiberling study and draw on these Beatitude verses for A.A.'s recovery program purposes?[91] We do not know.[92] But we do see some ideas

---

[89] Ethelbert W. Bullinger, *A Critical Lexicon and Concordance to the English and Greek New Testament* (Michigan: Zondervan Publishing House, 1981), p. 104.

[90] W. E. Vine, *Vine's Expository Dictionary of Old and New Testament Words*. Vol. I (New York: Fleming H. Revell, 1981), p. 133.

[91] Dr. Bob and his wife, and Bill and his wife, and Henrietta Seiberling all read Chambers' *My Utmost for His Highest*; and Chambers says at page 207, "the Beatitudes contain the dynamite of the Holy Ghost. . . . The Sermon on the Mount is not a set of

(continued...)

common to A.A.'s spiritual principles in the phrases: (1) Humility;[93] (2) Comfort for the suffering;[94] (3) Patience and tolerance to the end of eliminating resentment;[95] (4) Harmonizing actions with God's will;[96] (5) Compassion, which Webster defines as "sympathetic consciousness of others' distress together with a desire to alleviate;"[97] (6) "Cleaning house;"[98] (7) Making peace;[99] (8) Standing for and acting upon spiritual principles because they are God's principles, whatever the cost.[100] We see Twelve Step ideas in the Beatitudes; and A.A. founders probably saw them too.

2. *Letting your light shine.* Matthew 5:13-16 suggest glorifying your Heavenly Father by letting others *see* your good works. That is, "Letting your light shine" does not mean glorifying yourself, but

---

[91] (...continued)
rules and regulations: it is a statement of the life we will live when the Holy Spirit is getting His way with us." *The Upper Room* did a study of the Beatitudes in its devotionals for 7/17/38, 7/18/38, 7/19/38, 7/20/38, 7/21/38, 7/22/38.

[92] But see Dick B., *Anne Smith's Journal*, p. 133, which points out that Anne did speak of the Beatitudes in terms of Christ-like virtues to be cultivated.

[93] Big Book, pp. 59, 73.

[94] Big Book, pp. 20, 77, 97.

[95] Big Book, pp. 67, 70, 118.

[96] Big Book, p. 164.

[97] Big Book, p. 159.

[98] In *My Utmost for His Highest*, Chambers wrote: "the pure in heart see God. . . . If we are going to retain personal contact with the Lord Jesus Christ, it will mean there are some things we must scorn to do or to think, some legitimate things we must scorn to touch" (p. 86). Dr. Frank Buchman used the verse "blessed are the pure in heart, for they shall see God" in the context of getting people to change—to "hate sin, confess sin, and forsake sin." See A. J. Russell, *For Sinners Only* (London: Hodder & Stoughton, 1932), p. 63. This was part of the 5 C process of life-changing (As to the Five C's, see Dick B., *Design for Living*, pp. 175-79). For an additional reference to the "pure in heart," see *The Runner's Bible*, at page 77: "The pure in heart see only God . . . only Good, hence their conversation is not of evil, of imperfection, destruction, death; but of things that are perfect, that make for peace and happiness and spiritual growth." See Big Book, pp. 64, 98.

[99] Big Book, p. 103.

[100] Big Book, p. 77.

rather glorifying God by letting others see the spiritual walk in action—see the immediate results of surrender to the Master.[101] These ideas may be reflected in the Big Book's statement: "Our real purpose is to fit ourselves to be of maximum service to God . . ." (p. 77).

3. *The Law of Love in action*. In Matthew 5:17-47, Jesus confirms that the Law of Love fulfills the Old Testament Law. He rejects anger without cause, unresolved wrongs to a brother, quibbling with an adversary, lust and impurity, adultery, retaliation, and hatred of an enemy. Our title *Design for Living* covers many of these ideas as roots of A.A. principles.[102] And these verses may have influenced A.A. language such as: (1) Overcoming resentments;[103] (2) Making restitution;[104] (3) Avoidance of

---

[101] See *The Upper Room* for 5/2/35, 6/10/38; Holm, *The Runner's Bible*, pp. 74, 77.

[102] Dick B., *Design for Living*, pp. 149-297.

[103] Matthew 5:21-22. See Holm, *The Runner's Bible*, p. 82; *The Upper Room* for 10/18/35; E. Stanley Jones, *The Christ of the Mount*, p. 136.

[104] Matthew 5:23-24 reads: "Therefore if thou bring thy gift to the altar, and there rememberest that thy brother hath ought against thee; leave there thy gift before the altar, and go thy way; first be reconciled to thy brother, and then come and offer thy gift." Oxford Group and other writers commonly cited this verse in connection with their writings on restitution. See Clarence I. Benson, *The Eight Points of the Oxford Group* (London: Humphrey Milford, Oxford University Press, 1936), p. 30; Russell, *For Sinners Only*, p. 120; Weatherhead, *Discipleship*, p. 113; Macmillan, *Seeking and Finding*, p. 176; Shoemaker, *The Conversion of the Church*, pp. 47-48; *DR. BOB*, p. 308; Clark, *The Soul's Sincere Desire*, p. 57; *My Utmost for His Highest*, p. 46; E. Stanley Jones, *The Christ of the Mount*, pp. 133, 140. Matthew 5:25 says: "Agree with thine adversary quickly." As stated, Dr. Bob used and recommended Nora Smith Holm's *The Runner's Bible*; and Dr. Bob, Bill, and Henrietta all read and used Oswald Chambers' *My Utmost for His Highest*. Both *The Runner's Bible* at page 67, and *My Utmost for His Highest* at page 182, stressed Matthew 5:25 in connection with making amends. *My Utmost for His Highest* also referred to Matthew 5:26—paying "the uttermost farthing"—with regard to the amends concept (p. 183).

retaliation for wrongdoing by others;[105] and (4) Making peace with our enemies.[106]

Matthew Chapter 6

1. *Anonymity*. Matthew 6:1-8, 16-18, dealing with almsgiving "in secret," praying "in secret," fasting "in secret," avoidance of "vain repetitions," and hypocrisy, may, as mentioned earlier, possibly have played a role in the development of A.A.'s spiritual principle of anonymity. Jesus said, "your Father knoweth what things ye have need of, before ye ask him" and "thy Father, which seeth in secret, shall reward thee openly." The vain practices Jesus condemned focused on inflation of self—something A.A. disdains.[107] As we've discussed, we have located no direct tie between the teachings of Jesus on anonymity and A.A.'s traditions on this spiritual principle. But the concepts are parallel; and *The Runner's Bible* and other A.A. sources discuss their significance at some length.[108]

2. *Forgiveness*. Matthew 6:14-15 stressed forgiving men their trespasses; and Emmet Fox's emphatic statements about these verses which may well have influenced the A.A. amends process. He wrote:

> The forgiveness of sins is the central problem of life. . . . It is, of course, rooted in selfishness. . . . We must positively and definitely extend forgiveness to everyone to whom it is possible

---

[105] Matthew 5:38-41; See Chambers, *My Utmost for His Highest*, p. 196; Big Book, pp. 62, 77-78.

[106] Matthew 5:43-47; See *The Upper Room* for 5/22/35, 9/13/38; Big Book, pp. 77-78, 103, 135.

[107] Big Book, p. 62; compare p. 292. See Ernest Kurtz, *Not-God*. Expanded ed. (Minnesota: Hazelden, 1991), pp. 20-21.

[108] Holm, *The Runner's Bible*, pp. 61-62. See also Clark, *The Soul's Sincere Desire*, pp. 38, 53; Fosdick, *The Meaning of Prayer*, p. 57; E. Stanley Jones, *The Christ of the Mount*, pp. 202-07.

that we can owe forgiveness, namely, to anyone who we think can have injured us in any way. . . . When you hold resentment against anyone, you are bound to that person by a cosmic link, a real, tough metal chain. You are tied by a cosmic tie to the thing that you hate. The one person perhaps in the whole world whom you most dislike is the very one to whom you are attaching yourself by a hook that is stronger than steel.[109]

Did Fox's writing on this point influence the Big Book's emphasis on forgiveness? We do not know. But at least two writers have claimed that Fox's writings influenced Bill Wilson.[110] Other writers that were read by AAs used language similar to that used by Fox in his discussion of forgiveness of enemies.[111] And the Sermon on the Mount is not the only place in the New Testament where forgiveness is stressed. Thus, after Christ had accomplished remission of past sins, Paul wrote in Colossians 3:13:

Forbearing one another, and forgiving one another, if any man have a quarrel against any: even as Christ forgave you, so also *do ye*.

Henrietta Seiberling taught her children 1 John 4:20:

If a man say I love God, and hateth his brother, he is a liar: for he that loveth not his brother whom he hath seen, how can he love God whom he hath not seen.[112]

---

[109] Fox, *The Sermon on the Mount*, pp. 183-88. Cp. Big Book, page 66: "It is plain that a life which includes deep resentment leads only to futility and unhappiness. . . . We found that it is fatal. . . . If we were to live, we had to be free of anger. The grouch and the brainstorm were not for us. They may be the dubious luxury of normal men, but for alcoholics these things are poison."

[110] See Mel B., *New Wine*, p. 5; Igor Sikorsky, Jr., *A.A.'s Godparents* (Minnesota: CompCare Publishers, 1990). Compare Dick B., *Design for Living*, pp. 22-24.

[111] See, for example, Clark, *I Will Lift Up Mine Eyes*, p. 32: "Your first duty is to forgive others. Turn to all those who have trespassed against you and forgive them. . . . So, first of all, take up these sins that others have committed against you, and forgive them one by one. Forgive them completely and utterly."

[112] See Dick B., *The Akron Genesis*, p. 92.

In any event, the Big Book states at page 77:

> The question of how to approach the man we hated will arise. It
> may be he has done us more harm than we have done him and,
> though we may have acquired a better attitude toward him, we are
> still not too keen about admitting our faults. Nevertheless, with a
> person we dislike, we take the bit in our teeth. It is harder to go
> to an enemy than to a friend, but we find it more beneficial to us.
> We go to him in a helpful *and forgiving spirit*, confessing our
> former ill feeling and expressing our regret. Under no condition
> do we criticize such a person or argue. Simply we tell him that
> we will never get over drinking until we have done our utmost to
> straighten out the past (italics added).

3. *The "sunlight of the Spirit?"* Speaking of the futility and
unhappiness in a life which includes deep resentment, the Big
Book presents the interesting idea that "when harboring such
feelings we shut ourselves off from the sunlight of the Spirit."[113]
One often hears this idea quoted in A.A. meetings. Yet its origins
seem unreported and undocumented. Anne Smith referred
frequently in her journal to the verses in 1 John which had to do
with fellowship with God.[114] So did A.A.'s Oxford Group
sources.[115] And the following are the most frequently quoted
verses from 1 John having to do with God as "light" and the
importance of walking in the light to have fellowship with Him:

> That which we have seen and heard declare we unto you, that ye
> may have fellowship with us: and truly our fellowship *is* with the
> Father, and with his Son, Jesus Christ. And these things write we
> unto you, that your joy may be full. This then is the message
> which we have heard of him, and declare unto you, that God is
> light, and in him is no darkness at all. If we say that we have
> fellowship with him, and walk in darkness, we lie, and do not the

---

[113] Big Book, p. 66.

[114] Dick B., *Anne Smith's Journal*, pp. 71, 120, 130, 145.

[115] Dick B., *Design for Living*, pp. 104, 288-89, 329.

truth: But if we walk in the light, as he is in the light, we have
fellowship one with another, and the blood of Jesus Christ his Son
cleanseth us from all sin (1 John 1:3-7).[116]

We are dealing, in this portion, with the Sermon on the Mount.
But we also mention the foregoing verses from 1 John 1:3-7
(having to do with walking in God's light as against walking in
darkness). We believe the ideas in 1 John, together with the
following verses in the Sermon, may possibly have given rise to
Bill's references to the alcoholic's being blocked from the
"sunlight of the Spirit" when he or she dwells in such dark realms
as excessive anger. Matthew 6:22-24 state:

> The light of the body is the eye: if therefore thine eye be single,
> thy whole body shall be full of light. But if thine eye be evil, thy
> whole body shall be full of darkness. If therefore the light that is
> in thee be darkness, how great *is* that darkness! No man can serve
> two masters: for either he will hate the one, and love the other;
> or else he will hold to the one, and despise the other. Ye cannot
> serve God and mammon.

4. *Seek ye first the kingdom of God.* Matthew 6:24-34 seem to
have had tremendous influence on A.A. Their substance is that
man will be taken care of when he seeks first the kingdom of God
and His righteousness. Verse 33 says:

> But seek ye first the kingdom of God, and his righteousness; and
> all these things shall be added unto you.

As previously discussed, Dr. Bob specifically explained the A.A.
slogans "Easy Does It" and "First Things First."[117] When he
was asked the meaning of "First Things First," he replied, "Seek
ye first the kingdom of God and His righteousness, and all these

---

[116] See also Tileston, *Daily Strength for Daily Needs*, p. 165; Holm, *The Runner's Bible*, p. 7.

[117] *DR. BOB*, p. 192. See Big Book, p. 135.

things shall be added unto you."[118] He told his sponsee Clarence S. that "First Things First" came from Matthew 6:33 in the Sermon on the Mount. And this verse was widely quoted in the books that Dr. Bob and the Akron AAs read and recommended.[119]

On page 60, the Big Book states the A.A. solution to obtaining relief from alcoholism: "God could and would if He were sought." We believe the concept of "seeking" results by reliance on God instead of reliance on self is a bedrock idea in the Big Book.[120] And we believe the concept was much influenced by the "seeking the kingdom of God first" idea in Matthew 6:33.

Matthew Chapter 7

1. *Taking your own inventory.* Much of A.A.'s Fourth, Ninth, Tenth, and Eleventh Step procedures involve looking for your own part, for your own fault, in the house-cleaning and life-changing process which, in Appendix II of the Third Edition of the Big Book, became described as "the personality change sufficient to bring about recovery from alcoholism" (Big Book, p. 569).[121] Matthew 7:3-5 states:

And why beholdest thou the mote [speck] that is in thy brother's eye, but considerest not the beam [log] that is in thine own eye?

---

[118] *DR. BOB*, p. 144.

[119] Russell, *For Sinners Only*, p. 36; Clark, *The Soul's Sincere Desire*, pp. 16, 34; Shoemaker, *National Awakening*, p. 41; *A Young Man's View of the Ministry* (New York: Association Press, 1923), p. 80; Chambers, *My Utmost for His Highest*, p. 142; Holm, *The Runner's Bible*, p. 127; Tileston, *Daily Strength for Daily Needs*, p. 327; Jones, *The Christ of the Mount*, pp. 218-19; Glover, *The Jesus of History*, p. 111; Macmillan, *Seeking and Finding*, p. 226; *The Upper Room* for 9/4/35, 11/19/35, 5/20/37, 12/2/38; Chambers, *Studies in the Sermon on the Mount*, pp. 60-61.

[120] Big Book, pp. 11, 14, 25, 28, 43, 52-53, 57, 62, 68. Page 68 states: "Wasn't it because self-reliance failed us? Self-reliance was good as far as it went, but it didn't go far enough . . . we are now on a different basis; the basis of trusting and relying upon God. We trust infinite God rather than our finite selves."

[121] See the inventory procedures described in the Big Book, at pp. 67, 69-70, 76, 84, 86, 98.

Or how wilt thou say to thy brother, Let me pull the mote [speck] out of thine eye; and, behold, a beam [log] *is* in thine own eye. Thou hypocrite, first cast out the beam [log] out of thine own eye; and then shalt thou see clearly to cast out the mote [speck] out of thy brother's eye.

These verses were frequently cited by A.A.'s spiritual sources as Biblical authority for the requirement of self-examination and finding one's own part, one's own erroneous conduct, in a relationship problem.[122]

2. *Ask, seek, knock.* Matthew 7:7-11 states:

Ask, and it shall be given you; seek, and ye shall find; knock, and it shall be opened unto you;
For every one that asketh receiveth; and he that seeketh findeth; and to him that knocketh it shall be opened.
Or what man is there of you, whom if his son ask bread, will he give him a stone?
Or if he ask a fish, will he give him a serpent?
If ye then, being evil, know how to give good gifts unto your children, how much more shall your Father which is in heaven give good things to them that ask him?

Shoemaker wrote:

Our part [in the crisis of self-surrender] is to ask, to seek, to knock. His [God's] part is to answer, to come, to open.[123]

---

[122] Samuel M. Shoemaker, *God's Control* (New York: Fleming H. Revell, 1939), pp. 62-72; Chambers, *My Utmost for His Highest*, pp. 169, 174; Russell, *For Sinners Only*, pp. 309-16; Geoffrey Allen, *He That Cometh* (New York: The Macmillan Company, 1933), p. 139; Kitchen, *I Was a Pagan*, p. 110-11; Chambers, *Studies in the Sermon on the Mount*, p. 68; Clark, *The Soul's Sincere Desire*, p. 61; Jones, *The Christ of the Mount*, p. 244. See Dick B., *Anne Smith's Journal*, pp. 30-31

[123] Shoemaker, *Realizing Religion*, p. 32.

The Runner's Bible has an entire chapter titled, "Ask and Ye shall receive."[124] *My Utmost for His Highest* says about these verses beginning with Matthew 7:7

> The illustration of prayer that Our Lord uses here is that of a good child asking for a good thing. . . . It is no use praying unless we are living as children of God. Then, Jesus says—"Everyone that asketh receiveth."[125]

The foregoing verses indicate the importance of becoming a child of God, establishing a harmonious relationship with Him, and then expecting good results from the Father. We believe those verses influenced these similar ideas in the Big Book:

> If what we have learned and felt and seen means anything at all, it means that all of us, whatever our race, creed, or color are the children of a living Creator with whom we may form a relationship upon simple and understandable terms as soon as we are willing and honest enough to try (p. 28).

> God will constantly disclose more to you and to us. Ask Him in your morning meditation what you can do each day for the man who is still sick. The answers will come, *if your own house is in order*. But obviously you cannot transmit something you haven't got.[126] *See to it that your relationship with Him is right*, and great events will come to pass for you and countless others. This is the Great Fact for us (p. 164, italics added).

In this same vein, Dr. Bob's wife, Anne, had written in her workbook:

---

[124] Holm, *The Runner's Bible*, pp. 59-65. See also *The Upper Room* for 4/8/38; Jones, *The Christ of the Mount*, pp. 256-57; Clark, *I Will Lift Up Mine Eyes*, p. 30.

[125] Chambers, *My Utmost for His Highest*, p. 237. See also our discussion of James 4:3, as to asking amiss to consume it on self.

[126] For the teachings by Dr. Bob's wife and others that "we can't give away what we haven't got," see Dick B., *Anne Smith's Journal*, p. 69; *Design for Living*, p. 362.

We can't give away what we haven't got. We must have a genuine contact with God in our present experience. Not an experience of the past, but an experience in the present—actual, genuine.[127]

3. *"Do unto others."* The so-called "Golden Rule" cannot readily be identified in the Big Book though it certainly is a much-quoted portion of the Sermon on the Mount which Dr. Bob said underlies A.A.'s philosophy. The relevant verse is Matthew 7:12:

Therefore all things whatsoever ye would that men should do to you, do ye even so to them: for this is the law and the prophets.[128]

Perhaps the following two segments from the Big Book bespeak the philosophy:

We have begun to learn tolerance, patience and good will toward all men, even our enemies, for we look on them as sick people. We have listed the people we have hurt by our conduct, and are willing to straighten out the past if we can (p. 70).

Then you will know what it means to give of yourself that others may survive and rediscover life. You will learn the full meaning of "Love thy neighbor as thyself" (p. 153).

4. *He that doeth the will of my Father.* The author believes that the bottom line, in terms of what A.A. might have derived from the Sermon on the Mount, can be found in Matthew 7:21:

---

[127] Dick B., *Anne Smith's Journal*, p. 121.

[128] See discussion in Clark, *I Will Lift Up Mine Eyes*, p. 45; Jones, *The Christ of the Mount*, p. 295.

Not every one that saith unto me, Lord, Lord, shall enter into the kingdom of heaven; but he that doeth the will of my Father which is in heaven.[129]

Bill Wilson made the major point in the Big Book and in his other writings that the key to success in A.A. was doing the will of the Father—the Father Who is the subject of the Lord's Prayer, and the God upon whom early AAs depended. Wilson wrote:

I was to sit quietly when in doubt, asking only for direction and strength to meet my problems as He would have me (Bill's Story, Big Book, p. 13).

He humbly offered himself to his Maker—then he knew (Big Book, p. 57).

. . . praying only for knowledge of His will for us and the power to carry that out (Step Eleven, Big Book, p. 59).

May I do Thy will always (portion of "Third Step Prayer," Big Book, p. 63)!

Thy will be done (Big Book, pp. 67, 88).

Grant me strength, as I go out from here, to do your bidding. Amen (portion of "Seventh Step Prayer," Big Book, p. 76).

There is God, our Father, who very simply says, "I am waiting for you to do my will" (*Alcoholics Anonymous Comes of Age*, p. 105).

---

[129] See Henry Drummond, *The Ideal Life: Addresses Hitherto Unpublished* (New York: Hodder & Stoughton, 1897), p. 232-43; Wright, *The Will of God*, p. 43; Allen, *He That Cometh*, p. 139; Streeter, *The God Who Speaks*, p. 85; Jones, *The Christ of the Mount*, p. 300; Dick B., *Design for Living*, pp. 162, 259-60, 284; *The Upper Room* for 11/2/37; Fox, *The Sermon on the Mount*, pp. 146-48; Chambers, *Studies in the Sermon on the Mount*, p. 93.

5

The Good Book and the Twelve Steps

The first chapter highlights Bill Wilson's many statements that A.A. was not invented and borrowed all of its principles. Also that Dr. Bob specified the Bible as the source and Bill specified the Biblical principles of the Oxford Group. Yet that is as far as either went with details. At this point in our research, however, we believe it is possible to review all the sources that were read, listened to, and discussed by Dr. Bob, Bill, and the others in early A.A. and have a fairly good picture of what they took from the Bible. Our previous titles have already covered in great depth the Biblical A.A. ideas that seem to have originated with Sam Shoemaker, the Oxford Group, Henrietta Seiberling, and Dr. Bob's wife, Anne.[1]

---

[1] For details on the various other sources, see Dick B., *New Light on Alcoholism: The A.A. Legacy from Sam Shoemaker* (Corte Madera, CA: Good Book Publishing Company, 1994); *Design for Living: The Oxford Group's Contribution to Early A.A.* (San Rafael, CA: Paradise Research Publications, 1995), pp. 13-16, 24-29; *The Akron Genesis of Alcoholics Anonymous* (Corte Madera, CA: Good Book Publishing Company, 1994); *Anne Smith's Journal, 1933-1939: A.A.'s Principles of Success* (San Rafael, CA: Paradise Research Publications, 1995); *Dr. Bob's Library: Books for Twelve Step Growth* (San Rafael, CA: Paradise Research Publications, 1995); *Good Morning! Quiet Time,*

(continued...)

But the major problem in trying to *pinpoint* A.A.'s Biblical roots has to do with the difference between parallel language and borrowed language. Several writers and publishers have presented parallels between A.A. language and language found in the Bible.[2] But our concern is historical. We wish to pinpoint parallels between A.A. language and Biblical language *only* where the A.A. language appears actually to have been borrowed from the Bible. To do this, we frequently refer to the daily Bible devotionals, the general Christian literature of early A.A. days, Sam Shoemaker's teachings, and the Oxford Group writings to which early AAs were regularly exposed. We cannot always be sure that early AAs took a specific idea from a specifically quoted source; but we can say that AAs frequently used the named source and that the source relied on the Biblical segments to which we refer. We are concerned with what early AAs used that worked, not with what some writer or publisher believes AAs *should have* taken from the Bible. For A.A.'s own successful approach was to describe steps that were *taken* and the experiences that *occurred* by following the recovery program AAs borrowed from medicine, religion, and their own experience. Then to let others decide for themselves what they, as individuals, would do to further their own religious growth.[3]

---

[1] (...continued)

Morning Watch, Meditation, and Early A.A. (San Rafael, CA: Paradise Research Publications, 1996); *That Amazing Grace: The Role of Clarence and Grace S. in Alcoholics Anonymous* (San Rafael, CA: Paradise Research Publications, 1996); and *The Books Early AAs Read for Spiritual Growth*, 5th ed. (Kihei, HI: Paradise Research Publications, Inc, 1997).

[2] See, for example, Dr. Robert Hemfelt and Dr. Richard Fowler, *Serenity: A Companion for Twelve Step Recovery* (Nashville, Thomas Nelson Publishers, 1990); Paul Barton Doyle, *In Step with God: A Scriptural Guide for Practicing 12 Step Programs* (Tennessee: New Directions, 1989). Typical also of this approach are letters which came the author's way in 1995 in which two different correspondents likened the Steps to: (1) "a 5,000 year old Hebrew prayer called 'A Psalm for Serenity,' based on Psalm XIX;" and (2) "John Wesley's Decisions of Wholeness."

[3] Big Book, p. 28: "We think it no concern of ours what religious bodies our members identify themselves with as individuals. This should be an entirely personal affair which each one decides for himself in light of past associations or his present

(continued...)

We will now discuss each of the Twelve Steps AAs took to recover; and we will examine each Step in terms of relevant Bible verses AAs studied and/or the Biblical sources to which they were exposed as they put the Steps together.

Step One and Deflation at Depth

[Step One: We admitted we were powerless over alcohol—that our lives had become unmanageable.][4]

A.A.'s medical mentor, Dr. William D. Silkworth, chief psychiatrist at Towns Hospital in New York, and the man who treated Bill Wilson as Bill sought and attained recovery, said:

Men and women drink essentially because they like the effect produced by alcohol. The sensation is so elusive that, while they admit it is injurious, they cannot after a time differentiate the true from the false. To them, their alcoholic life seems the only normal one. They are *restless, irritable and discontented*, unless they can again experience the sense of ease and comfort which comes at once by taking a few drinks—drinks which they see others taking with impunity. After they have succumbed to the desire again, as so many do, and the phenomenon of craving develops, they pass through the well-known stages of a spree, emerging remorseful, with a firm resolution not to drink again. This is repeated over and over, and unless this person can experience an entire psychic change there is very little hope of his recovery (italics added).[5]

---

[3] (...continued)
choice." *Big Book* is a registered trademark of Alcoholics Anonymous World Services, Inc.; used here with permission of A.A.W.S.

[4] In this chapter and elsewhere in our book, *The Twelve Steps of Alcoholics Anonymous* are reprinted with permission of Alcoholics Anonymous World Services, Inc.

[5] Big Book, pp. xxvi-xxvii.

Silkworth thus concluded that the alcoholic is restless, irritable, and discontented unless and until he seeks and obtains the *illusory*, and *often fatal* solution of *peace through alcohol*.

Bill Wilson's principal religious teacher in the days before A.A.'s Big Book was published was the Reverend Sam Shoemaker, Jr., the rector of Calvary Episcopal Church in New York. And Shoemaker often wrote of a much deeper, spiritual problem causing irritability and discontent in most people of that day. Shoemaker's first title said:

> The modern mind is restless and easily bored. It is also intensely individualistic. . . . There has always been a large amount of unhappiness in the world, but it seems as if our modern America had got more than its share. Look at the sheer irritability you can find in any city you know! Can you count off half a dozen really happy, really peaceful people whom you know? So many "problems," so many "complex situations." Now the thing which is striking about much of the misery one sees is that it is *spiritual* misery. . . . It is the sadness of maladjustment to the eternal things, and this throws out the whole focus of life. Rest cures and exercise and motor drives will not help. The only thing that will help is religion. For the root of the malady is estrangement from God—estrangement from Him in people that were made to be His companions. . . . What you want is simply a vital religious experience. You need to find God. You need Jesus Christ.[6]

Bill Wilson seemed to cover this same religious territory when he wrote the following in A.A.'s Big Book:

> [W]e have been not only mentally and physically ill, we have been *spiritually sick*. When the *spiritual malady* is overcome, we straighten out mentally and physically.[7]

---

[6] Samuel M. Shoemaker, *Realizing Religion* (New York: Association Press, 1923), pp. 2-9.

[7] Big Book, p. 64 (italics added).

Remember that we deal with alcohol—cunning, baffling, powerful! Without help it is too much for us. But there is One who has all power—that One is God. May you find Him now![8]

There was, felt A.A.'s founders, a spiritual problem underlying the alcohol problem. Bill wrote in 1960:

Of course, we have since found that these awful conditions of mind and body invariably bring on the third phase of our malady. This is the sickness of the spirit; a sickness for which there must necessarily be a spiritual remedy. We AAs recognize this in the first five words of Step Twelve of the recovery program. Those words are: "Having had a spiritual awakening. . . ." Here we name the remedy for our threefold sickness of body, mind and soul. Here we declare the necessity for that all-important spiritual awakening.[9]

The spiritual problem, as Shoemaker characterized it, was estrangement from, and lack of contact with, God through Christ. And though others today have put a different interpretation on the *nature* of the "spiritual problem," there appears to be agreement with Bill Wilson's description of alcoholism as a three-part disease—physical, mental, and *spiritual*.[10]

Our question concerns the Biblical roots, if any, from which A.A.'s sources identified the spiritual problem—a problem epitomized by the Big Book's cry that there was a need for the seemingly hopeless alcoholic to find God. And to find Him *now*.[11]

Some of the early AAs (including Dr. Bob), and a good many religious writers of that day, read and quoted *The Confessions of*

---

[8] Big Book, pp. 58-59.

[9] *The Language of the Heart*, p. 297.

[10] Ernest Kurtz, *Not-God: A History of Alcoholics Anonymous*. Exp. ed (Minnesota: Hazelden, 1991), pp. 45, 199, 204, 381-82.

[11] See the comment by Harry Emerson Fosdick in the *Meaning of Faith* (New York: The Abingdon Press, 1917), p. 36: "*Men never really find God until they need him*; and some men never feel the need of him until life plunges them into a shattering experience (italics in original)."

St. Augustine.[12] Augustine wrote, "Thou madest us for Thyself, and our heart is restless, until it repose in Thee."[13] This idea struck several of A.A.'s root source writers as the real spiritual problem, for they frequently quoted the foregoing statement by Augustine.[14] Sam Shoemaker added, in connection with this Augustine quote, "The emptiness, loneliness, homesickness, wistfulness, wonderment which all men feel at some time is a hollow place in the human soul that God is meant to fill."[15]

Dr. Leslie D. Weatherhead—whose titles were read by many early AAs, including Henrietta Seiberling and Bill Wilson—quoted the Book of Job to describe man's despairing need to find God:

Even to day *is* my complaint bitter: my stroke is heavier than my groaning. Oh that I knew where I might find him! *that* I might come *even* to his seat![16]

In a book read by many early AAs, Dr. Harry Emerson Fosdick quoted Psalm 55:1-5 in describing man's plight without God's listening ear:

Give ear to my prayer, O God; and hide not thyself from my supplication. Attend unto me, and hear me: I mourn in my complaint, and make a noise. Because of the voice of the enemy, because of the oppression of the wicked: for they cast iniquity upon me, and in wrath they hate me. My heart is sore pained

---

[12] See Dick B., *Dr. Bob's Library: Books for Twelve Step Growth* (San Rafael, CA: Paradise Research Publications, 1994), p. 25; and *The Confessions of St. Augustine*, trans. by E. B. Pusey (New York: A Cardinal Edition, Pocket Books, 1952).

[13] *Confessions*, p. 1.

[14] See Harold Begbie, *Twice-Born Men* (New York: Fleming H. Revell, 1909), p. 263; Samuel M. Shoemaker, Jr., *National Awakening* (New York: Harper & Brothers, 1936), p. 46; T. R. Glover, *The Jesus of History* (New York: Association Press, 1919), pp. 97, 121; compare Emmet Fox, *The Sermon on the Mount: The Key to Success in Life* (New York: Harper & Row, 1938), pp. 111, 175.

[15] Shoemaker, *National Awakening*, p. 46.

[16] Job 23:2-3; Leslie D. Weatherhead, *How Can I Find God?* (London: Hodder & Stoughton, 1933), p. 1. See also *The Upper Room* for 7/2/35.

within me: and the terrors of death are fallen upon me. Fearfulness and trembling are come upon me, and horror hath overwhelmed me.[17]

The Reverend Sam Shoemaker quoted the Apostle Paul's description of man's spiritual problem and its solution:

O wretched man that I am! who shall deliver me from the body of this death? I thank God through Jesus Christ our Lord . . . (Romans 7:24-25).[18]

And one of the early A.A. pioneer stories in the Big Book's first edition quoted this segment of Romans and indicated the verses marked the turning point toward recovery. *Smile With Me, At Me* wrote:

One morning, after a sleepless night worrying over what I could do to straighten myself out, I went to my room alone—took my Bible in hand and asked Him, the One Power, that I might open to a good place to read—and I read. "For I delight in the law of God after the inward man. But I see a different law in my members, warring against the law of my mind and bringing me into captivity under the law of sin which is in my members. Wretched man that I am! Who shall deliver me out of the body of this death?" That was enough for me—I started to understand. Here were the words of Paul a great teacher. When, then if I had slipped? Now, I could understand. From that day I gave and still give and always will, time everyday to read the word of God and let Him do all the caring. Who am I to try to run myself or anyone else.[19]

---

[17] Fosdick, *The Meaning of Faith*, p. 184.

[18] Shoemaker, *National Awakening*, p. 48; *Religion That Works* (New York: Fleming H. Revell, 1928), p. 45. See also Glover, *The Jesus of History*, p. 149. This latter book was read and recommended by Dr. Bob and Anne Smith.

[19] Big Book, 1st edition, p. 347.

Dr. Carl G. Jung eventually gave AAs an even more specific Biblical picture of their spiritual problem and the necessary spiritual solution. Years after Bill Wilson had written the Big Book and the Twelve Steps, Jung responded to a letter from Bill and explained to Bill that he (Jung) had told one of Bill's Oxford Group mentors, Rowland Hazard, the solution to the alcoholic's spiritual problem. To his spiritual restlessness and discontent. And to his estrangement from God. Jung wrote:

> His [the alcoholic's] craving for alcohol was the equivalent on a low level of the spiritual thirst of our being for wholeness, expressed in medieval language: the union with God.[20]

Jung then referred Bill to Psalm 42:1:

> As the hart panteth after the water brooks, so panteth my soul after thee, O God.[21]

The bottom line in A.A.'s First Step, then, *was*, very possibly, biblical. AAs certainly needed to recognize the deadly physical and mental disease that medicine had revealed to them.[22] The alcoholic needed to know he or she was powerless over alcohol because of a mental obsession, coupled with a physical allergy.[23] And that life had become unmanageable.[24] But the alcoholic would never recover, found Bill and Dr. Bob, without spiritual wholeness, without finding God—without union *with* God, as Carl Jung put it. And the spiritual *problem*, which Jung described, had

---

[20] *Pass It On* (New York: Alcoholics Anonymous World Services, 1984), p. 384.

[21] *Pass It On*, p. 384-85.

[22] Bill wrote: "[Dr. Silkworth] was soon to contribute a very great idea without which AA could never have succeeded. For years he had been proclaiming alcoholism an illness, an obsession of the mind coupled with an allergy of the body. By now I knew this meant me. I also understood what a fatal combination these twin ogres could be." *The Language of the Heart: Bill W.'s Grapevine Writings* (New York: The A.A. Grapevine, Inc., 1988), p. 197.

[23] Big Book, pp. xxiv, 23, 37, 59.

[24] Big Book, p. 60: "That we were alcoholic and could not manage our own lives."

long before been defined in the Bible by Job, by David, and by Paul: Man was wretched of and by himself.[25] And man needed to learn and concede that spiritual fact, those Biblical writers said, in order to see his need for God as the solution to his seeming spiritual hopelessness.

Professor William James—whom Bill Wilson regarded as the father of modern psychology, "a founder" of A.A., and the author of the First Step's "deflation at depth" idea—had described the solution to every person's need for union with God via a conversion experience in the following terms:

> To be converted, to be regenerated, to receive grace, to experience religion, to gain an assurance, are so many phrases which denote the process, gradual or sudden, by which a self hitherto divided, and consciously wrong inferior and unhappy, becomes unified and consciously right superior and happy, in consequence of its firmer hold upon religious realities.[26]

And many of A.A.'s spiritual sources, including Anne Smith, quoted this William James definition as an example of man's divided self—which was consciously wrong, inferior, and unhappy—and which needed regeneration, change and conversion by the grace of God.[27]

---

[25] See also Paul's statement in Ephesians 2:12: "That at that time [when Gentiles were called Uncircumcision] ye were without Christ, being aliens from the commonwealth of Israel, and strangers from the covenants of promise, having no hope, and without God in the world."

[26] William James, *The Varieties of Religious Experience* (New York: Vintage Books/The Library of America Edition, 1990), p. 177. For Wilson's views of James as psychology's father, as an A.A. "founder," and as the source of A.A.'s "deflation at depth" idea, see *Pass It On*, pp. 124-25, 197; *Alcoholics Anonymous Comes of Age*, p. 64.

[27] Dick B., *Design for Living*, p. 60; *Anne Smith's Journal*, p. 101.

The solution to the divided self problem, said many of A.A.'s sources, was crucifixion of the big "I."[28] Surrender of self.[29] A turning point involving self-surrender of the ego.[30] And at least two of A.A.'s root sources referred to the turning point (which began with a divided, deflated self, requiring such a surrender) as "powerlessness" and loss of power.[31]

Many also declared the unmanageability of a spiritually sick life focused on self—a life of self-centeredness and ego-centricity, in which self constituted God.[32] A common prayer in use at that stage of the path was "O, God, manage me, because I cannot manage myself."[33] Dr. Bob's wife often recommended such a prayer at the point of powerlessness.[34]

Shoemaker summed up the spiritual problem as follows:

---

[28] Edgar J. Goodspeed, *The Wonderful Career of Moody and Sankey in Great Britain and America* (New York: Henry S. Goodspeed & Co., 1876), p. 46; Peter Howard, *Frank Buchman's Secret* (Garden City, NY: Doubleday & Company, 1961), p. 43; *The World Rebuilt: The True Story of Frank Buchman and the Achievements of Moral Re-Armament* (New York: Duell, Sloan and Pearce, 1951), p. 242; Paul Campbell and Peter Howard, *Remaking Men* (New York: Arrowhead Books, 1954), p. 75; The Layman with a Notebook, *What is the Oxford Group?* (London: Oxford University Press, 1933), pp. 23-24; A. J. Russell, *For Sinners Only* (London: Hodder & Stoughton, 1932), p. 60; Bremer Hofmeyr, *How to Change* (New York: Moral Re-Armament, n.d.), p. 3.

[29] Leslie D. Weatherhead, *Discipleship* (London: Student Christian Movement Press, 1934), p. 16. For the many discussions of the self-surrender idea in A.A. roots, see Dick B., *Design for Living*, pp. 170-75.

[30] *What Is the Oxford Group?*, pp. 23-24; Samuel M. Shoemaker, Jr., *If I Be Lifted Up* (New York: Fleming H. Revell, 1931), p. 28; Weatherhead, *How Can I Find God?*, p. 84; Dick B., *Design for Living*, pp. 47, 78, 334.

[31] Shoemaker, *If I Be Lifted Up*, pp. 131, 133; *How to Become a Christian* (New York: Harper & Brothers, 1953), p. 77; Dick B., *Anne Smith's Journal*, p. 22.

[32] Dick B., *Design for Living*, pp. 77, 79, 183, 299, 300, 347; *New Light on Alcoholism*, pp. 145, 230, 300; *Anne Smith's Journal*, pp. 19-21. See also Big Book, pp. 52, 53, 60-64, 71, 87-88.

[33] Dick B., *Design for Living*, pp. 77, 79, 182-83; *New Light on Alcoholism*, pp. 145, 230, 300.

[34] Dick B., *Anne Smith's Journal*, pp. 20-22.

God is God, and self is not God—that is the heart of it. It is an actual fact that we become God to ourselves unless we have God to believe in: the final reference becomes ourselves.[35]

My principles "listened" well but they worked like the devil's own. . . . I realized the horror I was passing through, and suddenly gave up that path because I saw it ending in a blank wall or worse. One is reminded of a very old verse: "There is a way which seemeth right unto a man, but the end thereof are the ways of death."[36]

The Big Book said:

So our troubles, we think, are basically of our own making. . . . Neither could we reduce our self-centeredness much by wishing or trying on our own power. We had to have God's help. This is the how and why of it. First of all, we had to quit playing God. It didn't work (p. 62).

In its chapter titled "Get Wisdom, Get Understanding," *The Runner's Bible* pointed to the reproof Jesus gave to the Sadducees:

Ye do err, not knowing the scriptures, nor the power of God.[37]

And we believe the early AAs, with their regular study of Scripture and their search for the power that God could provide, were following exactly the path Jesus suggested.[38] The early AAs studied the Good Book; and they sought the power of God for the solution to their spiritual misery and despair.

---

[35] Shoemaker, *National Awakening*, p. 48.

[36] Shoemaker, *Realizing Religion*, p. 7, quoting Proverbs 16:25.

[37] Matthew 22:29; Nora Smith Holm, *The Runner's Bible* (New York: Houghton Mifflin, 1915), p. 51.

[38] Note that the Big Book declared that probably no human power could relieve AAs of their alcoholism, but that "God could and would if He were sought" (p. 60).

Step Two, Willingness, Belief, and Seeking

[Step Two: Came to believe that a Power greater than ourselves could restore us to sanity.]

Reduced to its essence, and as described in A.A.'s Big Book, the Second Step required *"willingness* to believe," *belief* in a "Power, which is God," and *"seeking"* the power of God for relief from alcoholism. Some might disagree with our description of the Second Step requirements, but Bill Wilson put those ideas very explicitly in the following Big Book phrases:

> *It was only a matter of being willing to believe in a Power greater than myself. Nothing more was required of me to make my beginning.* I saw that growth could start from that point. Upon a foundation of complete willingness I might build what I saw in my friend [Bill's "sponsor," Ebby Thacher] (p. 12; italics in original).

> Its [the Big Book's] main object is to enable you to find a Power greater than yourself which will solve your problem . . . it means, of course, that *we are going to talk about God* . . . even though it was impossible for any of us to fully define or comprehend that *Power, which is God* (pp. 45-46; italics added).

> We needed to ask ourselves but one short question. "Do I now *believe, or am I even willing to believe*, that there is a Power greater than myself?" As soon as a man can say that he does believe, or is willing to believe, we emphatically assure him that he is on his way (p. 47; italics added).

> Circumstances made him willing to believe. He humbly offered himself to his Maker—then he knew. Even so has God restored us all to our right minds. . . . He has come to all who have honestly *sought* Him (p. 57; italics added).

[P]robably no human power could have relieved our alcoholism. . . . God could and would *if He were sought* (p. 60; italics added).

All three A.A. concepts—willingness, belief, and seeking—were borrowed by AAs from Bible verses A.A.'s sources had frequently quoted.

Concerning *willingness*, the Reverend Sam Shoemaker was A.A.'s most articulate Bible teacher.[39] Shoemaker said that if one wished to "come to believe," he or she should follow the injunction of Jesus Christ in John 7:17. The essence of Jesus's teaching as Shoemaker and others including early AAs interpreted it, was that if one obeyed the known commandments and doctrines of God by acting upon them, he or she would learn, believe, and know more about God and His will because God would then reveal more.[40] A.A.'s religious sources taught that *obedience* to God's will is the organ of spiritual *knowledge*.[41] They quoted John 7:17:

If any man will do his will, he shall know of the doctrine, whether it be of God, or *whether* I speak of myself.

Concerning *belief*, many of A.A.'s root sources quoted Hebrews 11:6. Oxford Group people, other A.A. sources, and

---

[39] See also the discussion by Shoemaker's Oxford Group friend, Philip Marshall Brown, *The Venture of Belief* (New York: Fleming H. Revell, 1935), pp. 29, 36.

[40] See, for example, Shoemaker, *Religion That Works*, p. 36; Russell, *For Sinners Only*, p. 211; Brown, *The Venture of Belief*, pp. 29, 36; Dick B., *Design for Living*, pp. 41, 50, 54-56, 70, 149, 164, 190, 217, 272-74, 313, 315-16, 333; *The Upper Room* for 4/26/35, 6/28/37, 12/1/37; Harry Emerson Fosdick, *The Meaning of Prayer* (New York: Association Press, 1915), p. 59; *The Meaning of Faith*, pp. 216-17; Glenn Clark, *I Will Lift Up Mine Eyes* (New York: Harper & Brothers, 1937), p. 27; Oswald Chambers, *Studies in the Sermon on the Mount* (London: Simpkin Marshall, n.d.), p. 37.

[41] See Henry Drummond, *The Ideal Life* (New York: Hodder & Stoughton, 1897), pp. 227-320; F. B. Meyer, *The Secret of Guidance* (New York: Fleming H. Revell, 1896), p. 11; Henry B. Wright, *The Will of God and a Man's Lifework* (New York: The Young Men's Christian Association, 1909), pp. 102-279; Clarence I. Benson, *The Eight Points of the Oxford Group* (London: Oxford University Press, 1936), pp. 134-42.

early AAs subscribed to the idea that they could not come to God
without believing that God is.[42] Hebrews 11:6 states:

> But without faith *it is* impossible to please *him*: for he that cometh
> to God must believe that He is, and *that* he is a rewarder of them
> that diligently seek him.

And concerning *seeking*, early AAs took their cue from the
Sermon on the Mount and religion's countless references to
seeking *first* the Kingdom of God. These references can be found
in Shoemaker's titles and the other Christian writings of the day
which were being studied by the AAs.[43] As we've mentioned, Dr.
Bob was very emphatic that A.A.'s well-known "First Things
First" slogan came from Matthew 6:33.[44] The verse declares:

> But seek ye first the kingdom of God, and his righteousness; and
> all these things [earthly needs for food, drink, clothing] shall be
> added unto you.

Step Three and the Decision to Surrender

[Step Three: Made a decision to turn our will and our lives over
to the care of God *as we understood Him.*]

---

[42] Weatherhead, *How Can I Find God?*, p. 72; Samuel M. Shoemaker, *The Gospel
According to You* (New York: Fleming H. Revell, 1934), p. 47; *National Awakening*,
pp. 40-41; *Religion That Works*, p. 55; *Confident Faith* (New York: Fleming H. Revell,
1932), p. 187; Oswald Chambers, *My Utmost for His Highest* (New Jersey: Barbour and
Company, 1963), p. 304; Fosdick, *The Meaning of Faith*, pp. 8, 92; Dick B., *Design
for Living*, pp. 165, 331; *New Light on Alcoholism*, p. 126; *DR. BOB and the Good
Oldtimers* (New York: Alcoholics Anonymous World Services, 1980), p. 144. The latter
title is hereinafter called *DR. BOB*.

[43] Shoemaker, *National Awakening*, p. 41; *The Upper Room* for 9/4/35; 11/19/35;
6/20/37; 12/2/38; Holm, *The Runner's Bible*, p. 127; Chambers, *My Utmost for His
Highest*, p. 142; *Studies in the Sermon on the Mount*, pp. 60-61; Fosdick, *The Meaning
of Faith*, pp. 192-93; Dick B., *Design for Living*, p. 284; *Anne Smith's Journal*, pp. 132,
140; *Dr. Bob's Library*, p. 93.

[44] *DR. BOB*, p. 144.

We have not, among A.A.'s religious sources, located any direct biblical references to the "decision" of Step Three. But, A.A. sources do discuss two verses which mandate a *decision*:

> That if thou shalt confess with thy mouth the Lord Jesus, and shalt believe in thine heart that God hath raised him from the dead, thou shalt be saved (Romans 10:9).[45]

> And be not conformed to this world: but be ye transformed by the renewing of your mind, that ye may prove what is that good, and acceptable, and perfect, will of God (Romans 12:2).[46]

And there are ample Bible verses, adopted by AAs from their root sources, which served as guides for their *making* their decision to surrender to God and to *entrust* their lives to His care.

The *decision* in early A.A.—and today in some cases—involved a surrender made on the knees.[47] The A.A. surrender language came from the Lord's Prayer—a part of the Sermon on the Mount. Several A.A. sources suggested *decision language* that declared simply and humbly, "Thy will be done."[48] A variant involved Jesus's other similar expression, "Not my will, but thine, be done."[49] The root language for these two "decision" expressions, as rendered in the King James Version of the Bible, came from:

---

[45] Shoemaker, *If I Be Lifted Up*, p. 83; Glenn Clark, *Touchdowns for the Lord: The Story of "Dad" A. J. Elliott* (Minnesota: Macalester Park Publishing Company, 1947), pp. 55-56.

[46] Dick B., *Anne Smith's Journal*, pp. 46, 77, 102, 132, 143; *Design for Living*, p. 171.

[47] For the history of the A.A. surrender "on the knees," see *Pass It On*, pp. 198-99.

[48] Big Book, pp. 67, 88; compare p. 443; Matthew 6:10; *What Is The Oxford Group*, p. 48; Samuel M. Shoemaker, Jr., *Children of the Second Birth* (New York: Fleming H. Revell, 1927), p. 175-87; *The Upper Room* for 12/3/37; Dick B., *Design for Living*, p. 181; *The Akron Genesis*, p. 96.

[49] Big Book, p. 85; compare pp. 229, 381; Mary Wilder Tileston, *Daily Strength for Daily Needs*, 1977 Printing (New York: Grosset & Dunlap, 1884), pp. 296, 146; *The Upper Room* for 6/21/38; *What is the Oxford Group?*, p. 48; Shoemaker, *Children of the Second Birth*, pp. 58, 182; Glenn Clark, *The Soul's Sincere Desire* (Boston: Little, Brown & Co., 1925), p. 40; *I Will Lift Up Mine Eyes*, p. 27.

Thy will be done in earth, as *it is* in heaven (Matthew 6:10).

[N]evertheless not my will, but thine, be done (Luke 22:42).

Sam Shoemaker cited Psalm 46:10 as to the *need* for surrendering and finding God. Shoemaker quoted Dr. Moffatt's translation of Psalm 46:10 as follows:

"Give in," he cries, "admit that I am God, high over nations, high over the world."[50]

Both the Big Book and Sam Shoemaker spoke of "abandoning yourself to God," and such language indicated the total surrender of the will that was expected.[51] The Third Step's actual surrender phraseology can be found in A.A. sources which used such language as "turned over to Him her life for His direction" and a "decision to cast my will and my life on God."[52]

Additional Bible verses which A.A.'s sources associated with a decision to surrender were:

I can of mine own self do nothing: as I hear, I judge: and my judgment is just; because I seek not mine own will, but the will of the Father which hath sent me (John 5:30).[53]

Know ye not, that to whom ye yield yourselves servants to obey, his servants ye are to whom ye obey; whether of sin unto death, or of obedience unto righteousness (Romans 6:16).[54]

---

[50] Shoemaker, *National Awakening*, pp. 45-54. The better known King James Version of Psalm 46:10 reads: "Be still, and know that I am God: I will be exalted among the heathen, I will be exalted in the earth."

[51] Big Book, pp. 164, 59, 63; Shoemaker, *Religion That Works*, p. 19.

[52] Samuel M. Shoemaker, Jr., *Children of the Second Birth*, p. 82; *Twice-Born Ministers* (New York: Fleming H. Revell, 1929), p. 134.

[53] Meyer, *The Secret of Guidance*, p. 11.

[54] Wright, *The Will of God and a Man's Lifework*, p. 31; Chambers, *My Utmost for His Highest*, p. 283.

Know ye not that ye are the temple of God, and *that* the Spirit of God dwelleth in you? (1 Corinthians 3:16).[55]

God *is* a Spirit: and they that worship him must worship *him* in spirit and in truth (John 4:24).[56]

For in him we live, and move, and have our being; as certain also of your own poets have said, For we are also his offspring (Acts 17:28).[57]

Repent ye therefore, and be converted, that your sins may be blotted out, when the times of refreshing shall come from the presence of the Lord (Acts 3:19).[58]

In connection with this Step, Clarence S. referred to 1 Thessalonians 1:9—"how ye turned to God from idols to serve the living and true God." Clarence also quoted Ephesians 4:22-24—putting off the old man by renewing your mind, and putting on the new man created in righteousness and true holiness.[59]

Step Four and Self-examination

[Step Four: Made a searching and fearless moral inventory of ourselves.]

---

[55] Holm, *The Runner's Bible*, p. 17; *What Is The Oxford Group?*, p. 39; Clark, *I Will Lift Up Mine Eyes*, p. 30.

[56] Fosdick, *The Meaning of Faith*, p. 85; *What Is the Oxford Group?*, p. 41; *The Upper Room* for 5/1/35; Holm, *The Runner's Bible*, p. 4.

[57] Fosdick, *The Meaning of Faith*, pp. 86-87; *What Is the Oxford Group?*, p. 42; R. C. Mowat, *Modern Prophetic Voices from Kierkegaard to Buchman* (Great Britain, New Cherwell Press, 1994), pp. 72-73; B. H. Streeter, *The God Who Speaks* (London: Macmillan & Co., Ltd., 1936), p. 12.

[58] Holm, *The Runner's Bible*, p. 88; *What Is The Oxford Group?*, p. 43. On repentance, see discussion in Benson, *The Eight Points*, pp. 7-9; *The Upper Room* for 6/1/37.

[59] See Dick B., *That Amazing Grace*, pp. 68-69.

A.A.'s root sources spoke of taking a *moral* inventory. One was to examine one's life in terms of how it measured up to the "Four Absolutes"—honesty, purity, unselfishness and love. More importantly, Oxford Group members wished to learn of any "sins" or "shortcomings" blocking them from God and from others.[60]

The basic idea that self-examination is required to establish a satisfactory relationship with God came from several verses in the Sermon on the Mount. These verses state that one should look for his own faults, his own part in difficulties, before looking at the faults of another. A.A. sources quoted Matthew 7:3-5:

> And why beholdest thou the mote [speck] that is in thy brother's eye, but considerest not the beam [log] that is in thine own eye? Or wilt thou say to thy brother, "Let me pull out the mote out of thine eye;" and, behold, a beam is in thine own eye? Thou hypocrite, first cast out the beam out of thine own eye; and then shalt thou see clearly to cast out the mote out of thy brother's eye.[61]

The Oxford Group's self-examination "yardsticks" were *positive*. The self-examination was to be in the context of how well a person was living up to the "absolute" moral standards taught by Jesus. The Oxford Group's standards were taken from Dr. Robert E. Speer's reconstruction of Jesus's uncompromising teachings on perfection.[62] Speer believed he had identified Jesus's four "absolute" moral standards in the following verses:

---

[60] See Dick B., *Design for Living*, pp. 166-70, for the varying Oxford Group definitions of sin, all of which characterized "sin" as that which blocks us from God and from others.

[61] Geoffrey Allen, *He That Cometh* (New York: The Macmillan Company, 1933), pp. 81, 140; Victor C. Kitchen, *I Was a Pagan* (New York: Harper & Brothers, 1934), p. 111; Samuel M. Shoemaker, Jr., *The Church Can Save the World*, 2d ed (New York: Harper & Brothers, 1938), pp. 88-121; *God's Control* (New York: Fleming H. Revell, 1939), pp. 62-72; Dick B., *Anne Smith's Journal*, pp. 30-31.

[62] Robert E. Speer, *The Principles of Jesus* (New York: Association Press, 1902). Speer discussed Jesus's standard of perfection at page 34 and quoted Matthew 5:48 from the Sermon on the Mount: "Be ye therefore perfect, even as your Father which is in heaven is perfect."

Honesty (which Speer spoke of as "an absolute standard of truth"). Speer urged, if Satan is the father of lies, how can any lie be justifiable? Speer's unmistakable reference is to John 8:44: "Ye are of *your* father the devil, and the lusts of your father ye will do. He was a murderer from the beginning, and abode not in the truth, because there is no truth in him. When he speaketh a lie, he speaketh of his own: for he is a liar, and the father of it."[63]

Unselfishness. Speer cited: (1) Mark 10:45: "For even the Son of man came not to be ministered unto, but to minister, and to give his life a ransom for many." (2) Luke 22:27: "For whether *is* greater, he that sitteth at meat, or he that serveth? *is* not he that sitteth at meat? but I am among you as he that serveth." (3) Luke 14:33: "So likewise, whosoever he be of you that forsaketh not all that he hath, he cannot be my disciple."[64]

Purity. Speer cited: (1) Mark 7:15: "There is nothing from without a man, that entering into him can defile him: but the things which come out of him, those are they that defile the man." (2) Matthew 5:29-30: "And if thy right eye offend thee, pluck it out, and cast *it* from thee: for it is profitable for thee that one of thy members should perish, and not *that* thy whole body should be cast into hell. And if thy right hand offend thee, cut it off, and cast *it* from thee: for it is profitable for thee that one of thy members should perish, and not *that* thy whole body should be cast into hell."[65]

Love. Speer basically cited (1) John 13:34: "A new commandment I give unto you, That ye love one another; as I have loved you, that ye also love one another." (2) John 13:1. "Now before the feast of the passover, when Jesus knew that his hour was come that he should depart out of this world unto the Father, having loved his own which were in the world, he loved them unto the end."[66]

---

[63] Speer, *The Principles of Jesus*, p. 35.

[64] Speer, *The Principles of Jesus*, p. 35. See also Streeter, *The God Who Speaks*, p. 84.

[65] Speer, *The Principles of Jesus*, p. 35.

[66] Speer, *The Principles of Jesus*, p. 35.

Later writers, including Sam Shoemaker, thought Speer's four
standards actually *came* from Jesus's teachings in the Sermon on
the Mount.[67] And the standards did, in the sense that they were
founded on the standard of perfection Jesus enunciated in the
Sermon. But the verses which Speer himself cited as authority
were not all from Matthew 5–7, though they *were* taught by Jesus
and were consistent *with* his Sermon on the Mount teachings.

Professor Henry B. Wright, who was a major influence on the
thinking of Oxford Group Founder Frank Buchman, examined
Speer's four absolute standards in light of the following Gospel
verses.[68] (Wright termed the principles in the verses the "Four
Absolutes."[69]):

Honesty. Luke 16:10-11: "He that is faithful in that which is least
is faithful also in much: and he that is unjust in the least is unjust
also in much. If therefore ye have not been faithful in the
unrighteous mammon, who will commit to your trust the true
riches?"[70]

Unselfishness. Luke 9:23-24: "And he said to *them* all, If any
man will come after me, let him deny himself, and take up his
cross daily, and follow me. For whosoever will save his life shall
lose it: but whosoever will lose his life for my sake, the same
shall save it."[71]

Purity. Matthew 5:8: "Blessed *are* the pure in heart: for they shall
see God."[72]

Love. Matthew 25:41-43, 45: ". . . Depart from me, ye cursed,
into everlasting fire, prepared for the devil and his angels; For I

---

[67] See Dick B., *Design for Living*, pp. 237-38.

[68] For a discussion of Wright's immense influence on Frank Buchman, see Dick B.,
Design for Living, pp. 67-72.

[69] Wright, *The Will of God*, pp. 167-218:

[70] Wright, *The Will of God*, p. 187.

[71] Wright, *The Will of God*, p. 197.

[72] Wright, *The Will of God*, p. 179. See also Russell, *For Sinners Only*, p. 63.

was an hungered, and ye gave me no meat: I was thirsty, and ye gave me no drink: I was a stranger, and ye took me not in: naked, and ye clothed me not: sick, and in prison, and ye visited me not. . . . Then shall he answer them, saying, Verily I say unto you, Inasmuch as ye did *it* not to one of the least of these, ye did *it* not to me."[73]

Unsurprisingly, A.A.'s other progenitors in the Oxford Group, including Wright himself, found the same four absolute moral principles in a good many other New Testament verses including the following: Mark 10:19-21; 1 Corinthians 13; Ephesians 4:15-16; Colossians 3:5-14; 1 Thessalonians 4:3-12; and James 3:17.[74]

In his last major address to AAs, Dr. Bob still spoke highly of the Oxford Group's "Four Absolutes" and said they were the "yardsticks" by which AAs could measure their conduct and, in effect, "take their inventory."[75] Dr. Bob's wife, Anne, frequently urged the Four Absolutes as moral standards for conduct.[76] In later years, A.A.'s other co-founder Bill Wilson became quite critical of the Four Absolutes, claiming they were too "absolute" for alcoholics to follow.[77] And perhaps in consequence, Wilson framed the Big Book's moral inventory in terms of *negatives*. AAs were enjoined to examine their lives for: (1) Resentments and grudges; (2) Fears; (3) Selfishness and self-seeking, particularly in the sex area; (4) Dishonesty; and (5) "Harms" they had caused others by their conduct.[78]

The Biblical roots which defined A.A.'s "negative" yardsticks were not as concisely and precisely defined in A.A.'s religious

---

[73] Wright, *The Will of God*, p. 207.

[74] Wright, *The Will of God*, p. 167; *What is the Oxford Group?*, p. 109; Harry J. Almond, *Foundations for Faith*. 2d ed (London: Grosvenor Books, 1980), p. 12; Benson, *The Eight Points*, pp. 44-57.

[75] *The Co-Founders of Alcoholics Anonymous: Biographical sketches Their last major talks* (New York: Alcoholics Anonymous World Services, 1972, 1975), pp. 12-14.

[76] Dick B., *Anne Smith's Journal*, pp. 31-34, 59-60, 104-06, 108, 115-20.

[77] *Alcoholics Anonymous Comes of Age*, pp. 74-75; *Pass It On*, pp. 171-74.

[78] See Big Book, pp. 64-70, 84, 86.

sources as were the four "positive" absolutes. But we believe those negative moral yardsticks do pop out rather clearly from the Bible verses early AAs studied or to which they were exposed.

In their search for objectionable conduct that blocked them from God, AAs were, in their Fourth Step, to *put on paper* their resentments, fears, selfish sex conduct, and harms to others.[79] And the underlying requirement was that they apply rigorous honesty in their inventory.[80]

And we believe the following Biblical teachings by A.A.'s sources had a major influence in defining the negatives AAs were to search for, list in writing, and root out. We believe this because of the pervasive A.A. source teachings *about* these spiritual problems, and the similarity between A.A. language and the Biblical root teachings:

Resentments and grudges: "Grudge not one against another, brethren, lest ye be condemned: behold, the judge standeth before the door" (James 5:9). "But I say unto you, That whosoever is angry with his brother without a cause shall be in danger of the judgment: and whosoever shall say to his brother, Raca, shall be in danger of the council: but whosever shall say, Thou fool, shall be in danger of hell fire" (Matthew 5:22—in the Sermon on the Mount).[81]

Fears: "The Lord *is* my light and my salvation; whom shall I fear? the Lord *is* the strength of my life; of whom shall I be afraid?" (Psalm 27:1); "Yea, though I walk through the valley of the shadow of death, I will fear no evil: for thou *art* with me; thy rod

---

[79] Big Book p. 64 (resentments); p. 68 (fears); p. 69 (selfish sex conduct); p. 70 (people hurt by the conduct).

[80] Big Book, pp. 58, 65, 67, 69. See also pp. 84, 86.

[81] See *The Upper Room* for 10/18/35; Holm, *The Runner's Bible*, p. 82; Shoemaker, *Twice-Born Ministers*, p. 182; *How to Become a Christian*, pp. 55-64; Harold Begbie, *Life Changers* (London: Mills & Boon, Ltd., 1923), p. 38; Ebenezer Macmillan, *Seeking and Finding* (New York: Harper & Brothers, 1933), pp. 96-98; E. Stanley Jones, *The Christ of the Mount* (New York: The Abingdon Press, 1931), p. 136; Dick B., *Anne Smith's Journal*, pp. 34-36.

and thy staff they comfort me" (Psalm 23:4); "Fear not: for I *am*
with thee" (Isaiah 43:5); "Be not afraid, only believe" (Mark
5:36); "For God hath not given us the spirit of fear; but of power,
and of love, and of a sound mind" (2 Timothy 1:7); "There is no
fear in love; but perfect love casteth out fear: because fear hath
torment" (1 John 4:18).[82]

Selfishness. "Charity . . . seeketh not her own" (1 Cor. 13:4-5).[83]

Dishonesty. "Charity . . . rejoiceth not in iniquity, but rejoiceth in
the truth" (1 Corinthians 13:4, 6); "Finally, brethren, whatsoever
things are true, whatsoever things *are* honest, whatsoever things
are just . . . if *there be* any virtue, and if *there be* any praise, think
on these things" (Philippians 4:8).[84]

Harms caused. Oxford Group writer Olive Jones succinctly defined
"restitution" from the Oxford Group viewpoint as follows:
"*Restitution*, by which we make amends, restore, so far as human
power permits, for the wrong done."[85] The four principal sets of
Bible verses from which came the A.A. suggestions as to amends
for harm done were: Numbers 5:6-7; Matthew 5:23-24; and Luke,
Chapter 15, and 19:1-10. We will quote and discuss these verses
at a later point in connection with Step Nine.[86]

---

[82] Holm, *The Runner's Bible*, pp. 41-44, 132; *The Upper Room* for 7/11/35, 8/22/35,
5/2/37, 8/2/37, 8/6/37, 7/1/38; Tileston, *Daily Strength for Daily Needs*, p. 228;
Fosdick, *The Meaning of Faith*, pp. 191-92, 240; Clark, *The Soul's Sincere Desire*, pp.
8-9, 14; *What is the Oxford Group?*, p. 2; Streeter, *The God Who Speaks*, p. 68; Stephen
Foot, *Life Began Yesterday* (New York: Harper & Brothers, 1935), p. 35; Dick B., *The
Akron Genesis*, p. 94.

[83] Henry Drummond, *The Greatest Thing in the World*, 2d ed (World Bible
Publishers), pp. 26, 32, 33; *DR. BOB*, pp. 96, 310; Dick B., *Anne Smith's Journal*, p.
131.

[84] Drummond, *The Greatest Thing in the World*, pp. 27, 39; *DR. BOB*, pp. 96, 310;
Clark, *I Will Lift Up Mine Eyes*, pp. 54, 93; *The Upper Room* for 9/12/35, 5/14/36,
7/20/37; Tileston, *Daily Strength for Daily Needs*, p. 364; Holm, *The Runner's Bible*,
p. 116; Fosdick, *The Meaning of Prayer*, p. 72.

[85] Olive M. Jones, *Inspired Children* (New York: Harper & Brothers, 1933), p. 136.

[86] See also Weatherhead, *Discipleship*, pp. 114-23; Benson, *The Eight Points*, pp.
30-43.

Clarence S. emphasized Mark 7:18-23 and Galatians 5:16-26, both of which segments emphasize the nature of a person's shortcomings—defiling, defeating, evil things people nurture inside themselves and which need purging.[87]

Step Five and Confession

[Step Five: Admitted to God, to ourselves, and to another human being the exact nature of our wrongs.]

Except for scattered mention of a few other verses, AAs and their sources very consistently mentioned James 5:16 as the root of their "confession" step.[88] James 5:16 states:

Confess *your* faults one to another, and pray for one another, that ye may be healed. The effectual fervent prayer of a righteous man availeth much.

Step Six, Conviction and Readiness to Change

[Step Six: Were entirely ready to have God remove all these defects of character.]

It is difficult to pinpoint the Sixth's Step's Biblical link to A.A. The link, if any, was never discussed by Bill Wilson; and apparently it was not discussed either by Dr. Bob or his wife,

---

[87] Dick B., *That Amazing Grace*, pp. 69-71.

[88] J. P. Thornton-Duesbury, *Sharing* (Pamphlet of The Oxford Group, published at Oxford University Press, no date), p. 5; Sherwood Sunderland Day, *The Principles of the Group* (Oxford: University Press, n.d.), p. 6; *What is the Oxford Group?*, pp. 29, 31; Streeter, *The God Who Speaks*, p. 125; Weatherhead, *Discipleship*, p. 32; Almond, *Foundations for Faith*, p. 13; Garth Lean, *Cast Out Your Nets* (London: Grosvenor, 1990), p. 48; Samuel M. Shoemaker, Jr., *The Conversion of the Church* (New York: Fleming H. Revell, 1932), p. 35; Fosdick, *The Meaning of Faith*, p. 190; *The Meaning of Prayer*, pp. 157-58; *The Upper Room* for 12/4/35; *Pass It On*, p. 128; Dick B., *Anne Smith's Journal*, pp. 36, 38, 40, 99, 129, 131-32, 142, 144.

Anne. However, A.A.'s link to the Oxford Group's "Five C's" and their "soul-surgery" art is very clear.[89] And the third "C" in the Oxford Group formula for life-change was "Conviction."[90] "Conviction" was mentioned *by name and by concept* by Bill Wilson's wife, Lois, in Lois's "Oxford Group Notes" and subsequent 1937 diary entries.[91] Dr. Bob's wife, Anne Smith, addressed the "conviction" subject quite frequently in the spiritual journal she kept between 1933 and 1939.[92]

Shoemaker's Oxford Group colleague Olive M. Jones defined "conviction" as follows: "*Conviction*, by which we come to a conscious realization of our sins which shut God away from us."[93]

Understood from the vantage point of its Oxford Group roots in the Five C's, the Step Six "conviction" idea could have come from several Biblical roots. Repentance or dying to self, is the way Glenn Clark summarized the conviction concept.[94] And note that the Biblical source verses progress from the idea that one must convict himself or herself of sin to the idea that *God* brings people to conviction:

"Against thee, thee only, have I sinned, and done *this* evil in thy sight . . ." (Psalm 51:4); "Iniquities prevail against me: as *for* our transgressions, thou shalt purge them away" (Psalm 65:3); "And

---

[89] See Dick B., *Design for Living*, pp. 175-79; *New Light on Alcoholism*, p. 64; *Anne Smith's Journal*, pp. 96-97; and see also *DR. BOB*, p. 54.

[90] Dick B., *Design for Living*, pp. 192-97; Howard A. Walter, *Soul Surgery: Some Thoughts on Incisive Personal Work*, 6th ed. (Oxford: University Press, 1940), pp. 64-78.

[91] Dick B., *New Light on Alcoholism*, pp. 337-41; *The Akron Genesis*, p. 155. For example, during one of his two visits to Stepping Stones Archives at Bedford Hills, New York, the author was allowed by the archivist to inspect and copy entries from Lois Wilson's diary for 1937. That diary contained an entry for February 8, 1937, which stated, "Convicted of trying to be a fixer . . ." For February 13, 1937, Lois wrote, "Convicted of being put out when my personal things have been mishandled . . ."

[92] Dick B., *Anne Smith's Journal*, pp. 41-45, 100-01.

[93] Olive Jones, *Inspired Children*, pp. 135-36.

[94] Clark, *I Will Lift Up Mine Eyes*, p. 77.

the son said unto him, Father, I have sinned against heaven, and in thy sight, and am no more worthy to be called thy son" (Luke 15:21); "For we know that the law is spiritual: but I am carnal, sold under sin" (Romans 7:14); "Who is weak, and I am not weak? who is offended, and I burn not?" (2 Corinthians 11:29); "And when he [the Comforter] is come, he will reprove [convict] the world of sin, and of righteousness, and of judgment" (John 16:8). "But God commendeth his love toward us, in that, while we were yet sinners, Christ died for us" (Romans 5:8).[95]

Step Seven, Humble Submission and Rebirth

[Step Seven: Humbly asked Him to remove our shortcomings.]

Early AAs believed God was willing and able to change them. They expected the change to occur if they asked Him for it. In his correspondence with Dr. Carl Jung, Bill Wilson wrote the great psychiatrist about "conversion" and "conversion experiences." As to Rowland Hazard and the "conversion experience that released him for the time being from his compulsion to drink," Bill wrote:

> This concept [a spiritual experience] proved to be the foundation of such success as Alcoholics Anonymous has since achieved. This has made conversion experience . . . available on an almost wholesale basis.[96]

A *conversion experience* certainly meant, among other things, to Bill and to Bill's spiritual teachers, that one had been "born again of the spirit."[97]

---

[95] Walter, *Soul Surgery*, pp. 64-78; Fosdick, *The Meaning of Faith*, pp. 54, 146; *The Upper Room* for 6/2/37; Chambers, *My Utmost for His Highest*, p. 324; Glover, *The Jesus of History*, p. 149.

[96] *Pass It On*, p. 383.

[97] Shoemaker, *Realizing Religion*, pp. 21, 35; *Children of the Second Birth*, p. 32; *Religion That Works*, p. 14; *Twice-Born Ministers*, pp. 10, 56; *Confident Faith*, pp. 137, 140; *National Awakening*, pp. 55-66; Allen, *He That Cometh*, pp. 19, 32, 48-49; Jones,
(continued...)

In an early Big Book manuscript which the author found at Bill's home at Stepping Stones in Bedford Hills, New York, Bill spoke of his *own* conversion experience. He proclaimed of that experience, "For sure, I'd been born again;" and he repeated that "born again" conclusion in another early manuscript.[98] Neither of Bill's explicit observations about his rebirth was included in A.A.'s Conference Approved literature. However, Bill reached his conclusion after he had made a decision for Christ at Shoemaker's Calvary Rescue Mission in New York, just prior to Bill's entering Towns Hospital for the last time.[99]

This early A.A. idea that one needed to be "converted" and "born again" by the power of God seemed to vanish in later A.A. language. Yet the early A.A. concept that one achieves freedom from sin by the grace of God was firmly rooted in John 3 and the new birth principle. Hence even the third edition of the Big Book—seemingly almost by oversight—proclaimed, "as we became conscious of His presence, we began to lose our fear of today, tomorrow or the hereafter. We were reborn" (p. 63).

The following were the verses most frequently cited by A.A. sources in connection with the conversion experiences to which AAs had been led in their early days:

Jesus answered and said unto him, Verily, verily, I say unto thee, Except a man be born again, he cannot see the kingdom of God. . . . Jesus answered, Verily, verily, I say unto thee, Except a man be born of water and of the Spirit, he cannot enter the kingdom *of* God. . . . Marvel not that I said unto thee, Ye must be born again (John 3:3, 3:5, 3:7).[100]

---

[97] (...continued)
Inspired Children, p. 136; Drummond, *The Ideal Life*, pp. 212-26; Frank Buchman, *Remaking The World* (London: Blandford, 1961), p. 23; Begbie, *Life Changers*, p. 117.

[98] Dick B., *New Light on Alcoholism*, p. 55.

[99] Dick B., *New Light on Alcoholism*, pp. 55-56.

[100] See Olive Jones, *Inspired Children*, which states at page 136: "*Conversion*, which means simply a changed life. 'Ye must be born again,' said Christ." See also
(continued...)

Submit yourselves therefore to God. Resist the devil, and he will flee from you (James 4:7).[101]

Humble yourselves in the sight of the Lord, and he shall lift you up (James 4:10).[102]

Clarence S. illustrated the Seventh Step process by characterizing it as the Step where the New Manager (God) got out the tape eraser and erased the defects identified in Step Four, confessed in Step Five, and renounced in Step Six. He said the assurance of God's help was given in the Sermon on the Mount (Matthew 7:7-11). The fullness of God's forgiveness was set forth in Psalm 103:10-12. And the procedure for praying with other believers to secure removal was set forth in James 5:13-16.[103]

Step Eight, Willingness to Make Amends

[Step Eight: Made a list of all persons we had harmed, and became willing to make amends to them all.]

The Big Book states:

We have made a list of all persons we have harmed and to whom we are willing to make amends. . . . Now we go out to our fellows and repair the damage done in the past. We attempt to sweep away the debris which has accumulated out of our effort to live on self-will and run the show ourselves (p. 76).

---

[100] (...continued)
Shoemaker, *Twice-Born Ministers*, pp. 56, 10; *National Awakening*, pp. 55, 57, 58; Buchman, *Remaking the World*, p. 23; Begbie, *Life Changers*, p. 117; Allen, *He That Cometh*, pp. 19-43; Chambers, *My Utmost for His Highest*, pp. 228, 333; *Studies in the Sermon on the Mount*, pp. 16, 31; *The Upper Room* for 6/8/37, 5/22/38.

[101] Holm, *The Runner's Bible*, pp. 59, 94, 112, 115.

[102] Samuel M. Shoemaker, *Those Twelve Steps as I Understand Them*; Volume II, *Best of the Grapevine* (New York: The A.A. Grapevine, Inc., 1986), p. 130.

[103] Dick B., *That Amazing Grace*, pp. 72-74.

In discussing the approach to others and the reason for making amends even to those we dislike, A.A.'s sources emphasized the following verses:

Agree with thine adversary quickly, whiles thou art in the way with him; lest at any time the adversary deliver thee to the judge, and the judge deliver thee to the officer, and thou be cast into prison (Matthew 5:25).[104]

If a man say, I love God, and hateth his brother, he is a liar: for he that loveth not his brother whom he hath seen, how can he love God whom he hath not seen? (1 John 4:20).[105]

Step Nine, Restitution

[Step Nine: Made direct amends to such people wherever possible, except when to do so would injure them or others.]

Four sets of verses captured the attention of A.A.'s root sources in connection with straightening out the wreckage of the past and making restitution for harms done to others:

Therefore if thou bring thy gift to the altar, and there rememberest that thy brother hath ought against thee; leave there thy gift before the altar, and go thy way; first be reconciled to thy brother, and then come and offer thy gift (Matthew 5:23-24).[106]

---

[104] Holm, *The Runner's Bible*, p. 67; Chambers, *My Utmost for His Highest*, p. 182; Benson, *The Eight Points*, p. 32; Weatherhead, *Discipleship*, p. 112. See also *The Upper Room* for 1/12/36 or 1/12/39.

[105] Clark, *I Will Lift Up Mine Eyes*, p. 32; Benson, *The Eight Points*, pp. 36-37; Macmillan, *Seeking and Finding*, p. 99; Tileston, *Daily Strength for Daily Needs*, p. 103; Dick B., *The Akron Genesis*, p. 92, n. 10; *New Light on Alcoholism*, p. 272.

[106] Benson, *The Eight Points*, p. 30; MacMillan, *Seeking and Finding*, p. 176; Russell, *For Sinner's Only*, p. 120; Weatherhead, *Discipleship*, p. 113; Shoemaker, *The Conversion of the Church*, pp. 47-48; *The Gospel According to You*, p. 149; Holm, *The Runner's Bible*, p. 82; Chambers, *My Utmost for His Highest*, p. 268; *DR. BOB*, p. 308; *RHS* (the dedication page); E. Stanley Jones, *The Christ of the Mount*, p. 140.

Speak unto the Children of Israel, when a man or a woman shall commit any sin that men commit, to do a trespass against the Lord, and that soul shall be guilty; Then they shall confess their sin which they have done: and he shall make restitution for his guilt in full, and add unto it the fifth part thereof, and give it unto him in respect of whom he hath been guilty (Numbers 5:6-7, as the translation is rendered in Russell, *For Sinners Only*, p. 119).

For Sinners Only also referred to the Prodigal Son story in Luke, chapter 15. Russell said, "Sending prodigal sons back to their earthly as well as their Heavenly Father is a specialty of the Oxford Group."[107]

For Sinners Only also cited the conversation between Jesus and Zacchaeus recorded in Luke 19:1-10. Zacchaeus had told Jesus that if he had taken anything from any man by false accusation, he had restored the man fourfold. Jesus responded approvingly, "This day is salvation come to thy house."[108]

Step Ten and Daily Corrective Action

[Step Ten: Continued to take personal inventory and when we were wrong promptly admitted it.]

The elements of the Tenth Step can be found on page 84 of the Big Book. The Tenth Step instructions call primarily for a daily application of the spiritual principles learned in the previous nine steps; and the instructions add that AAs should strive to be helpful, loving, and tolerant toward others.

Thus the Big Book's Tenth Step directions state the alcoholic is to *continue* to watch for resentment, selfishness, dishonesty, and fear (tests derived from Step Four). If the "defects of character"

---

[107] Russell, *For Sinners Only*, p. 129. See also *What is the Oxford Group?*, pp. 63-64.

[108] Russell, *For Sinners Only*, p. 135; Lean, *Cast out Your Nets*, pp. 87-88; Macmillan, *Seeking and Finding*, p. 111; Weatherhead, *Discipleship*, pp. 115-16; Almond, *Foundations for Faith*, p. 13.

are encountered, he or she is to confess the problem to another (derived from Step Five). Then God is to be asked for help in eliminating the shortcoming (derived from Steps Six and Seven). If harm has been caused, amends are to be made promptly (derived from Steps Eight and Nine). The alcoholic is then to think of, and help others (derived from Steps Nine and Twelve). And a code of love and tolerance is proclaimed. In short, continuing surrender, continuing recourse to God for help, and continuing corrective behavior are specified as the elements for taking this step.

These ideas involving daily inventory and housecleaning can be found in the Oxford Group concept of "Conservation."[109] Later, Oxford Group writers began speaking of "Continuance" as their Fifth "C," rather than "Conservation."[110] They called for *continuing* repentance, "dying of self," as A.A.'s religious sources might have put it.[111] And the significant Bible verses from which continuance ideas seem to have come are these:

I am crucified with Christ: nevertheless I live; yet not I, but Christ liveth in me: and the life which I now live in the flesh I live by the faith of the Son of God, who loved me, and gave himself for me (Galatians 2:20).[112]

Watch and pray, that ye enter not into temptation: the spirit indeed *is* willing, but the flesh *is* weak (Matthew 26:41).[113]

---

[109] Dick B., *Design for Living*, pp. 221-24; *New Light on Alcoholism*, p. 66; *Anne Smith's Journal*, pp. 49-53, 107, 143; Walter, *Soul Surgery*, 89-100.

[110] The Five C's have alternately been said to include either Conservation or Continuance. But Oxford Group historian and writer K. D. Belden of Great Britain recently wrote the author and explained that the later and preferred usage had become "Continuance." "Continuance" had supplanted "conservation" in usage; and this change may explain A.A.'s emphasis on the word "continued" in connection with the Tenth Step.

[111] Clark, *I Will Lift Up Mine Eyes*, p. 77.

[112] Howard J. Rose, *The Quiet Time* (Sussex, England, n.d.), p. 3; Streeter, *The God Who Speaks*, p. 92; Fosdick, *The Meaning of Faith*, p. 269; *The Upper Room* for 3/27/36 or 3/27/39 and 5/30/36 or 5/30/39.

[113] Rose, *The Quiet Time*, p. 3; Tileston, *Daily Strength for Daily Needs*, p. 100. See also Luke 21:36 and Holm, *The Runner's Bible*, p. 61; *The Upper Room* for 6/13/35.

Howbeit when he, the Spirit of truth, is come, he will guide you into all truth: for he shall not speak of himself; but whatsoever he shall hear, *that* shall he speak: and he will shew you things to come. He shall glorify me: for he shall receive of mine, and shall shew *it* unto you. All things that the Father hath are mine: therefore said I, that he shall take of mine, and shall shew *it* unto you (John 16:13-15).[114]

If ye continue in the faith grounded and settled, and *be* not moved away from the hope of the gospel, which ye have heard, *and* which was preached to every creature which is under heaven; whereof I Paul am made a minister (Colossians 1:23).[115]

Being confident of this very thing, that he which hath begun a good work in you will perform *it* until the day of Jesus Christ (Philippians 1:6).[116]

Step Eleven, Prayer, Guidance, Growth, Power

[Step Eleven: Sought through prayer and meditation to improve our conscious contact with God *as we understood Him*, praying only for knowledge of His will for us and the power to carry that out.]

The Effectiveness of Prayer

The Big Book states: "*Step Eleven* suggests prayer and meditation. We shouldn't be shy on this matter of prayer. Better men than we are using it constantly. It works, if we have the proper attitude and work at it."[117] And many A.A. sources quoted the verse in the Book of James which confirmed the effectiveness of prayer:

---

[114] Rose, *The Quiet Time*, p. 3; Holm, *The Runner's Bible*, pp. 16, 129; Clark, *I Will Lift Up Mine Eyes*, p. 134; Streeter, *The God Who Speaks*, p. 113; Dick B., *The Akron Genesis*, p. 93; *New Light on Alcoholism*, p. 271.

[115] Dick B., *Anne Smith's Journal*, p. 52.

[116] Benson, *The Eight Points*, pp. 162-63.

[117] Big Book, pp. 85-86.

The effectual fervent prayer of a righteous man availeth much (James 5:16).[118]

A.A. sources also quoted from 1 John:

And this is the confidence that we have in him, that, if we ask any thing according to his will, he heareth us: And if we know that he hear us, whatsoever we ask, we know that we have the petitions that we desired of him (1 John 5:14-15).[119]

Eleventh Step Guidance Elements

In one sense, the Eleventh Step (as the Big Book presents the instructions for taking it) contains four elements: (1) *In the evening, before retiring* the alcoholic is to review his or her day, essentially to see how well the Tenth Step was practiced. Then ask forgiveness where there were mistakes or failures. And see what can be done to improve the situation for the future. (2) *In the morning, on awakening*, he or she is to ask for the guidance of God at that time *and* for the rest of the day. (3) *For spiritual growth*, there is to be prayer, meditation, study of "helpful books," and religious observances if the latter are part of one's belief system. (d) *In times of stress throughout the day*, he or she is to deal with agitation and doubt by turning to God for direction and strength.

1. *The End of Day Review.*

We have already dealt with what we believe were A.A.'s Tenth Step Biblical origins and here need only to point to 1 John 1:9 as

---

[118] Holm, *The Runner's Bible*, p. 62; *The Upper Room* for 8/19/35; Fosdick, *The Meaning of Faith*, p. 190; *The Meaning of Prayer*, pp. 157-58; Walter, *Soul Surgery*, p. 29; Macmillan, *Seeking and Finding*, p. 128; Roger Hicks, *How to Read the Bible* (London: Moral Re-Armament, n.d.), p. 35; Dick B., *Anne Smith's Journal*, pp 36-37.

[119] Holm, *The Runner's Bible*, p. 64; Clark, *I Will Lift Up Mine Eyes*, p. 24; Dick B., *Design for Living*, p. 162.

a source for the idea that God will forgive *future* shortcomings as they occur. In its Eleventh Step instructions, the Big Book states: "After making our review we ask God's forgiveness and inquire what corrective measures should be taken."[120] On this subject of forgiveness, the Good Book states:

> And the prayer of faith shall save the sick, and the Lord shall raise him up; and if he have committed sins, they shall be forgiven him (James 5:15).[121]

> But if we walk in the light, as he is in the light, we have fellowship one with another, and the blood of Jesus Christ his Son cleanseth us from all sin (1 John 1:7).[122]

> If we confess our sins, he is faithful and just to forgive us *our* sins, and to cleanse us from all unrighteousness (1 John 1:9).[123]

2. *Morning Quiet Time and Guidance.*

The "Morning Watch," or "Quiet Time," as it was called in the Oxford Group, had ancient origins in the Book of Psalms. The verse most commonly said to be the origin of the "morning watch" idea was Psalm 5:3:

> My voice shalt thou hear in the morning, O Lord; in the morning will I direct *my prayer* unto thee, and will look up.[124]

---

[120] Big Book, p. 86. See also the Big Book discussion on page 70 concerning sex conduct which falls "short of the chosen ideal." The text adds: "If we are sorry for what we have done, and have the honest desire to let God take us to better things, we believe we will be forgiven and will have learned our lesson."

[121] Holm, *The Runner's Bible*, p. 114; Fosdick, *The Meaning of Faith*, p. 190.

[122] Chambers, *My Utmost for His Highest*, p. 361; Howard, *Frank Buchman's Secret*, p. 109; Miles Phillimore, *Just for Today*, (Privately published pamphlet, 1940) p. 7; Almond, *Foundations for Faith*, p. 15.

[123] Almond, *Foundations for Faith*, p. 13.

[124] Holm, *The Runner's Bible*, p. 158; *The Upper Room* for 5/9/35, 7/1/35, 7/22/37; Fosdick, *The Meaning of Prayer*, p. 75.

There was another verse from the Book of James that was frequently quoted concerning the importance of going to God for wisdom and guidance:

> If any of you lack wisdom, let him ask of God, that giveth to all *men* liberally, and upbraideth not; and it shall be given him (James 1:5).[125]

And there were an immense number of Bible verses, segments, and ideas that supported the belief that God does guide and provide when His will is sought in the Bible or listened to.[126]

The following are precise biblical references to revelation from God:

> For I [the Apostle Paul] neither received it [my gospel] of man, neither was I taught *it*, but by revelation of Jesus Christ (Galatians 1:12).[127]

> All scripture *is* given by inspiration of God . . . (2 Timothy 3:16).[128]

> For to one is given by the Spirit the word of wisdom; to another the word of knowledge by the same Spirit . . . (1 Corinthians 12:8).[129]

---

[125] Holm, *The Runner's Bible*, p. 51; Fosdick, *The Meaning of Prayer*, p. 118; *The Meaning of Faith*, p. 239; Clark, *I Will Lift Up Mine Eyes*, p. 137.

[126] Oxford Group Founder Frank Buchman's biographer said, for example: "To Sam Shoemaker in 1920, Buchman wrote a seven-page foolscap letter, citing a formidable array of Biblical and theological authority for the practice" [listening to God]. Garth Lean, *On the Tail of a Comet: The Life of Frank Buchman* (Colorado Springs, CO: Helmers & Howard, 1988), p. 75

[127] Streeter, *The God Who Speaks*, p. 91; Macmillan, *Seeking and Finding*, p. 140.

[128] See discussion as to Dwight L. Moody, the evangelist, in Dick B., *Design for Living*, p. 44.

[129] Streeter, *The God Who Speaks*, p. 123; compare Holm, *The Runner's Bible*, p. 138

For the prophecy came not in old time by the will of man: but holy men of God spake *as they were* moved by the Holy Ghost (2 Peter 1:21).[130]

The following were the better known verses quoted to show that God guides and provides:

Trust in the Lord with all thine heart; and lean not unto thine own understanding. In all thy ways acknowledge him, and he shall direct thy paths (Proverbs 3:5-6).[131]

I will instruct thee and teach thee in the way which thou shalt go: I will guide thee with mine eye (Psalm 32:8).[132]

Commit thy way unto the Lord; Trust also in him; and he shall bring *it* to pass (Psalm 37:5).[133]

For as many as are led by the Spirit of God, they are the sons of God (Romans 8:14).[134]

But as it is written, Eye hath not seen, nor ear heard, neither have entered into the heart of man, the things which God hath prepared for them that love him (1 Corinthians 2:9).[135]

---

[130] Holm, *The Runner's Bible*, p. 18.

[131] *The Upper Room* for 5/15/35, 10/17/35; Holm, *The Runner's Bible*, pp. 39, 41, 61, 126; Tileston, *Daily Strength for Daily Needs*, p. 31; Clark, *The Soul's Sincere Desire*, p. 10; *I Will Lift Up Mine Eyes*, pp. 9, 28, 89, 151; Brown, *The Venture of Belief*, p. 40; Streeter, *The God Who Speaks*, p. 135; Benson, *The Eight Points*, p. 81.

[132] Drummond, *The Ideal Life*, p. 282; Wright, *The Will of God*, p. 9; Streeter, *The God Who Speaks*, p. 115; Benson, *The Eight Points*, p. 80; Holm, *The Runner's Bible*, p. 128; Tileston, *Daily Strength for Daily Needs*, p. 184; *The Upper Room* for 4/22/35.

[133] Holm, *The Runner's Bible*, pp. 127, 136; Clark, *I Will Lift Up Mine Eyes*, p. 28; Benson, *The Eight Points*, p. 81; Samuel M. Shoemaker, Jr., *The Experiment of Faith* (New York: Harper & Brothers, 1957), pp. 28-29; *How You Can Find Happiness* (New York: E. P. Dutton, 1947), p. 149; *The Upper Room* for 11/9/35, 9/25/38, 11/3/38.

[134] *What is the Oxford Group?*, p. 65; Jack C. Winslow, *Why I Believe in the Oxford Group* (London: Hodder & Stoughton, 1934), p. 39.

[135] *What is the Oxford Group?*, p. 65; Lean, *Cast Out Your Nets*, p. 30; Dick B., *The Akron Genesis*, p. 100; Holm, *The Runner's Bible*, p. 142.

For we walk by faith, not by sight (2 Corinthians 5:7).[136]

But the wisdom that is from above is first pure, then peaceable, gentle, *and* easy to be intreated, full of mercy and good fruits, without partiality, and without hypocrisy (James 3:17).[137]

As to receiving God's wisdom, A.A.'s sources suggested getting quiet, listening, and expecting to *receive*: i.e., "Speak, Lord, thy servant heareth." Not "Hear Lord, thy servant speaketh."[138]

The Big Book said: "We relax and take it easy. We don't struggle. We are often surprised how the right answers come . . ." (p. 86). A.A.'s sources for these ideas were:

Be still, and know that I *am* God (Psalm 46:10).[139]

Speak, Lord; for thy servant heareth (1 Samuel 3:9).[140]

Lord, what wilt thou have me to do? (Acts 9:6).[141]

---

[136] *What is the Oxford Group?*, p. 67.

[137] Holm, *The Runner's Bible*, p. 46; Wright, *The Will of God*, p. 167; Clark, *I Will Lift Up Mine Eyes*, p. 63; *The Upper Room* for 9/25/35.

[138] See Shoemaker, *National Awakening*, p. 86; Benson, *The Eight Points*, p. 66.

[139] Chambers, *My Utmost for His Highest*, p. 53; Holm, *The Runner's Bible*, p. 112; Howard Rose, *The Quiet Time*; Brown, *The Venture of Belief*, p. 37; Benson, *The Eight Points*, pp. 63, 68, 72, 87; *The Upper Room* for 6/23/35, 9/7/35, 1/16/36 or 1/16/39, 3/20/36 or 3/20/39, 4/10/37, 7/3/37, 12/13/38.

[140] Tileston, *Daily Strength for Daily Needs*, p. 157; Fosdick, *The Meaning of Prayer*, p. 66; Shoemaker, *Children of the Second Birth*, p. 16; *The Church Can Save the World*, p. 30; *National Awakening*, pp. 78, 83, 86, 88; *God's Control*, pp. 115-16; 121; Cecil Rose, *When Man Listens* (New York: Oxford University Press, 1937), p. 30; Foot, *Life Began Yesterday*, p. 4; Jack C. Winslow, *When I Awake* (London: Hodder & Stoughton, 1938), p. 48; Bremer Hofmeyr, *How to Listen* (New York: Moral Re-Armament, n.d.), p. 1; K. D. Belden, *Reflections on Moral Re-Armament* (London: Grosvenor, 1983), p. 35; Benson, *The Eight Points*, p. 66; *The Upper Room* for 4/2/37; Dick B., *The Akron Genesis*, pp. 95-96.

[141] Drummond, *The Ideal Life*, p. 306; Shoemaker, *A Young Man's View of the Ministry*, p. 80; *Religion That Works*, p. 65; Dick B., *Anne Smith's Journal*, p 124; *The Upper Room* for 6/5/36 or 6/5/39.

What shall I do, Lord? (Acts 22:10).[142]

3. *Further Work for Spiritual Growth.*

Big Book "spirituality" did not end with surrender, prayer, or meditation. It suggested spiritual *growth*—through work with one's priest, minister, or rabbi; and study of "helpful books" (p. 87). Anne Smith mentioned these.[143] For her, the Bible was "the main Source Book of all."[144] Support for these aids to growth was certainly suggested by the following source verses:

> Study to shew thyself approved unto God, a workman that needeth not to be ashamed, rightly dividing the word of truth (2 Timothy 2:15).[145]

> Search the scriptures . . . (John 5:39).[146]

> And ye shall know the truth, and the truth shall make you free (John 8:32).[147]

4. *When Agitated and Doubtful.*

The Big Book did not end its Eleventh Step instructions with the end-of-the-day review, morning prayer and meditation, and suggestions for spiritual growth. For the major spiritual battles

---

[142] Shoemaker, *Confident Faith*, pp. 107, 110, 115; *How to Find God*, p. 10; *Extraordinary Living for Ordinary Men* (Michigan: Zondervan, 1965), pp. 40-44, 46, 48.

[143] Dick B., *Anne Smith's Journal*, p. 83.

[144] Dick B., *Anne Smith's Journal*, p. 60.

[145] Tileston, *Daily Strength*, p. 68; *The Upper Room* for 4/27/38, 9/20/38. *Going through the Steps* said: "Read the Bible . . . know the Word of God so that you will understand it when you meditate." Clarence S., (NV: Roger Bunn, n.d.), p. 7.

[146] Holm, *The Runner's Bible*, p. 51; *The Upper Room* for 8/12/38; Dick B., *New Light on Alcoholism*, p. 270.

[147] Holm, *The Runner's Bible*, pp. 46, 107; Clark, *I Will Lift Up Mine Eyes*, p. 58; *The Upper Room* for 5/20/36, 6/28/36.

occur *all through the day*.[148] As to these situations, the Big Book suggested continued reliance on the guidance of God, stating:

> As we go through the day we pause, when agitated or doubtful, and ask for the right thought or action. We constantly remind ourselves we are no longer running the show, humbly saying to ourselves many times each day "Thy will be done." We are then in much less danger of excitement, fear, anger, worry, self-pity, or foolish decisions. We become much more efficient. We do not tire so easily, for we are not burning up energy foolishly as we did when we were trying to arrange life to suit ourselves (pp. 87-88).

And there were some well-accepted and much relied upon Biblical precedents for this thinking:

> Be careful [anxious] for nothing; but in everything by prayer and supplication with thanksgiving let your requests be made known unto God. And the peace of God, which passeth all understanding, shall keep your hearts and minds through Christ Jesus (Philippians 4:6-7).[149]

> Take no thought for [be not anxious about] your life, what ye shall eat, or what ye shall drink; nor yet for your body, what ye shall put on. . . . for your heavenly Father knoweth that ye have need of all these things. But seek ye first the kingdom of God, and his righteousness; and all these things shall be added unto you (Matthew 6:25, 32-33).[150]

---

[148] See Ephesians 6:10-18; and discussion of the spiritual battle by Shoemaker, *God's Control*, pp. 27-32; and Clark, *I Will Lift Up Mine Eyes*, p. 38.

[149] Holm, *The Runner's Bible*, pp. 61, 115, 147, 155; Tileston, *Daily Strength for Daily Needs*, pp. 53, 361; *The Upper Room* for 10/7/35, 10/20/35, 11/24/35; Fosdick, *The Meaning of Prayer*, p. 72; Clark, *I Will Lift Up Mine Eyes*, p. 93.

[150] Tileston, *Daily Strength for Daily Needs*, p. 61; Chambers, *My Utmost for His Highest*, p. 144; *Studies in the Sermon on the Mount*, pp. 54-57; Fosdick, *The Meaning of Faith*, pp. 192-93; Holm, *The Runner's Bible*, p. 144; *The Upper Room* for 5/10/37; Glover, *The Jesus of History*, p. 91; Streeter, *The God Who Speaks*, p. 81; E. Stanley Jones, *The Christ of the Mount*, p. 200; Dick B., *The Akron Genesis*, pp. 91-92.

Thou wilt keep *him* in perfect peace, *whose* mind *is* stayed on *thee*: because he trusteth in thee (Isaiah 26:3).[151]

Step Twelve, Awakening, Witness, Practice of Principles

[Step Twelve: Having had a spiritual awakening as the result of these steps, we tried to carry this message to alcoholics, and to practice these principles in all our affairs.]

In one sense, the Twelfth Step has three elements: (1) The spiritual awakening which occurs when the alcoholic has taken the previous eleven Steps; (2) The message of hope as to such a spiritual awakening that he or she is to carry to another alcoholic; (3) The practice of the principles he or she has learned from the Steps and is to apply in all of life's affairs.

The Spiritual Awakening

There are many possible definitions of A.A.'s "spiritual awakening." It was described as a spiritual "experience" in the First Edition of the Big Book.[152] And the terms "spiritual experience" and "spiritual awakening" are both Oxford Group expressions.[153] For the author, at least, based on his own experience and much language in the Big Book, a spiritual experience has meant to him consciousness and *knowledge* of the power and presence of God in his life.[154] Another less easily

---

[151] Holm, *The Runner's Bible*, pp. 112, 145; Tileston, *Daily Strength for Daily Needs*, p. 321; *The Upper Room* for 6/30/35, 7/13/35; 9/15/35; 10/22/35; 10/20/37; Clark, *The Soul's Sincere Desire*, pp. 10, 83; *I Will Lift Up Mine Eyes*, p. 93; Dick B., *The Akron Genesis*, pp. 91-92.

[152] See discussion in Appendix II of the Third Edition, pp. 569-70.

[153] Dick B., *Design for Living*, pp. 276-77.

[154] See Big Book, pp. 25, 47, 51, 56, 63, 130, 162, 164; Kitchen, *I Was a Pagan*, pp. 157, 68; Brown, *The Venture of Belief*, pp. 24-26; Samuel M. Shoemaker, Jr., *With*

(continued...)

understood expression for this consciousness was "God Consciousness."[155]

Early AAs and their spiritual sources referred to several Biblical segments dealing with the change in attitude and receipt of power that had entered their lives as the result of their conversion experiences:

> But ye shall receive power, after that the Holy Ghost is come upon you: and ye shall be witnesses unto me both in Jerusalem, and in all Judaea, and in Samaria, and unto the uttermost part of the earth (Acts 1:8).[156]

> And when they had prayed, the place was shaken where they were assembled together; and they were all filled with the Holy Ghost, and they spake the word of God with boldness. . . . And with great power gave the apostles witness of the resurrection of the Lord Jesus: and great grace was upon them all (Acts 4:31, 33).[157]

> I beseech you therefore, brethren, by the mercies of God, that ye present your bodies a living sacrifice, holy, acceptable unto God, *which is* your reasonable service. And be not conformed to this world: but be ye transformed by the renewing of your mind, that

---

[154] (...continued)
the Holy Spirit and with Fire (New York: Harper & Brothers, 1960), p. 27. For other Oxford Group ideas expressions for the experience, see Dick B., *Design for Living*, pp. 276-77.

[155] Big Book, p. 570; Begbie, *Life Changers*, pp. 41, 20; Philip Leon, *The Philosophy of Courage or the Oxford Group Way* (New York: Oxford University Press, 1939), pp. 110-11; Kitchen, *I Was a Pagan*, pp. 41, 75; Robert H. Murray, *Group Movements Throughout the Ages* (New York: Harper & Brothers, 1935), p. 349; Shoemaker, *Twice-Born Ministers*, p. 123; *How to Become a Christian*, p. 52; Clark, *The Soul's Sincere Desire*, p. 47.

[156] Holm, *The Runner's Bible*, p. 16; *The Upper Room* for 6/9/35, 11/12/35, 4/23/37, 10/29/37, 6/6/38, 12/31/38; Benson, *The Eight Points*, p. 101; Streeter, *The God Who Speaks*, p. 111; compare Dick B., *Anne Smith's Journal*, p. 22.

[157] Shoemaker, *Religion That Works*, pp. 66-76; Macmillan, *Seeking and Finding*, pp. 162-63.

ye may prove what *is* that good, and acceptable, and perfect, will of God (Romans 12:1-2).[158]

Therefore if any man *be* in Christ, *he is* a new creature: old things are passed away; behold, all things are become new (2 Corinthians 5:17).[159]

Now unto him that is able to do exceeding abundantly above all that we ask or think, according to the power that worketh in us (Ephesians 3:20).[160]

Carrying the Message

As part of the AA's Twelfth Step, there was the critical importance of witnessing, of carrying to another the message of deliverance. "You have to give it away to keep it," said the early AAs and their sources.[161] Action was called for; and the following Bible verses spelled out the duty to get into action and witness:

And he [Jesus] saith unto them, Follow me, and I will make you fishers of men (Matthew 4:19).[162]

---

[158] *The Upper Room* for 12/17/35, 4/18/63, 4/4/38; Tileston, *Daily Strength for Daily Needs*, pp. 98, 196; Holm, *The Runner's Bible*, p. 106; Fosdick, *The Meaning of Faith*, p. 219; Phillimore, *Just for Today* (portion containing a study of Romans chapter 12); Hicks, *How to Read the Bible*, p. 32; Dick B., *Anne Smith's Journal*, pp. 46, 77-78, 108, 132; Chambers, *Studies in the Sermon on the Mount*, pp. 23, 60.

[159] *The Upper Room* for 7/16/35, 5/1/38, 7/29/38; Holm, *The Runner's Bible*, p. 93; Chambers, *My Utmost for His Highest*, pp. 297, 317; Hicks, *How to Read the Bible*, p. 32; Streeter, *The God Who Speaks*, p. 111; E. Stanley Jones, *The Christ of the Mount*, p. 107. See also Dick B., *The Akron Genesis*, p. 205, containing a discussion of the verse by early AA, William V. H. in *Going through the Steps*, Clarence S. quoted this verse—saying, "You are Reborn." (NV: Roger Bunn, n.d.), pp. 6-7.

[160] For the frequency of Oxford Group founder Frank Buchman's reference to this verse, see Dick B., *Design for Living*, pp. 369-70; Phillimore, *Just for Today*, pp. 12-13.

[161] See Dick B., *Design for Living*, p. 294; *Anne Smith's Journal*, pp. 69, 65, 72-73, 85, 121, 138; *New Light on Alcoholism*, pp. 272-74.

[162] Shoemaker, *Realizing Religion*, p. 82; *Twice-Born Ministers*, p. 16; Almond, *Foundations for Faith*, 2d ed., p. 25; Glenn Clark, *Fishers of Men* (Boston: Little, Brown, 1928); Dick B., *New Light on Alcoholism*, p. 272.

But wilt thou know, O vain man, that faith without works is dead? (James 2:20).[163]

Having therefore obtained the help of God, I continue unto this day, witnessing both to small and great, saying none other things than those things which the prophets and Moses did say should come: That Christ should suffer, *and* that he should be the first that should rise from the dead, and shew light unto the people, and to the Gentiles (Acts 26:22-32).[164]

Now then we are ambassadors for Christ, as though God did beseech *you* by us: we pray *you* in Christ's stead, be ye reconciled to God (2 Corinthians 5:20).[165]

Practicing the Principles

Finally, there were spiritual principles to be practiced in daily living. Principles from the Sermon on the Mount, from 1 Corinthians 13, from the Book of James, from the Oxford Group's Four Absolutes, and from a number of other biblical sources as well.

The Big Book really does not specifically list the "principles" or describe the "works" that are to the follow the attaining of "faith." But we believe the following are *among* the principles the Big Book suggests should be practiced: (1) Relying upon God (Big Book, pp. 46, 50, 51-53, 68, 80, 98, 100, 120); (2) Being rigorously honest (pp. 58, 64, 67, 69, 73, 84, 86); (3) Eliminating selfishness and self-centeredness (pp. 67-68, 84, 86, 145); (4) Eliminating resentment, jealousy, and envy (pp. 64-67, 84, 86, 145); (5) Eliminating fear (pp. 67-68, 84, 86, 145); (6) Practicing patience, tolerance, kindliness, understanding, love, forgiveness,

---

[163] Big Book, pp. 14-15, 76, 88, 93; *What Is The Oxford Group?*, p. 36; *DR. BOB*, p. 71; *Pass It On*, p. 147; Nell Wing, *Grateful to Have Been There*, pp. 70-71.

[164] *What Is The Oxford Group?*, p. 25; Dick B., *Anne Smith's Journal*, p. 131.

[165] *What Is The Oxford Group?*, p. 35; *The Upper Room* for 8/28/38; Dick B., *Anne Smith's Journal*, p. 131.

and helpfulness to others (pp. 20, 77, 83, 84, 97, 118, 153). And there are additional Twelfth Step principles embodying ideas of humility, forgiveness, and service (Big Book, pp. 73, 77). Also, stressing overcoming the bondage of self, sharing by confession, making restitution, reconciling, seeking guidance, and so on (Big Book, pp. 63, 73, 76, 77, 85-88).

The Rev. Harry Almond said, of the biblical principles of the Oxford Group (which contained many of A.A.'s roots): "A good place to start is with the Ten Commandments." In modern words, Almond summarized them as follows: (1) You shall have no other gods before me. (2) You shall not make for yourself a graven image . . . or . . . likeness. You shall not bow down to them or serve them. (3) You shall not take the name of the Lord your God in vain. (4) Remember the sabbath day, to keep it holy. (5) Honor your father and mother. (6) You shall not kill. (7) You shall not commit adultery. (8) You shall not steal. (9) You shall not bear false witness against your neighbor. (10) You shall not covet.[166]

And there were the Oxford Group's own spiritual principles of absolute honesty, purity, unselfishness, and love from the Oxford Group's Four Absolutes, which we have already discussed.

As we have also discussed at length, Professor Drummond in his *The Greatest Thing in the World*—which was widely read and recommended in early A.A.—summarized the "love elements" of 1 Corinthians 13 as follows: (1) *Patience.* (2) *Kindness.* (3) *Generosity.* (4) *Humility.* (5) *Courtesy.* (6) *Unselfishness.* (7) *Good Temper.* (8) *Guilelessness.* (9) *Sincerity.*[167] These, said Drummond *and* Dr. Bob, were vital elements in living the

---

[166] Almond, *Foundations for Faith*, 2d ed., p. 10. For the Ten Commandments themselves, see Exodus 20:3-17; Deuteronomy 5:6-21.

[167] Drummond, *The Greatest Thing in the World*, pp. 26-27; 1 Corinthians 13:4-6. See comment in Benson, *The Eight Points*, p. 47: "The perfect life is simply a life of perfect love. Love is all in all. Jesus said that the whole law is summed up in the one word *love*. It embraces everything, as St. Paul teaches in his glorious hymn to love" (1 Corinthians 13). See similar discussions in Clark, *I Will Lift Up Mine Eyes*, pp. 65-66; Dick B., *Anne Smith's Journal*, p. 131.

principles which Dr. Bob said could be simmered down to "love and service."[168]

Many A.A. principles, detailed elsewhere, came from the Book of James and include: (1) Patience. (2) Seeking the wisdom of God. (3) Avoiding temptation. (4) Telling the truth. (5) Avoiding anger. (6) Studying the word of God and "doing" it. (7) Helping the unfortunate. (8) Loving your neighbor. (9) Avoiding adultery and killing. (10) Backing up faith with works. (11) Bridling the tongue. (12) Avoiding envy and strife. (13) Avoiding lying. (14) Avoiding selfish lusts. (15) Avoiding pride. (16) Submitting to God. (17) Purifying hearts. (18) Being humble. (19) Avoiding speaking evil of another. (20) Doing good. (21) Avoiding riches for the sake of riches. (22) Avoiding grudges. (23) Avoiding swearing and false oaths. (24) Relying on prayer. (25) Confessing faults. (26) Converting sinners from the error of their ways.

The following A.A. principles, detailed elsewhere, seem to have come from the Sermon on the Mount: (1) Humility. (2) Compassion. (3) Meekness. (4) Spotless conduct. (5) Making peace with enemies. (6) Harmonizing actions with God's will. (7) Overcoming resentments. (8) Making restitution. (9) Avoiding retaliation. (10) Conducting prayers and good works anonymously. (11) Forgiving. (12) Seeking God first. (13) Utilizing self-examination. (14) Doing the will of God. (15) Being rigorously honest. (16) Avoiding evil. (17) Being unselfish. (18) Loving.[169]

---

[168] *DR. BOB*, p. 338.

[169] See also Almond, *Foundations for Faith*, pp. 10-11, setting forth additional Oxford Group views of "Sin—the Disease" and urging avoidance of conduct such as murder, adultery, deceit, envy, slander, pride, theft, and greed.

6

Keeping It Simple

Dr. Bob was often credited with the A.A. concept of "Keeping It Simple."[1] In fact, when Bill Wilson had been trying in Akron to sell some of his more grandiose plans prior to the writing of the Big Book, Dr. Bob said, "For God's sake, Billy, keep it simple."[2] In his final address to A.A., Dr. Bob again cautioned AAs to keep their program simple and "not louse it up with freudian complexes and things that are interesting to the scientific mind, but have very little to do with our actual A.A. work."[3] We believe, however, that Dr. Bob was not referring to spiritual study or spiritual growth, but rather to business ventures, complex organizational ideas, and psychological explorations.

Dr. Bob *never* "kept it simple" in his search for spiritual truth. He frequently stayed up late into the night studying the Bible and

---

[1] *Alcoholics Anonymous Comes of Age* (New York: Alcoholics Anonymous World Services, 1957), p. 9; *Pass It On* (New York: Alcoholics Anonymous World Services, 1984), p. 339; Ernest Kurtz, *Not-God: A History of Alcoholics Anonymous*, exp. ed. (Minnesota: Hazelden, 1991), pp. 42, 321 n. 17; *DR. BOB and the Good Oldtimers* (New York: Alcoholics Anonymous World Services, Inc., 1980), pp. 227, 338. Hereinafter, this latter title is called *DR. BOB*.

[2] Dick B., *The Akron Genesis of Alcoholics Anonymous* (Corte Madera, CA: Good Book Publishing Company, 1994), pp. 11, 224-26; Robert Thomsen, *Bill W.* (New York: Harper & Row, 1975), pp. 266-71.

[3] *DR. BOB*, p. 338.

stressed it as the place to find the answers.[4] He read it cover to cover three times, could quote favorite verses verbatim, and devoted about twenty minutes each day to study of a familiar verse.[5] He studied an immense amount of religious literature.[6] He prayed during the day and sought God's guidance in his daily life.[7] And he said, in describing A.A.'s development period, that it involved *study* of the Good Book which later enabled AAs to reduce their recovery ideas to "terse and tangible form."[8]

The Original Six Steps

Once the basic ideas had been refined from the Bible, Dr. Bob apparently focused on six of them and utilized a very simple recovery program consisting of six steps.[9] So did Bill Wilson.[10] And the following were the six steps the co-founders developed and used:

1. We admitted that we were licked, that we were powerless over alcohol.
2. We made a moral inventory of our defects or sins.
3. We confessed or shared our shortcomings with another person in confidence.
4. We made restitution to all those we had harmed by our drinking.
5. We tried to help other alcoholics, with no thought of reward in money or prestige.

---

[4] Dick B., *Dr. Bob's Library: Books for Twelve Step Growth* (San Rafael, CA: Paradise Research Publications, 1994), pp. 12-13.

[5] Dick B., *Dr. Bob's Library*, p. 14; *DR. BOB*, pp. 310, 314.

[6] Dick B., *Dr. Bob's Library*, pp. 13-15; *DR. BOB*, pp. 310-15.

[7] DR. BOB, pp. 314-15.

[8] *DR. BOB*, pp. 96-97.

[9] Big Book, p. 291. **Big Book** is a registered trademark of Alcoholics Anonymous World Services, Inc.; used here with permission of A.A.W.S.

[10] *Pass It On*, p. 197.

6. We prayed to God to help us do these things as best we could.[11]

We have listed in the following footnote some very limited references to the Bible segments upon which the six steps were based; but the reader should realize from this entire work that there were many specific Bible verses, chapters, and segments which contributed to the simplified statement of the basic ideas.[12]

---

[11] For the variant ways in which these original six steps have been expressed, see Dick B., *The Akron Genesis*, pp. 256-60. Note that with reference to the Sixth Step, Bill wrote in July, 1953, shortly after Dr. Bob died: "6. We prayed to God to help us do these things as best we could." See *The Language of the Heart: Bill W.'s Grapevine Writings* (New York: The AA Grapevine, Inc., 1988), p. 200. In the foregoing list of six steps, we chose the form for the sixth step as Bill expressed that form in 1953. As to the first five steps, we chose the form as expressed in *Pass It On* at page 197. That form said, as to the sixth step: "6. We prayed to whatever God we thought there was for power to practice these precepts." We think that was an edited version. We believe, despite the variance, that the more common usage, in A.A.'s earliest and highly successful years, was based on the unabridged reference to "God" rather than "whatever God we thought there was." We base this on Bill's statement that when "God *as we understood Him*" was added to the Twelve Steps, when they were being written, "God was certainly there in the Twelve Steps, but He was now expressed in terms that anybody—*anybody at all*—could accept and try." See *Alcoholics Anonymous Comes of Age*, p. 167. See our discussion of "God" in Chapter Two of this title; and also refer to the unqualified reference to "GOD" in capital letters on page 69 of the First Edition of the Big Book. Recall too that there are over 400 unqualified references to "God" even in the Third Edition of the Big Book.

[12] For six, out of many basic segments of the Bible, consider the following: (1) Step One: "we were licked . . . [and] we were powerless." See Romans 7:24—"O wretched man that I am! who shall deliver me?" Big Book 1st Edition, p. 347; also Dick B., *Anne Smith's Journal, 1933-1939: A.A.'s Principles of Success* (San Rafael, CA: Paradise Research Publications, 1994), p. 22. (2) Step Two: "a moral inventory." See Matthew 7:1-5—"first cast the beam out of thine own eye." (3) Step Three: "We confessed." See James 5:16—"Confess your faults one to another." (4) Step Four: "We made restitution." See Matthew 5:23-25—"first be reconciled to thy brother, and then come and offer thy gift." (5) Step Five: "We tried to help other alcoholics." See James 2:26—"faith without works is dead;" Acts 26:22—"Having therefore obtained help of God, I continue unto this day, witnessing." (6) Step Six: "We prayed to God to help us." See James 5:13-16—"Is any among you afflicted? let him pray. . . . Is any sick among you? let him call for the elders of the church; and let them pray over him. . . . And the prayer of faith shall save the sick. . . . pray for one another, that ye may be healed."

A Summary of A.A.'s Basic Ideas from the Bible

Just as the early A.A. recovery program could be simply expressed in six steps, so, we believe, can the basic biblical ideas—upon which the recovery program was based—be simply expressed. Expressed in terms of some fourteen concepts early AAs took from the Bible. We do not necessarily subscribe to these basic ideas as representing our own biblical beliefs or our own views on religious ideas. But the following do seem to represent a simply statement of where early AAs were coming from when they took their basic spiritual ideas from the Bible and embodied them in their program of recovery. We list fourteen principal A.A. concepts we believe were taken from the Bible; and, in the footnotes, quote the portions of the Bible from which the ideas came, as well as the way the biblical idea was expressed in A.A. language. As we have progressed with our discussion in this book, we have shown the sources from which, or by which, the principles reached A.A.

Conceptions of God:

1. God is a loving God, the Creator, who wants all of us to become his children.[13]

---

[13] From the Bible: "God is love" (1 John 4:8, 16). "For God so loved the world, that he gave his only begotten Son, that whosoever believeth in him should not perish, but have everlasting life" (John 3:16). "Whosoever believeth that Jesus is the Christ is born of God" (1 John 5:1). "Being born again [from above—of the spirit], not of corruptible seed, but of incorruptible, by the word of God, which liveth and abideth for ever" (1 Peter 1:23). "Beloved, now are we the sons of God" (1 John 3:2). See Big Book, p. 28: "If what we have learned and felt and seen means anything at all, it means that all of us, whatever our race, creed, or color are children of a living Creator with whom we may form a relationship upon simple and understandable terms as soon as we are willing and honest enough to try." Discussing the first two Traditions of A.A., Bill also wrote: "Our whole AA program is securely founded on the principle of humility. . . . Which implies, among other things, that we relate ourselves rightly to God and to our fellows. . . . we of Alcoholics Anonymous are certain that there is but one ultimate authority, "a loving God as he may express himself in our group conscience." *The Language of the Heart* (New York: The AA Grapevine, 1988), pp. 76, 78.

Blocks to a relationship with God and His children:

2. "Sin," or as AAs came to say, "self-will" and its manifested "shortcomings," block us from a relationship with God and our fellow man and leave us spiritually sick.[14]

Beginning the path to a restored relationship:

3. The *path* begins with belief that God is and rewards those who diligently seek Him.[15]

4. The *search* begins when we seek God's kingdom *first* through a rebirth and becoming *willing to do His known will*.[16]

---

[14] "For all have sinned, and come short of the glory of God" (Romans 3:23). "Wherefore, as by one man sin entered into the world, and death by sin; and so death passed upon all men, for that all have sinned" (Romans 5:12). "For if by one man's offense death reigned by one; much more they which receive abundance of grace and of the gift of righteousness shall reign in life by one, Jesus Christ. . . . That as sin hath reigned unto death, even so might grace reign through righteousness unto eternal life by Jesus Christ our Lord" (Romans 5:17, 21). Big Book, pp. 70-71: "In this book you read again and again that faith did for us what we could not do for ourselves. We hope you are convinced that God can remove whatever self-will has blocked you off from Him."

[15] "But without faith, *it is* impossible to please *him*: for he that cometh to God must believe that he is, and *that* he is a rewarder of them that diligently seek him" (Hebrews 11:6). Big Book, p. 60: "That probably no human power could have relieved our alcoholism. . . . That God could and would if He were sought."

[16] "Marvel not that I said unto thee, Ye must be born again" (John 3:7). "If any man will do his will, he shall know of the doctrine, whether it be of God, or *whether* I speak of myself (John 7:17). "Not every one that saith unto me, Lord, Lord, shall enter into the kingdom of heaven; but he that doeth the will of my Father which is in heaven" (Matthew 7:21). "But seek ye first the kingdom of God, and his righteousness; and all these things shall be added unto you" (Matthew 6:33). Big Book, p. 76: "Are we now ready to let God remove from us all the things which we have admitted are objectionable? . . . I pray that you now remove from me every single defect of character which stands in the way of my usefulness to you and my fellows. Grant me strength, as I go out from here, to do your bidding."

5. The spiritual *walk* commences with "giving in," "admitting that God is God and self is not God," and then, on one's knees, surrendering through saying in some form, Thy will be done.[17]

Eliminating the barriers to God with God's help:

6. Self-examination for shortcomings is the first requirement.[18]

7. Confession is required to overcome egos, fear, and dishonesty.[19]

---

[17] "Give in . . . admit that I am God . . ." (Moffatt's Translation of Psalm 46:10). "Thy will be done . . ." (Matthew 6:10). "Nevertheless not my will, but thine, be done" (Luke 22:42). "Lord, what wilt thou have me to do?" (Acts 9:6). Big Book, p. 59: "We asked His protection and care with complete abandon." Big Book, p. 164: "Abandon yourself to God as you understand God."

[18] **Self-examination**—"Thou hypocrite, first cast out the beam out of thine own eye; and then shalt thou see clearly to cast out the mote out of thy brother's eye" (Matthew 7:5). **Measure the shortcomings** by seeing where you fall short of the Four Absolutes—**Honesty:** Matthew 5:33-37; Ephesians 4:25-28. **Unselfishness:** Matthew 5:38-42. **Purity:** Matthew 5:27-28. **Love:** Matthew 5:43-47; 1 Corinthians 13; James 2:8. **Or measure the shortcomings** by seeing where they resemble the "old man" biblical nature that is to be put off—**Resentment and grudges:** Matthew 5:22; Ephesians 4:26; Colossians 3:8; James 5:9. **Fear:** Proverbs 29:25; Luke 8:50; 2 Timothy 1:7; 1 John 4:18. **Self-seeking:** 1 Corinthians 13:5; Philippians 2:4. **Dishonesty:** 1 Corinthians 13:6; Ephesians 4:25; Philippians 4:8. **Harm to others:** Exodus 20:1-17; 1 Corinthians 13:4-5; James 3:8; 4:11-17; 5:1-6. Big Book, p. 84: "Continue to watch for selfishness, dishonesty, resentment, and fear. When these crop up, we ask God at once to remove them."

[19] James 5:16: "Confess *your* faults one to another, and pray for one another, that ye may be healed." Big Book, p. 73: "But they had not learned enough of humility, fearlessness and honesty, in the sense we find it necessary, until they told someone else *all* their story."

8. Next there must be "conviction" that the shortcomings are contrary to God's will and need, with His help, to be hated and forsaken.[20]

9. The conversion experience, which occurs through the power of God and eliminates the sin, requires humble submission to God and His Will.[21]

Eliminating the barriers to others with God's help:

10. Loving others requires a review of the conduct that has harmed them, *and* willingness to correct the harms.[22]

11. Action in the form of restitution must follow—by making amends.[23]

---

[20] Acts 3:19: "Repent ye therefore, and be converted, that your sins may be blotted out, when the times of refreshing shall come from the presence of the Lord." Big Book, p. 76: "Are we now ready to let God remove from us all the things which we have admitted are objectionable?" See also Nora Smith Holm, *The Runner's Bible* (New York: Houghton Mifflin Co., 1915), p. 88; Mel B., *New Wine: The Spiritual Roots of the Twelve Step Miracle* (Minnesota: Hazelden, 1991, pp. 34-35, 42.

[21] "Know ye not, that to whom ye yield yourselves servants to obey, his servants ye are to whom ye obey; whether of sin unto death, or of obedience unto righteousness" (Romans 6:16). "Submit yourselves therefore to God . . ." (James 4:7). "Humble yourselves in the sight of the Lord, and he shall lift you up" (James 4:10). Big Book, p. 76: "My Creator, I am now willing that you should have all of me, good and bad."

[22] "Agree with thine adversary quickly . . . " (Matthew 5:25). "If a man say, I love God, and hateth his brother, he is a liar; for he that loveth not his brother whom he hath seen, how can he love God, whom he hath not seen" (1 John 4:20)? Big Book, p. 76: "We have a list of all persons we have harmed and to whom we are willing to make amends. . . . Now we go out to our fellows and repair the damage done. . . . If we haven't the will to do this, we ask until it comes."

[23] "Therefore if thou bring thy gift to the altar, and there rememberest that thy brother hath ought against thee; Leave there thy gift before the altar, and go thy way; first be reconciled to thy brother, and then come and offer thy gift" (Matthew 5:23-24). Big Book, p. 77: "At the moment we are trying to put our lives in order. But that is not an end in itself. Our real purpose is to fit ourselves to be of maximum service to God and the people about us."

Daily walking in harmony with God's will:

12. The walk of love requires efforts toward spiritual growth
    and a walk in accordance with God's will.[24]

13. Growth means *daily* prayer to God; meditation on, and study
    of His Word and Will; seeking His guidance and direction;
    and turning to Him for peace.[25]

Being transformed through taking the Twelve Steps:

14. The result of taking the Steps is power *and* consciousness of
    God's presence—which is to be followed by love and
    service to Him and others through sharing about one's
    deliver ance. The spiritual transformation enables one, with
    the power and guidance of God, to practice God's
    commandments, walk in love, and conform one's life to

---

[24] Matthew 26:41: "Watch and pray that ye enter not into temptation: the spirit
indeed *is* willing, but the flesh *is* weak." Big Book, p. 84: "Our next function is to grow
in understanding and effectiveness. This is not an overnight matter. It should continue
for our lifetime."

[25] 1 John 5:14-15: "And this is the confidence that we have in him, that, if we asking
anything according to his will, he heareth us: And if we know that he hear us,
whatsoever we ask, we know that we have the petitions we desired of him." James 1:5:
"If any of you lack wisdom, let him ask of God, that giveth to all *men* liberally, and
upbraideth not; and it shall be given him." Proverbs 3:5-6: "Trust in the Lord with all
thine heart; and lean not unto thine own understanding. In all thy ways acknowledge him,
and he shall direct thy paths." 1 Samuel 3:9: "Speak, Lord, for thy servant heareth."
Philippians 4:6-7: "Be careful [anxious] for nothing; but in everything by prayer and
supplication with thanksgiving let your requests be made known unto God. And the peace
of God, which passeth all understanding, shall keep your hearts and minds through Christ
Jesus." Big Book, pp. 85-87: "prayer . . . works if we have the proper attitude and work
at it. . . . When we retire at night, we constructively review our day. . . . After making
our review we ask God's forgiveness and inquire what corrective measures should be
taken. On awakening . . . we consider our plans for the day . . . [and] ask God to direct
our thinking. . . . Be quick to see where religious people are right. Make use of what
they offer. As we go through the day we pause, when agitated or doubtful, and ask for
the right thought or action."

declarations of God's will such as those found in the
Sermon on the Mount, Corinthians, and James.[26]

Simmered Down to the Last

Bill and Bob both had the capacity to keep it simple when it came
to describing the *essence* of their spiritual program of recovery. In
his chapter "Working with Others," Bill wrote:

> Burn the idea into the consciousness of every man that he can get
> well regardless of anyone. The only condition is that he trust in
> God and clean house.[27]

In his last address to AAs, Dr. Bob said:

> Our Twelve Steps, when simmered down to the last, resolve
> themselves into the words "love" and "service." We understand

---

[26] (1) **The transformation:** "Tarry ye in the city of Jerusalem, until ye be endued
with power from on high" (Luke 24:49); "ye shall receive power, after that the Holy
Ghost is come upon you" (Acts 1:8). See B. H. Streeter, *The God Who Speaks* (London:
Macmillan & Co., 1943), pp. 111, 125. "And be not conformed to this world: but be
ye transformed by the renewing of your mind that ye may prove what *is* that good, and
acceptable, and perfect, will of God" (Romans 12:2). See Mary W. Tileston, *Daily
Strength for Daily Needs* (Boston: Roberts Brothers, 1893), pp. 98, 196. (2) **The
message must be shared:** "But be ye doers of the word, and not hearers only, deceiving
your own selves. For if any be a hearer of the word, and not a doer, he is like unto a
man beholding his natural face in a glass" (James 1:22-23). See Tileston, *Daily Strength
for Daily Needs*, p. 272. "Faith without works is dead" (James 2:20; 2:26). (3) **The
love we must practice:** "Thou shalt love the Lord thy God with all thy soul, and with
all thy mind. . . . And . . . Thou shalt love thy neighbor as thyself" (Deuteronomy 6:5;
Leviticus 19:18; Matthew 22:36-40; Mark 12:28-31; Luke 10:25-28; Romans 13:8-10;
James 2:8; 1 John 4:7; 4:11-12; 4:20-21). See T. R. Glover, *The Jesus of History* (New
York: Association Press, 1919), p. 60. Big Book, pp. 14-15: "My friend [Ebby Thacher]
had emphasized the absolute necessity of demonstrating these principles in all my affairs.
Particularly was it imperative to work with others as he had worked with me. Faith
without works was dead, he said . . . . For if an alcoholic failed to perfect and enlarge
his spiritual life through work and self-sacrifice for others, he could not survive the
certain trials and low spots ahead.

[27] Big Book, p. 98.

what love is, and we understand what service is. So let's bear those two things in mind.[28]

Simmered down to the last, then, Bill and Bob reduced their program to four basic ideas that would enable the alcoholic to get well: (1) *Trust in God*; (2) *Cleaning house*; (3) *Love*; and (4) *Service*. And we believe they acquired those ideas in their earliest days of studying the Good Book.

Let's consider again those four ideas as they were expressed in the Good Book and appear to have been transported to the Big Book:

Trust God:

The Good Book said:

Trust in the Lord with all thine heart; and lean not unto thine own understanding. In all thy ways acknowledge him, and he shall direct thy paths (Proverbs 3:5-6).

The Big Book said:

For we are now on a different basis; the basis of trusting and relying upon God. We trust infinite God rather than our finite selves (p. 68).

Clean house:

The Good Book said:

Draw nigh to God, and he will draw nigh to you. Cleanse *your* hands, *ye* sinners; and purity *your* hearts, *ye* double minded. . . . Humble yourselves in the sight of the Lord, and he shall lift you up (James 4:8, 10).

---

[28] *DR. BOB*, p. 338.

The Big Book said:

> Above everything, we alcoholics must be rid of this selfishness. We must, or it kills us! God makes that possible. And there often seems no way of entirely getting rid of self without His aid (p. 62).

Love:

The Good Book said:

> If ye fulfil the royal law according to the scripture, Thou shalt love thy neighbor as thyself, ye do well. . . . What *doth it* profit, my brethren, though a man say he hath faith, and have not works? can faith save him? . . . Even so faith, if it hath not works, is dead, being alone (James 2:8, 14, 17).

> And now abideth faith, hope, charity [love], these three; but the greatest of these *is* charity [love] (1 Corinthians 13:13).

The Big Book said:

> But that is not all. There is action and more action. "Faith without works is dead." The next chapter is entirely devoted to *Step Twelve* (p. 88).

> Then you will know what it means to give of yourself that others may survive and rediscover life. You will learn the full meaning of "Love thy neighbor as thyself" (p. 153).

Serve:

The Good Book said:

> And whosoever of you will be the chiefest, shall be servant of all. For even the Son of man came not to be ministered unto, but to

minister, and to give his life a ransom for many (Mark 10:44-45).[29]

Is any sick among you? let him call for the elders of the church; and let them pray over him, anointing him with oil in the name of the Lord: And the prayer of faith shall save the sick, and the Lord shall raise him up; and if he have committed sins, they shall be forgiven him (James 5:14-15).

The Big Book said:

These men had found something brand new in life. Though they knew they must help other alcoholics if they would remain sober, that motive became secondary. It was transcended by the happiness they found in giving themselves for others (p. 159).

Note that, in his last major address to AAs, Dr. Bob said:

I think the kind of service that really counts is giving of yourself, and that almost invariably requires effort and time . . . giving of our own effort and strength and time is quite a different matter. And I think that is what Bill learned in New York and I didn't learn in Akron until we met.[30]

Trust God, clean house, love, serve. In their simplest form, those were the four spiritual challenges to AAs from the Good Book and the Big Book! The AAs' own spiritual roots gave them these ideas from the Bible.

---

[29] See Robert E. Speer, *Studies of the Man Christ Jesus* (New York: Fleming H. Revell, 1896), p. 72; Dick B., *Anne Smith's Journal, 1933-1939: A.A.'s Principles of Success* (San Rafael, CA: Paradise Research Publications, 1994), p. 83.

[30] The Co-Founders of Alcoholics Anonymous: Biographical sketches Their last major talks (New York: Alcoholics Anonymous World Services, 1972, 1975), p. 12.

7

The Good Book and A.A. Today

Some in today's A.A. are scared to death to mention the Bible.

Is this because they resent it? Don't know what's in it? Are intimidated by its subject matter? Have no idea where and how A.A. got its recovery ideas? Believe A.A.'s Traditions forbid discussion of its history? Or fear what others might think?

Possibly a bit of each.

The author has personally heard the following comments within the A.A. Fellowship: (1) "I resent anyone's mentioning the bible in a meeting of Alcoholics Anonymous." (2) "I will not allow anyone I sponsor to come to an A.A. meeting which discusses its origins in Christianity and the Bible." (3) "A.A. left the Bible behind in Akron." (4) "You should not mention the Bible in your books about A.A. history because that is not what it is about." (5) "A.A.'s program is 'spiritual, not religious.'" (6) "Mentioning either the Bible or God at an A.A. meeting will scare away the newcomer."

And this brings to mind three of our personal experiences.

The first concerns a wonderful old gal in the A.A. area where the author got sober. The author had seizures in her arms at a huge A.A. meeting seven days after he entered the rooms of Alcoholics Anonymous. It was she who summoned an ambulance and very probably saved his life. She now has well over twenty years of sobriety. She often talks in A.A. meetings about God and prayer. And though she sometimes causes discomfort, we've never seen her shouted down or ejected. She frequently says: "If the word *God* scares you out of these rooms, a bottle of booze will bring you back *if you don't die first.*" The woman seems undeterred by A.A.'s "Conference Approved" issues when it comes to mentioning God and prayer. Nor has she seemed concerned that she addresses "religious" rather than "spiritual" matters when she speaks of God and her regular attendance at a Roman Catholic Church. She's not afraid to mention Christianity in an A.A. meeting; and she is well known for the expression: "If you don't have a god in your life, you damn well better get one." She's outspoken. Yet her words have given many of the author's own sponsees the courage to pursue Bible study as part of their spiritual growth in A.A., to pray in a manner consistent with their own beliefs, and, yes, even to mention God and the Scriptures at meetings *when sharing their own experience.* And our point is that this lady knows where A.A. came from, knows how she got sober, knows Who made that possible, and feels quite comfortable sharing *her* experience without being inhibited by someone else's religious convictions, hangups, prejudices, or ignorance.

Perhaps the lady is of a dying breed is today's A.A. At least it sometimes seems that way to the author.

The author's next experience began during his very first days in A.A. To his surprise, the author found himself listening to a sponsor (his sponsor) who kept telling him not to read the Bible. Telling him he should read nothing but the Big Book for six months. And commenting that people who read the Bible in A.A. frequently get drunk. In fact, as he was writing this present title, the author received a phone call from an A.A. newcomer in Atlanta, Georgia, who was hearing the same kind of comments from some AAs there—that he (the newcomer) should refrain from reading the Bible in order to get sober and focus on recovery.

Our readers might think these are isolated cases limited to individual people in A.A. with whom the author has had some personal contact. But it's a long way from Atlanta, Georgia, to Maui, Hawaii. And the author's last experience was a recent one that occurred in California. It involved a very large and highly successful A.A. program where some distinguished A.A. oldtimers had traveled from afar to share about A.A.'s beginnings in Akron, the Oxford Group, and the Bible. Following the program, the author heard one of the local A.A. "gurus" start and spread the rumor that AAs who read the Bible often get drunk. The gentleman said A.A. had left the Bible behind in Akron. He said to the author and to many others that he had been most distressed that the Bible had been mentioned at an A.A. Conference. And this influential person's comments have so intimidated several of those who organized the California spiritual roots programs that similar programs, which were scheduled for the future, have never been held. When asked, the man said he had never read the Bible. He never shared where or how he had acquired the idea that those in A.A. who read the Bible get drunk. But the man was totally successful in his efforts to terminate meetings on A.A.'s early spiritual history. For there has never been another meeting.

Which brings us to this question: Just where *do* A.A.'s Bible roots belong in today's A.A.?

By now, our readers should be clear that early AAs studied and used the Bible and read a good many books about it. And they recorded a remarkable success rate—unequaled today.[1]

We have shown that early A.A. was part of "A First Century Christian Fellowship" and was sometimes described by AAs as a "Christian Fellowship."[2] Yet somehow those historical facts have

---

[1] See discussion of today's low success *rate* in Dick B., *Design for Living: The Oxford Group's Contribution to Early A.A.* (San Rafael, CA: Paradise Research Publications, 1995), pp. 3-8. Refer also to our own prior discussion in this book of A.A.'s 1989 membership survey. Today's picture should be compared with that described in the annual meeting of the American Psychiatric Association at Detroit, Michigan, in May of 1943. There Bill Wilson's friend Dr. Harry M. Tiebot was still reporting, as of 1943: "Alcoholics Anonymous claims a recovery rate of 75% of those who really try their methods." See *Alcoholics Anonymous Comes of Age* (New York: Alcoholics Anonymous World Services, Inc., 1957), p. 310.

[2] *DR. BOB and the Good Oldtimers* (New York: Alcoholics Anonymous World Services, 1980), pp. 118, 129, 136—this title hereinafter being called *DR. BOB*; Dick
(continued...)

slipped through the cracks in the rooms of today's A.A. In a sense, the slippage began in 1937 when Bill Wilson's resentments against Oxford Group attitudes at Calvary Episcopal Church in New York culminated in his leading his handful of New York AAs away from the Oxford Group fellowship there.[3] In a sense, it continued in 1939 when one of Dr. Bob's sponsees, Clarence S., feared Roman Catholics could not attend Akron A.A. and get help because of A.A.'s early involvement with Protestant practices in the Oxford Group—following which Clarence led his group of AAs to form "Alcoholics Anonymous" in Cleveland.[4]

Yet neither event actually resulted in A.A.'s abandoning the *Bible*.

Akron AAs published, in the 1940's, and still publish, such pamphlets as *Spiritual Milestones in Alcoholics Anonymous*.[5] The *Spiritual Milestones* pamphlet refers to the Ten Commandments; to 1 Corinthians 15:9; to Philippians 4:13; to Matthew 22:37-38; to "God as Christ teaches us;" to 1 Corinthians 15:33; to the newcomer's learning that "THERE IS A GOD" (capitals in original); to the story of Paul's conversion in the ninth chapter of the Book of Acts; to Romans 13:13, 14; and to James 1:27.

In the 1940's, Clarence S.'s Cleveland AAs often spoke of the "Four Absolutes" and included Bible verses and comments about

---

[2] (...continued)
B., *Anne Smith's Journal, 1933-1939: A.A.'s Principles of Success* (San Rafael, CA: Paradise Research Publications, 1994), pp. 119-20; *Pass It On* (New York: Alcoholics Anonymous World Services, 1984), p. 130.

[3] For two versions of the circumstances surrounding Bill's departure, see *Pass It On*, pp. 169-74; Ernest Kurtz, *Not-God: A History of Alcoholics Anonymous*, exp. ed. (Minnesota: Hazelden, 1991), pp. 44-45.

[4] For two versions of the Akron/Cleveland split, see *DR. BOB*, pp. 161-69, Kurtz, *Not-God*, pp. 77-82.

[5] For a discussion of the origin and content of these pamphlets and of their having been written at the instigation of A.A. co-founder Dr. Bob, see Wally P., *But, for the Grace of God . . . How Intergroups & Central Offices Carried the Message of Alcoholics Anonymous in the 1940's* (West Virginia: The Bishop of Books, 1995), pp. 30-46.

the Bible in their Central Bulletin.[6] And Clarence himself continued, to the date of his death, using with the hundreds of AAs he helped, the anointing-with-oil practices adopted from James 5:13-16.[7] Clarence also used Scripture guides in taking his sponsees through the Twelve Steps.[8]

We have already covered Bill Wilson's statement to the Yale Summer School of Alcohol Studies in 1945 that "in his second, third, or fourth year, the A.A. will be founding reading his Bible quite as often—or more—as he will a standard psychological work."

Finally, Akron AAs, led by Dr. Bob, continued to emphasize prayer, Bible study, and spiritual reading as an integral part of their program, at least to the date of Dr. Bob's death on November 16, 1950.

Perhaps it is time for AAs and others to appreciate just how important the Bible was in early A.A. and how useful a knowledge of the Bible's explanations of the existence, will, and power of God can be today. Surely, if one tries to evaluate A.A.'s program in terms of a "higher power" that is a chair, a bulldozer, a lightbulb, or even the A.A. "group," there is little of a spiritual nature left in the A.A. which originally said the alcoholic was 100% hopeless apart from "divine help."[9] *Divine help* is not

---

[6] The author has in his possession a number of issues of this Cleveland A.A. publication for the early 1940's. See also Clarence's comment to Dr. Bob: "We have a book now [the Big Book], the Steps, the absolutes. Anyone can live by that program. We can start our own meetings." *DR. BOB*, p. 163. *Big Book* is a registered trademark of Alcoholics Anonymous World Services, Inc.; used with permission of A.A.W.S.

[7] See Dick B., *The Akron Genesis of Alcoholics Anonymous* (Corte Madera, CA: Good Book Publishing Company, 1994), pp. 194-97, 284-85.

[8] the author was provided by Mitch K., one of Clarence's A.A. sponsees, with materials showing how Clarence led sponsees through the Steps. Danny W., another AA who is sponsored by Clarence's widow (Grace), provided the author with a copy of the scriptural guide to the Twelve Steps that Clarence used with sponsees; and Danny also provided copies of materials showing how Clarence took sponsees through the Third and Seventh Steps with reference to Jesus Christ.

[9] Big Book, p. 43.

available from a chair, a lightbulb, or simply through the ministrations of a "self help" group.

And the Big Book established, from A.A.'s very beginnings, the clear distinction between: (1) the *fellowship* of alcoholics who had shared in, and supported each other during, a common peril, and (2) the *common solution* which had given them all "a way out on which . . . [they could] absolutely agree"—namely, the religious, spiritual, or conversion experience which is the subject of the Big Book's "solution" chapter (pp. 17-29). This solution reaches its culmination when an AA completes the Twelve Steps.

No person in recent years has contended that atheists or agnostics are or should be excluded from A.A. In fact, the Big Book makes clear that these people can, if they choose to do so, and within the rooms of Alcoholics Anonymous, "come to believe" in, and recover through, the power of God. Moreover, no AA today could successfully contend that a Moslem, a Hindu, or a Jew is, can be, or should be excluded from A.A. because that person might hold religious beliefs contrary to those in the New Testament which so greatly influenced early A.A. ideas, recovery principles, and successes.[10]

But note the boldness with which Dr. Bob wrote the following at the close of his own story in the Big Book—a story that still heads those in the personal narrative portion of the Big Book's Third Edition:

> If you think you are an atheist, an agnostic, a skeptic, or have any other form of intellectual pride which keeps you from accepting what is in this book, I feel sorry for you. If you still think you are strong enough to beat the game alone, that is your

---

[10] In a Foreword at page xx, the Big Book now states: "By personal religious affiliation, we include Catholics, Protestants, Jews, Hindus, and a sprinkling of Moslems and Buddhists."

affair. But . . . we know that we have an answer for you. . . .
Your Heavenly Father will never let you down (p. 181)![11]

What is important, we believe, is that the Bible is an ancient
and respected religious document. For those who take its words to
be truth, it is the product of divine revelation.[12] Its vital moral
principles and spiritual truths have guided, inspired, and delivered
hundreds of millions of people throughout the ages. More
important to AAs themselves, it guided, inspired, and made
deliverance available to some seventy-five percent of the early
AAs who really tried to recover.

Though some may conclude that the Bible is no longer an
appropriate part of an AA's recovery process, there is no reason
why knowledge of early A.A.'s biblical principles still cannot
show AAs with no faith, little faith, or of other persuasions that it
was belief in a power greater than themselves—the power of God
as He is described in the Bible—which insured that early AAs
recovered from their seemingly hopeless disease of mind, body,
and spirit.[13] And belief in the necessity for such *power* is what
today distinguishes A.A.'s recovery program from "self-help" and
"mutual support" groups which might resemble A.A. itself were
A.A. to forget its own early emphasis on God and His Word.

A.A.'s Big Book *still* emphatically declares:

Remember that we deal with alcohol—cunning, baffling,
powerful! Without help it is too much for us. But there is One

---

[11] In the Sermon on the Mount, which was so important in early A.A. and which Dr.
Bob quoted with frequency, Jesus said: "for your heavenly Father knoweth that ye have
need of all these things. But seek ye first the kingdom of God, and his righteousness; and
all these things shall be added unto you" (Matthew 6:32-33).

[12] See Galatians 1:11-12; 2 Timothy 3:16-17; 2 Peter 1:20-21; also our discussions
in various parts of this book on these verses and on the writings of Shoemaker and other
A.A. root sources to the effect that the Bible contains the "universal" or "general" will
of God and is divinely inspired.

[13] For the many Big Book statements that people who have taken the Twelve Steps
have *recovered*, as distinguished from their "being in recovery," see Big Book, pp. xiii,
17, 20, 98.

who has all power—that One is God. May you find Him now!
(pp. 58-59).

To which we would add that the "One who has all power" cannot
be understood by reading a catalog on chairs, a manual on
lightbulbs, or an analysis of the techniques of *self help* groups.

In the earliest days of his sobriety, the author was physically
and mentally sick; desperately trying to deal with the wreckage of
the past; focusing his efforts on staying sober; and beset by
confused, disoriented, frightened thinking. His psychiatrist and his
Bible fellowship friends had supported his entry into A.A. But his
psychiatrist then seemed overwhelmed by the immensity of the
author's withdrawal, the depth of his spiritual sickness, and the
persistence of his need for something more than therapy. The
physician was able to provide very little in the way of either of a
solution or comfort.

Finally, and almost despairingly, this fine professional said:
"Dick, why don't you get a Bible and a Big Book, put a rubber
band around both, keep them with you at all times, and study them
both." And eventually, that is just what the author did. In fact,
that's the experience he has shared with the more than sixty men
he had sponsored in their recovery. Eventually, he discovered that
the results for these men very much resembled the 4, 2, 1 success
rate and experiences of early A.A.

And these are some important *Bible verses* which have helped
the author and the men he sponsored when they were confronted
in A.A. with what Sam Shoemaker called "absurd modern names
of God," "half-baked prayers," and "self-made religion."[14] These
verses illustrate the kind of guidance the Bible can still provide for

---

[14] For Shoemaker's comments made directly to AAs and also in Shoemaker's
writings, see Dick B., *New Light on Alcoholism: The A.A. Legacy from Sam Shoemaker*
(Corte Madera, CA: Good Book Publishing Company, 1994), pp. 219, 303-04. See also:
(1) *Alcoholics Anonymous Comes of Age*, p. 265—"half-baked prayers;" (2) Dick B.,
New Light on Alcoholism, p. 222—"absurd modern names of God;" (3) Samuel M.
Shoemaker, Jr., *Realizing Religion* (New York: Association Press, 1923), p. 2—one's
"own religion," or self-made religion.

escaping the labyrinth of confusion one finds in present-day chatter about a "higher power," fatalistic prayer, and the vices of religion. Whether used as a spiritual starting point or as a guide to life, the Bible offers much to any AAs who *wish to use it* for deliverance and spiritual growth. We have listed below some of the helpful Bible verses; and we have given some footnote references which indicate where the verses can also be found discussed in *The Runner's Bible, The Upper Room, The Meaning of Prayer*, and other devotionals Dr. Bob used while he was working with the more than 5,000 alcoholics he personally helped:

Jesus answered and said unto them, Ye do err, not knowing the scriptures, nor the power of God.[15]

Search the scriptures; for in them ye think ye have eternal life: and they are they which testify of me.[16]

Study to shew thyself approved unto God, a workman that needeth not to be ashamed, rightly dividing the word of truth.[17]

And ye shall know the truth, and the truth shall make you free.[18]

Be careful for [anxious about] nothing; but in everything by prayer and supplication with thanksgiving let your requests be made known unto God. And the peace of God, which passeth all understanding, shall keep your hearts and minds through Christ Jesus.[19]

---

[15] Matthew 22:29; Nora Smith Holm, *The Runner's Bible* (New York: Houghton Mifflin Company, 1915), p. 51.

[16] John 5:39; Holm, *The Runner's Bible*, p. 51; *The Upper Room* for 8/12/38.

[17] 2 Timothy 2:15; Mary Wilder Tileston, *Daily Strength for Daily Needs*, 1977 printing (New York: Grosset & Dunlap, 1884), p. 68; Oswald Chambers, *My Utmost for His Highest* (New Jersey: Barbour & Company, 1963), p. 350.

[18] John 8:32; Holm, *The Runner's Bible*, p. 107; *The Upper Room* for 5/20/36, 6/28/36.

[19] Philippians 4:6-7; Holm, *The Runner's Bible*, p. 61; *The Upper Room* for 10/7/35, 10/20/35, 11/24/35.

God is love.[20]

There is no fear in love; but perfect love casteth out fear; because fear hath torment. He that feareth is not made perfect in love.[21]

Stand fast therefore in the liberty wherewith Christ hath made us free, and be not entangled again with the yoke of bondage.[22]

As we reviewed the daily Bible devotionals that Dr. Bob, Anne, Bill, and the early AAs read, as well as the immense amount of religious literature circulated in early A.A., we saw the message of the foregoing verses over and over again.

The message could be found in *The Runner's Bible*, which Dr. Bob and his wife, Anne, consulted frequently for study and inspiration. It could be found in *The Upper Room*, which was so widely read and used in the homes and meetings of early A.A. It could be found in *My Utmost for His Highest*, a devotional read by both the Smiths and the Wilsons, and utilized by Henrietta Seiberling in the early A.A. meetings in Akron. It could be found in *Daily Strength for Daily Needs* by Tileston, and *The Meaning of Faith* and *The Meaning of Prayer* by Fosdick—books recommended and used by Dr. Bob and Anne Smith. It could be found in *Victorious Living* by E. Stanley Jones, a book used by the AAs in the first years. And it could be found in the Glenn Clark books so widely read in the beginnings of A.A.

Given the striking parallels in A.A. language, we believe it very probable that AAs studied, and certainly were much exposed to, the biblical language and ideas in the Bible verses and biblical sources we have covered in so much detail in this present work.

---

[20] 1 John 4:8, 16; Holm, *The Runner's Bible*, pp. 6, 27; *The Upper Room* for 5/24/36, 5/4/37, 8/27/37.

[21] 1 John 4:18; Holm, *The Runner's Bible*, p. 42; *The Upper Room* for 5/2/37; Glenn Clark, *The Soul's Sincere Desire* (Boston: Little, Brown, and Company, 1927), p. 59.

[22] Galatians 5:1; Tileston, *Daily Strength for Daily Needs*, p. 221; Chambers, *My Utmost for His Highest*, p. 127.

We are certain it was his Good Book orientation that caused Dr. Bob, at the end of his personal story in the Big Book, to state emphatically, "Your Heavenly Father will never let you down!"[23] We believe that same early biblical emphasis has led most A.A. meetings, *even today*, to close those meetings with a recital of the Lord's Prayer from the Sermon on the Mount. And though the religions and denominations of the world may disagree over who God is and what faith is, it is difficult to make a case that AAs today no longer need to believe in the power of God in order to recover.

As Bill Wilson himself wrote:

Actually we were fooling ourselves, for deep down in every man, woman, and child, is the fundamental idea of God. It may be obscured by calamity, by pomp, by worship of other things, but in some form or other it is there. For faith in a Power greater than ourselves, and miraculous demonstrations of that power in human lives, are facts as old as man himself. . . . When we drew near to Him He disclosed Himself to us![24]

The author has little doubt that the roots which gave Bill Wilson the strength and courage to write those words came directly from the materials early AAs saw, gathered, and studied in the Good

---

[23] See the Sermon on the Mount, Matthew 6:6: "thy Father which seeth in secret shall reward thee openly;" Matthew 6:14: "your heavenly Father will forgive your trespasses;" Matthew 6:33: "But seek ye first the kingdom of God and his righteousness; and all these things shall be added unto you;" Matthew 7:11: "If ye then, being evil, know how to give good gifts unto your children, how much more shall your Father which is in heaven give good things to them that ask him?" See also James 1:17: "Every good gift and every perfect gift is from above, and cometh down from the Father of lights, with whom is no variableness, neither shadow of turning;" James 3:17: "But the wisdom that is from above is first pure, then peaceable, gentle, *and* easy to be intreated, full of mercy and good fruits, without partiality, and without hypocrisy;" Holm, *The Runner's Bible*, pp. 46, 54, 61-62, 65, 140; Chambers, *My Utmost for His Highest*, pp. 142, 198, 236, 260; Harry Emerson Fosdick, *The Meaning of Prayer* (New York: Association Press, 1915), pp. 175-76.

[24] Big Book, pp. 55, 57; Chambers, *My Utmost for His Highest*, p. 309.

Book and, in the foregoing case, from the much favored Book of James.[25]

We believe the Bible today can be of invaluable assistance in gaining a meaningful understanding of many A.A. terms. We believe it offers some vital spiritual truths that explain how A.A.'s principles can still produce the same splendid results they produced in A.A.'s formative years between 1935 and 1939. We believe the Bible can enable many to avoid the confused floundering heard in today's A.A. meetings over the will of God, how to pray about and deal with the life problems of men and women, and how to harness the power of God to solve those problems. Our belief is buttressed by the fact that bill Wilson referred so many times to the fact that A.A.'s spiritual ideas were rooted in sources outside of A.A. itself. Speaking of A.A.'s most basic spiritual principles, Bill said they "were ancient and universal ones, the common property of mankind."[26] Bill also said, "Everything in A.A. is borrowed from somewhere else."[27] And, "We represent no particular faith or denomination. We are dealing only with general principles common to most denominations" (Big Book, pp. 93-94). Bill humbly explained, "We have no monopoly on God; we merely have an approach that worked with us."[28] And Bill frequently made the point that A.A. is merely a *spiritual kindergarten*. In so stating, he impliedly called for every AA to pursue his or her *own* theological quest for spiritual growth.[29]

And now we will conclude with some specific examples in the A.A. scene where we believe the Bible can have great utility today.

---

[25] See James 4:8: "Draw nigh to God, and he will draw nigh to you."

[26] *Alcoholics Anonymous Comes of Age*, p. 39.

[27] Nell Wing, *Grateful to Have Been There* (Illinois: Parkside Publishing Corporation, 1992), p. 25.

[28] Big Book, p. 95.

[29] Dick B., *New Light on Alcoholism*, pp. 12-13; *As Bill Sees It: The A.A. Way of Life . . . selected writings of A.A.'s co-founder* (New York: Alcoholics Anonymous World Services, Inc., 1967), p. 45; *DR. BOB*, p. 315.

1. **Formulating a rational conception and understanding of God**: The Big Book states: "When, therefore, we speak to you of God, we mean your own conception of God" (p. 47). We believe such language contains an open invitation to see in the Bible the rational conception and understanding of God that Bill, Dr. Bob, and the Big Book itself adopted when they spoke of their "Creator," "Almighty God," and "God of love." Furthermore, Bible basics immediately eliminate from consideration absurd ideas about a "god" or a delivering "Power" that can be described as a lightbulb, a bulldozer, or an A.A. group.

2. **Determining whether God exists at all**: The Big Book declares quite bluntly, "God either is, or He isn't" (p. 53). Sam Shoemaker said, "God is and is a Rewarder of them that seek Him."[30] Hebrews 11:6 told AAs: "he that cometh to God must believe that he is, and *that* he is a rewarder of them that diligently seek him."

3. **Acquiring faith in God**: The Big Book says: "Arrived at this point, we were squarely confronted with the question of faith. We couldn't duck the issue" (Big Book, p. 53). "Imagine life without faith! Were nothing left but pure reason, it wouldn't be life" (Big Book, p. 54). "[D]eep down in every man, woman, and child is the fundamental idea of God" (Big Book, p. 55). The Good Book explained to AAs how faith in God is attained:

So then faith *cometh* by hearing, and hearing by the word of God (italics in original).[31]

For the word of God *is* quick and powerful, and sharper than any two-edged sword, piercing even to the dividing asunder of soul

---

[30] Samuel M. Shoemaker, Jr., *The Gospel According to You and Other Sermons* (New York: Fleming H. Revell, 1934), p. 47.

[31] Romans 10:17; See, as an example, Samuel M. Shoemaker, *How to Become a Christian* (New York: Harper & Brothers, 1953), p. 92.

and spirit, and of the joints and marrow, and *is* a discerner of the thoughts and intents of the heart (italics in original).[32]

But the scripture hath concluded all under sin, that the promise by faith of Jesus Christ might be given to them that believe. . . . For ye are all the children of God by faith in Christ Jesus.[33]

4. **Relying upon the effectiveness of prayer**: The Big Book said of prayer: "It works, if we have the proper attitude and work at it" (p. 86). Shoemaker said: "Whatever be one's theories about prayer, two things stand: man will pray as long as God and he exist, and the spiritual life cannot be lived without it."[34] James 5:16 assured AAs: "The effectual fervent prayer of a righteous man availeth much."[35]

5. **Approaching prayer by assuming the goodness of God**: The Big Book said: "What seemed at first a flimsy reed, has proved to be the loving and powerful hand of God" (Big Book, p. 28). "He stood in the Presence of Infinite Power and Love. He had stepped from bridge to shore. For the first time, he lived in conscious companionship with his Creator" (Big Book, p. 56). "For our group purpose there is but one ultimate authority—a loving God as He may express Himself in our group conscience" (Big Book, p. 565). And the Good Book confirmed for AAs these assumptions about a loving God:

---

[32] Hebrews 4:12.

[33] Galatians 3:22, 26.

[34] Samuel M. Shoemaker, Jr., *Realizing Religion* (New York: Association Press, 1923), p. 63.

[35] Holm, *The Runner's Bible*, p. 114; Fosdick, *The Meaning of Prayer*, pp. 157-58.

Beloved, let us love one another; for love is of God; and every one that loveth is born of God, and knoweth God. He that loveth not knoweth not God; for God is love.[36]

Herein is love, not that we loved God, but that he loved us, and sent his son *to be* the propitiation for our sins.[37]

For this is the love of God, that we keep his commandments: and his commandments are not grievous.[38]

And the Bible also confirmed for AAs a good many other ideas about this loving God's nature: God as Creator, God as Almighty, God as Lord—the God of peace, grace, patience and consolation, hope, all comfort, mercies, and love.[39]

6. **Basing prayer on the sufficiency of God**: The Big Book said: "We agnostics and atheists were sticking to the idea that self-sufficiency would solve our problems. When others showed us that "God-sufficiency" worked with them, we began to feel like those who had insisted the Wrights would never fly" (Big Book, pp. 52-53).[40] As to which, the Good Book offered these powerful promises:

---

[36] 1 John 4:7-8. See also 1 John 4:16—"God is love;" Holm, *The Runner's Bible*, pp. 27, 29; Glenn Clark, *I Will Lift Up Mine Eyes* (New York: Harper & Row, 1937), pp. 93, 132.

[37] 1 John 4:10.

[38] 1 John 5:3.

[39] Dick B., *Design for Living*, pp. 152-53; 1 Peter 5:10; Romans 15:5; 15:13; 16:20; 2 Corinthians 1:3; 1 John 4:8.

[40] Compare Samuel M. Shoemaker, Jr., *National Awakening* (New York: Harper & Brothers, 1936), p. 54: "God give us all grace today to still the other voices and influences about us, to look in the one necessary direction, to leave behind us self-sufficiency and pride, to 'give in' to Him with all our hearts."

And such trust have we through Christ to God-ward. Not that we are sufficient to think any thing as of ourselves; but our sufficiency *is* of God (italics in original).[41]

And God *is* able to make all grace abound toward you; that ye, always having all sufficiency in all *things*, may abound to every good work (italics in original).[42]

7. **Basing prayer on the will of God as expressed in the Bible**: Possibly no issue in the spiritual realm gives rise to more speculation and confusion in today's A.A. than the question: What is the will of God?

Bill Wilson said: "There is God, our Father, who very simply says, 'I am waiting for you to do my will.'"[43] A.A.'s Eleventh Step suggests, "Sought through prayer and meditation to improve our conscious contact with God *as we understood Him*, praying only for knowledge of His will for us and the power to carry that out" (Big Book, p. 59). And the Big Book several times proclaims: "Thy will be done," which comes from a phrase in the Lord's Prayer.[44]

We therefore believe A.A.'s own spiritual roots *should have* pointed present-day AAs directly to the Bible for some important history as to where early AAs found God's will. Jesus had taught that only those would enter the kingdom of heaven who did the will of his Father which is in heaven.[45] Jesus made several statements about his brethren and mother which established Jesus's belief that the word of God is the will of God.[46] And there were a steady stream of declarations by A.A.'s spiritual root sources

---

[41] 2 Corinthians 3:4-5.

[42] 2 Corinthians 9:8.

[43] *Alcoholics Anonymous Comes of Age*, p. 105.

[44] Big Book, pp. 67, 88; Matthew 6:10.

[45] Matthew 7:21; B. H. Streeter, *The God Who Speaks* (London: Macmillan and Company, 1943), p. 85.

[46] Matthew 12:50; Mark 3:35; Luke 8:21; Henry Drummond, *The Ideal Life: Addresses Hitherto Unknown* (New York: Hodder & Stoughton, 1897), p. 235.

that the Bible contains God's "universal" or "general" written will in words, in formal thoughts, and in grace.[47] Why present-day AAs began *ignoring* the Bible as a primary source of information as to God's will is very hard to understand. For it is one thing to renounce affiliation with a particular sect, denomination, or religion; but it is quite another to omit or delete the history of religious sources that explain the language, ideas, and practices of a highly successful program that became the foundation for the basic text on recovery. Furthermore, as we will discuss in a moment, AAs turned to the bible for information on how to learn God's *particular* will through guidance; yet their literature left in the dust source attributions for such clear and ancient statements of God's will as the Ten Commandments, the bible's two great commandments about love of God and love of neighbor (commandments found in the Old and New Testaments). And their literature also left unmentioned the Beatitudes and a host of other biblical verses that were the source of their principles.[48]

This was strange indeed considering the daily bible study that went on in early A.A. and its parent entity, the Oxford Group. Anne Smith had taught early AAs for years that "the Bible ought

---

[47] Horace Bushnell, *The New Life* (London: Strahan & Co., 1868), pp. 3, 11; Drummond, *The Ideal Life*, pp. 231, 235, 239, 243, 264, 268, 271, 304; William R. Moody, *The Life of D. L. Moody* (New York: Fleming H. Revell, 1900), p. 497; James F. Findlay, Jr., *Dwight L. Moody American Evangelist* (Chicago: University of Chicago Press, 1969), pp. 257-58, 409; f. B. Meyer, *The Secret of Guidance* (New York: Fleming H. Revell, 1896), pp. 6, 12-13, 16, 28-29; Robert E. Speer, *The Principles of Jesus Applied to Some Questions Today* (New York: Association Press, 1902), pp. 211-12; Henry B. Wright, *The Will of God and a Man's Lifework* (New York: The Young Men's Christian Association Press, 1909), pp. 135, 137, 139, 149; Samuel M. Shoemaker, Jr., *The Conversion of the Church* (New York: Fleming H. Revell, 1932), p. 49; *Twice-Born Ministers* (New York: Fleming H. Revell, 1919), p. 184; *A Young Man's View of the Ministry* (New York: Association Press, 1923), p. 78. And for a discussion of these writings as root sources of A.A.'s basic spiritual ideas, see Dick B., *Design for Living: The Oxford Group's Contribution to Early A.A.* (San Rafael, CA: Paradise Research Publications, 1995), pp. 39-72; Mel B., *New Wine: The Spiritual Roots of the Twelve Step Miracle* (Minnesota: Hazelden, 1991), pp. 28-32, 41, 127-41.

[48] See, for example, Harry J. Almond, *Foundations for Faith* (London: Grosvenor, 1980), pp. 10, 12; Dick B., *Anne Smith's Journal*, pp. 78, 133.

to be the main Source Book of all."[49] And we believe the large
Roman Catholic contingent in A.A. probably never contested the
concept that the Bible contains the will of God. As an example,
one Roman Catholic evangelist, who had respected and belonged
to the Oxford Group and then converted to Roman Catholicism,
said this:

> The Catholic Church holds the Scriptures in the highest regard,
> for she positively insists that they are sacred and inspired by God.
> The Vatican Council holds—as the Church has ever held—that the
> books of the Old and the New Testaments, having been written
> under the inspiration of the Holy Ghost, have God as their
> Author. This pronouncement is an article of faith and
> consequently the Church excommunicates any one of her children,
> priest or layman, who dares to impugn the Divine origin or
> authority of the Bible. The rule of faith for Catholics has a first
> and a second term—the Church and the Bible; the Bible
> interpreted by an infallible interpreter, i.e., the Church. Catholics
> believe the Bible to be God's word—the truth. . . . Clearly the
> Crux of the matter is to make plain that the Bible is God's word;
> to show that it is only upon God's own testimony that the
> Christian world can reasonably accept belief in the Bible as God's
> Word.[50]

8. **Praying for guidance as to God's particular will**: While
discarding mention of the Bible as the authority for God's
universal will, Bill nonetheless adopted biblical ideas from the
Oxford Group, Shoemaker, and other religious writers that god
discloses his *particular* will when a person seeks such guidance.
That is the essence of the Eleventh Step's language. And we have

---

[49] Dick B., *Anne Smith's Journal*, p. 60.

[50] Theodore H. Dorsey, *From a Far Country: The Conversion Story of a Campaigner for Christ* (Huntington, Indiana: Our Sunday Visitor Press, n.d.,), pp. 173-74.

pointed to its biblical roots in such verses as John 7:17; Acts 9:6; Psalm 46:10; Psalm 32:8; Proverbs 3:6; and 1 Samuel 3:9.[51]

9. **Aligning one's requests with the will of God**: The Big Book said: "In meditation, we ask God what we should do about each specific matter. The right answer will come, if we want it" (p. 69); "'How can I best serve Thee—Thy will (not mine) be done.' These are thoughts which must go with us constantly. We can exercise our will power along this line all we wish. It is the proper use of the will" (p. 85). "See to it that your relationship with Him is right, and great events will come to pass for you and countless others" (p. 164). The most reassuring Bible verses on this topic are these:

> And this is the confidence that we have in him, that if we ask anything according to his will, he heareth us: And if we know that he hear us whatsoever we ask, we know that we have the petitions we desired of him.[52]

The author believes great confidence, power, and deliverance—all items consistent with the path of the Twelve Steps—can be achieved by using the biblical principles of early A.A. These biblical principles can enable people to learn God's will, to pray in accordance with God's will, to receive the power God promised to His children, and to claim the promises God made in His word.

We believe the following promises from God's own word are among the most compelling in offering deliverance to a desperately sick new member of A.A. We list the promises and then some of

---

[51] See Dick B., *Design for Living* pp. 227-69; and the guidance books, Eleanor Napier Forde, *The Guidance of God* (Oxford: Printed at the University Press, 1930); Bremer Hofmeyr, *How to Listen* (New York: Moral Re-Armament, n.d.); Cecil Rose, *When Man Listens* (New York: Oxford University Press, 1937); Howard J. Rose, *The Quiet Time* (New York: The Oxford Group at 61 Gramercy Park, North, 1937); Streeter, *The God Who Speaks*; Jack C. Winslow, *When I Awake* (London: HOdder & Stoughton, 1938).

[52] 1 John 5:14-15; Holm, *The Runner's Bible*, p. 64; Clark, *I Will Lift Up Mine Eyes*, p. 24.

A.A.'s root sources which probably tendered these promises to early AAs:

Bless the Lord, O my soul, And forget not all his benefits: Who forgiveth all thine iniquities; who healeth all thy diseases; Who redeemeth thy life from destruction; who crowneth thee with lovingkindness and tender mercies (Psalm 103:2-4).[53]

Beloved, I wish above all things that thou mayest prosper and be in health, even as thy soul prospereth (3 John 2).[54]

In all thy ways, acknowledge him, and he shall direct thy paths (Proverbs 3:6).[55]

But my God shall supply all your need according to his riches in glory by Christ Jesus (Philippians 4:19).[56]

The Lord *is* my shepherd; I shall not want. He maketh me to lie down in green pastures: he leadeth me beside the still waters. He restoreth my soul: he leadeth me in the paths of righteousness for his name's sake. Yea, though I walk through the valley of the shadow of death, I will fear no evil: for *thou* art with me; thy rod and thy staff *they* comfort me. Thou preparest a table before me

---

[53] These verses are contained in *Just for Today*, a privately published pamphlet, compiled by Miles G. W. Phillimore in 1940, and containing the favorite and most frequently quoted verses and ideas of Oxford Group founder Dr. Frank N. D. Buchman. See also Glenn Clark, *I Will Lift Up Mine Eyes* (New York: Harper & Row, 1937), p. 147.

[54] This was a verse quoted by Anne Smith in her journal—as to which Anne added: "Imagine the President speaking over a nation-wide hookup saying: My fellow citizens, my best wish for you is that your material prosperity and your physical health may be just in proportion to your spiritual well-being." See Dick B., *Anne Smith's Journal*, pp. 71, 131.

[55] *The Upper Room* for May 15, 1935; Clark, *I Will Lift Up Mind Eyes*, pp. 28, 89, 151. for the many other A.A. root sources that quoted this verse, see Dick B., *Dr. Bob's Library: Books for Twelve Step Growth* (San Rafael, CA: Paradise Research Publications, 1994), p. 97.

[56] Fosdick, *The Meaning of Prayer*, p. 131; Holm, *The Runner's Bible*, p. 98; Clark, *I Will Lift Up Mine Eyes*, p. 143; Joel 2:21-27.

in the presence of mine enemies: thou anointest my head with oil; my cup runneth over. Surely goodness and mercy shall follow me all the days of my life: and I will dwell in the house of the Lord for ever (Psalm 23).[57]

The fear of man bringeth a snare; but whose putteth his trust in the Lord shall be safe (Proverbs 29:25).[58]

We believe such verses provided pillars of strength for early AAs. We also believe they still can offer tremendous hope and power to the confused, despairing, and often fatalistic new AA as he or she begins the quest for sobriety—barraged by the realities of an unmanaged, and what eventually became an unmanageable, past.

New AAs commonly face devastating marriage and relationship issues, huge debts, unpaid taxes, revoked or suspended licenses, non-existent insurance capability, physical impairment, and seemingly inevitable depression, shame, anxiety, guilt, and fear.

For such newcomers, the Big Book suggested these two vital helps: (1) "There is one who has all power—that One is God" (p. 59). (2) "God ought to be able to do anything" (p. 158).

And we should add that A.A. Number Three, the man who made the second statement, went on to lead early A.A. meetings with passages from the Scriptures. And the words which inspired that man can also offer hope to all those who have come after him and who today are commencing the journey to a new and sober life through Alcoholics Anonymous.

These new people may, if they choose, believe that the Bible accurately records what god can do for those who hear His word, believe it, and conform their lives to His principles. We have previously referred to a story in the First Edition of the Big Book which story is not included in the Third Edition. How interesting

---

[57] See *A Manual for Alcoholics Anonymous*, 6th rev. ed. (Akron, OH: AA of Akron, 1989), p. 8; Clark, *The Soul's Sincere Desire*, pp. 5, 14; Phillimore, *Just for Today*, p. 29; Holm, *The Runner's Bible*, p. 132.

[58] Holm, *The Runner's Bible*, p. 42.

it would be if newcomers could *still* refer to the following portion
of that First Edition story, which says at page 347:

> One morning, after a sleepless night worrying over what I could
> do to straighten myself out, I went to my room alone—took my
> Bible in hand and asked Him, the One Power, that I might open
> to a good place to read—and I read "Wretched man that I am!
> Who shall deliver me out of the body of this death?" That was
> enough for me—I started to understand. Here were th words of
> Paul a great teacher. When [sic] then if I had slipped? Now I
> could understand. Here were the words of Paul a great teacher.
> When [sic] then if I had slipped? Now, I could understand. From
> that day I gave and still give and always will, time everyday to
> read the word of God and let Him do all the caring.

And 1 Thessalonians 2:13 expresses quite convincingly the profit
of believing that word of God:

> For this cause also thank *we* God without ceasing, because when
> ye received the word of God which ye heard of us, ye received *it*
> not *as* the word of men, but as it is in truth, the word of God,
> which effectually worketh also in you that believe (italics in
> original).

THE END

Bibliography

Alcoholics Anonymous

Publications About

A Guide to the Twelve Steps of Alcoholics Anonymous. Akron: A.A. of Akron, n.d.

A Program for You: A Guide to the Big Book's Design for Living. Minnesota: Hazelden, 1991.

Alcoholics Anonymous. (multilith volume). New Jersey: Works Publishing Co., 1939.

Alcoholics Anonymous: An Interpretation of Our Twelve Steps. Washington, D.C.: "The Paragon" Creative Printers, 1944.

A Manual for Alcoholics Anonymous. Akron: A.A. of Akron, n.d.

B., Dick. *Anne Smith's Journal, 1933-1939: A.A.'s Principles of Success*. San Rafael, CA: Paradise Research Publications, 1994.

———. *Dr. Bob's Library: Books for Twelve Step Growth*. San Rafael, CA: Paradise Research Publications, 1994.

———. *Good Morning!: Quiet Time, Morning Watch, Meditation, and Early A.A.*. San Rafael, CA: Paradise Research Publications, 1996.

———. *New Light on Alcoholism: The A.A. Legacy from Sam Shoemaker*. Corte Madera, CA: Good Book Publishing Company, 1994.

———. *That Amazing Grace: The Role of Clarence and Grace S. in Alcoholics Anonymous*. San Rafael, CA: Paradise Research Publications, 1996.

———. *The Akron Genesis of Alcoholics Anonymous: An A.A.-Good Book Connection*. Corte Madera, CA: Good Book Publishing Company, 1994.

———. *The Books Early AAs Read for Spiritual Growth*. San Rafael, CA: Paradise Research Publications, 1994.

———. *The Good Book and The Big Book: A.A.'s Roots in the Bible*. San Rafael, CA: Paradise Research Publications, 1995.

———, and Bill Pittman. *Courage to Change: The Christian Roots of the 12-Step Movement*. Grand Rapids, MI: Fleming H. Revell, 1994.

B., Jim. *Evolution of Alcoholics Anonymous*. New York: A.A. Archives.

B. Mel. *New Wine: The Spiritual Roots of the Twelve Step Miracle*. Minnesota: Hazelden, 1991.

Bishop, Charles, Jr. *The Washingtonians & Alcoholics Anonymous*. WV: The Bishop of Books, 1992.

———, and Bill Pittman. *To Be Continued . . . . . The Alcoholics Anonymous World Bibliography: 1935-1994*. Wheeling W. VA: The Bishop of Books, 1994.

Bufe, Charles. *Alcoholics Anonymous: Cult or Cure*. San Francisco: Sharp Press, 1991.

C., Stewart. *A Reference Guide To The Big Book of Alcoholics Anonymous*. Seattle: Recovery Press, 1986.

Central Bulletin, Volumes I-II. Cleveland: Central Committee, Oct. 1942-Sept. 1944.

Clapp, Charles, Jr. *Drinking's Not the Problem*. New York: Thomas Y. Crowell, 1949.

Cutten, C. B. *The Psychology of Alcoholism*. New York: Scribner's & Sons, 1907.

Conrad, Barnaby. *Time Is All We Have*. New York: Dell Publishing, 1986.

Darrah, Mary C. *Sister Ignatia: Angel of Alcoholics Anonymous*. Chicago: Loyola University Press, 1992.

Doyle, Paul Barton. *In Step with God*. Tennessee: New Directions, 1989.

E., Bob. *Handwritten note to Lois Wilson on pamphlet entitled "Four Absolutes."* (copy made available to the author at Founders Day Archives Room in Akron, Ohio, in June, 1991).

———. Letter from Bob E. to Nell Wing. Stepping Stones Archives.

First Steps: Al-Anon . . . 35 Years of Beginnings. New York: Al-Anon Family Group Headquarters, 1986.

Ford, John C. *Depth Psychology, Morality and Alcoholism*. Massachusetts: Weston College, 1951.

Gray, Jerry. *The Third Strike*. Minnesota: Hazelden, 1949.

Hunter, Willard, with assistance from M. D. B. *A.A.'s Roots in the Oxford Group*. New York: A.A. Archives, 1988.

K., Mitch. "How It Worked: The Story of Clarence H. Snyder and the Early Days of Alcoholics Anonymous in Cleveland, Ohio." New York, 1991-1992.

Kessell, Joseph. *The Road Back: A Report on Alcoholics Anonymous*. New York: Alfred A. Knopf, 1962.

Knippel, Charles T. *Samuel M. Shoemaker's Theological Influence on William G. Wilson's Twelve Step Spiritual Program of Recovery*. Ph. D. dissertation. St Louis University, 1987.

Kurtz, Ernest. *Not-God: A History of Alcoholics Anonymous*. Expanded Edition. Minnesota: Hazelden, 1991.

———. *Shame and Guilt: Characteristics of the Dependency Cycle*. Minnesota: Hazelden, 1981.

———, and Katherine Ketcham. *The Spirituality of Imperfection: Modern Wisdom from Classic Stories*. New York: Bantam Books, 1992.

McQ, Joe. *The Steps We Took*. Arkansas: August House Publishing, 1990.

Morreim, Dennis C. *Changed Lives: The Story of Alcoholics Anonymous*. Minneapolis: Augsburg Fortress, 1991.

Morse, Robert M., M.D., and Daniel K. Flavin, M.D. "The Definition of Alcoholism." *The Journal of the American Medical Association*. August 26, 1992, pp. 1012-14.

Peale, Norman Vincent. *The Power of Positive Thinking*. New York: Prentice-Hall, 1952.

Pittman, Bill. *AA The Way It Began*. Seattle: Glen Abbey Books, 1988.

Poe, Stephen E. and Frances E. *A Concordance to Alcoholics Anonymous*. Nevada: Purple Salamander Press, 1990.

Playfair, William L., M.D. *The Useful Lie*. Illinois: Crossway Books, 1991.

Robertson, Nan. *Getting Better Inside Alcoholics Anonymous*. New York: William Morrow & Co., 1988.

Second Reader for Alcoholics Anonymous. Akron: A.A. of Akron, n.d.

Seiberling, John F. "Origins of Alcoholics Anonymous." (A transcript of remarks by Henrietta B. Seiberling: transcript prepared by Congressman John F. Seiberling of a telephone conversation with his mother, Henrietta, in the spring of 1971): *Employee Assistance Quarterly*, 1985, (1), pp. 8-12.

Sikorsky, Igor I., Jr. *AA's Godparents*. Minnesota: CompCare Publishers, 1990.

Smith, Bob and Sue Smith Windows. *Children of the Healer*. Illinois: Parkside Publishing Corporation, 1992.

Spiritual Milestones in Alcoholics Anonymous. Akron: A.A. of Akron, n.d.

Stafford, Tim. "The Hidden Gospel of the 12 Steps." *Christianity Today*, July 22, 1991.

The Four Absolutes. Cleveland: Cleveland Central Committee of A.A., n. d.

Thomsen, Robert. *Bill W.* New York: Harper & Row, 1975.

Walker, Richmond. *For Drunks Only*. Minnesota: Hazelden, n.d.

———. *The 7 Points of Alcoholics Anonymous*. Seattle: Glen Abbey Books, 1989.

Wilson, Bill. *How The Big Book Was Put Together*. New York: A.A. Archives. Transcript of Bill Wilson Speech delivered in Fort Worth, Texas, 1954.

———. *Bill Wilson's Original Story*. N.d. Stepping Stones Archives. Bedford Hills, New York, a manuscript whose individual lines are numbered 1 to 1180.

———. "Main Events: Alcoholics Anonymous Fact Sheet by Bill." November 2, 1954. Archives Room. Stepping Stones Archives. Bedford Hills, New York.

———. "The Fellowship of Alcoholics Anonymous." *Quarterly Journal of Studies on Alcohol*. Yale University, 1945, pp. 461-73.

———. *W. G. Wilson Recollections*. Bedford Hills, New York: Stepping Stones Archives, September 1, 1954 transcript of Bill's dictations to Ed B.

Wilson, Jan R., and Judith A. Wilson. *Addictionary: A Primer of Recovery Terms and Concepts from Abstinence to Withdrawal*. New York: Simon and Schuster, 1992.

Wilson, Lois. *Lois Remembers*. New York: Al-Anon Family Group Headquarters, 1987.

———. Article in *The Junction* [New York A.A. newsletter for June, 1985].

Windows, Sue Smith. (daughter of AA's Co-Founder, Dr. Bob). Typewritten Memorandum entitled, *Henrietta and early Oxford Group Friends*, by Sue Smith Windows. Delivered to the author of this book by Sue Smith Windows at Akron, June, 1991.

Wing, Nell. *Grateful to Have Been There: My 42 Years with Bill and Lois, and the Evolution of Alcoholics Anonymous*. Illinois: Parkside Publishing Corporation, 1992.

Publications Approved by Alcoholics Anonymous

Alcoholics Anonymous. 3rd Edition. New York: Alcoholics Anonymous World Services, Inc., 1976.

Alcoholics Anonymous. 1st Edition. New Jersey: Works Publishing, 1939.

Alcoholics Anonymous Comes of Age. New York: Alcoholics Anonymous World Services, Inc., 1979,

As Bill Sees It: The A.A. Way of Life . . . selected writings of A.A.'s Co-Founder. New York: Alcoholics Anonymous World Services, Inc., 1967.

Best of the Grapevine. New York: The A.A. Grapevine, Inc., 1985.

Best of the Grapevine, Volume II. New York: The A.A. Grapevine, Inc., 1986.

Came to Believe. New York: Alcoholics Anonymous World Services, Inc., 1973.

Daily Reflections. New York: Alcoholics Anonymous World Services, Inc., 1991.

DR. BOB and the Good Oldtimers. New York: Alcoholics Anonymous World Services, Inc., 1980.

Members of the Clergy Ask about Alcoholics Anonymous. New York: Alcoholics Anonymous World Services, 1961, 1979-revised 1992, according to 1989 Conference Advisory Action.

Pass It On. New York: Alcoholics Anonymous World Services, Inc., 1984.

*The A.A. Grapevine: "RHS"—*issue dedicated to the memory of the Co-Founder of Alcoholics Anonymous, DR. BOB. New York: A.A. Grapevine, Inc., 1951.

The A.A. Service Manual. New York: Alcoholics Anonymous World Services, Inc., 1990-1991.

The Co-Founders of Alcoholics Anonymous: Biographical Sketches; Their Last Major Talks. New York: Alcoholics Anonymous World Services, Inc., 1972, 1975.

The Language of the Heart. Bill W.'s Grapevine Writings. New York: The A.A. Grapevine, Inc., 1988.

Twelve Steps and Twelve Traditions. New York: Alcoholics Anonymous World Services, Inc., 1953.

The Bible—Versions of and Books About

Authorized King James Version. New York: Thomas Nelson, 1984.

Bullinger, Ethelbert W. *A Critical Lexicon and Concordance to the English and Greek New Testament.* Michigan: Zondervan, 1981.

Burns, Kenneth Charles. "The Rhetoric of Christology: A Content Analysis of Texts Which Discuss Titus 2:13." Master's thesis, San Francisco State University, 1991.

Harnack, Adolph. *The Expansion of Christianity in the First Three Centuries.* New York: G. P. Putnam's Sons, Volume I, 1904; Volume II, 1905.

Jukes, Andrew. *The Names of GOD in Holy Scripture.* Michigan: Kregel Publications, 1967.

Moffatt, James. *A New Translation of the Bible.* New York: Harper & Brothers, 1954.

New Bible Dictionary. 2nd Edition. Wheaton, Illinois: Tyndale House Publishers, 1987.

Revised Standard Version. New York: Thomas Nelson, 1952.

Serenity: A Companion for Twelve Step Recovery. Nashville: Thomas Nelson, 1990.

Strong, James. *The Exhaustive Concordance of the Bible.* Iowa: Riverside Book and Bible House, n.d.

The Abingdon Bible Commentary. New York: Abingdon Press, 1929.

The Companion Bible. Michigan: Zondervan Bible Publishers, 1964.

The Revised English Bible. Oxford: Oxford University Press, 1989.

Vine, W. E. *Vine's Expository Dictionary of Old and New Testament Words.* New York: Fleming H. Revell, 1981.

Young's Analytical Concordance to the Bible. New York: Thomas Nelson, 1982.

Zodhiates, Spiros. *The Hebrew-Greek Key Study Bible.* 6th ed. AMG Publishers, 1991.

Bible Devotionals

Chambers, Oswald. *My Utmost for His Highest*. London: Simpkin Marshall, Ltd., 1927.

Clark, Glenn, *I Will Lift Up Mine Eyes*. New York: Harper & Brothers, 1937.

Dunnington, Lewis L. *Handles of Power*. New York: Abingdon-Cokesbury Press, 1942.

Fosdick, Harry Emerson. *The Meaning of Prayer*. New York: Association Press, 1915.

Holm, Nora Smith. *The Runner's Bible*. New York: Houghton Mifflin Company, 1915.

Jones, E. Stanley. *Abundant Living*. New York: Abingdon-Cokesbury Press, 1942.

————. *Victorious Living*. New York: Abingdon Press, 1936.

The Upper Room: Daily Devotions for Family and Individual Use. Quarterly. 1st issue: April, May, June, 1935. Edited by Grover Carlton Emmons. Nashville: General Committee on Evangelism through the Department of Home Missions, Evangelism, Hospitals, Board of Missions, Methodist Episcopal Church, South.

The Two Listeners. *God Calling*. Edited by A. J. Russell. Australia: DAYSTAR, 1953.

Tileston, Mary W. *Daily Strength for Daily Needs*. Boston: Roberts Brothers, 1893.

Publications by or about the Oxford Group & Oxford Group People

A Day in Pennsylvania Honoring Frank Nathan Daniel Buchman in Pennsburg and Allentown. Oregon: Grosvenor Books, 1992.

Allen, Geoffrey Francis. *He That Cometh*. New York: The Macmillan Company, 1933.

Almond, Harry J. *Foundations for Faith*. 2d ed. London: Grosvenor Books, 1980.

————. *Iraqi Statesman: A Portrait of Mohammed Fadhel Jamali*. Salem, OR: Grosvenor Books, 1993.

Austin, H. W. "Bunny". *Frank Buchman As I Knew Him*. London: Grosvenor Books, 1975.

————. *Moral Re-Armament: The Battle for Peace*. London: William Heineman, 1938.

Begbie, Harold. *Life Changers*. New York: G. P. Putnam's Sons, 1927.

————. *Souls in Action*. New York: Hodder & Stoughton, 1911.

————. *Twice-Born Men*. New York: Fleming H. Revell, 1909.

Belden, David C. *The Origins and Development of the Oxford Group (Moral Re-Armament)*. D. Phil. Dissertation, Oxford University, 1976.

Belden, Kenneth D. *Is God Speaking-Are We Listening?* London: Grosvenor Books, 1987.

————. *Meeting Moral Re-Armament*. London: Grosvenor Books, 1979.

————. *Reflections on Moral Re-Armament*. London: Grosvenor Books, 1983.

————. *The Hour of the Helicopter*. Somerset, England: Linden Hall, 1992.

Bennett, John C. *Social Salvation*. New York: Charles Scribner's Sons, 1935.

Benson, Clarence Irving. *The Eight Points of the Oxford Group*. London: Humphrey Milford, Oxford University Press, 1936.

Blair, David. *For Tomorrow-Yes!* Compiled and edited from David Blair's Notebook by Jane Mullen Blair & Friends. New York: Exposition Press, 1981.

Blake, Howard C. *Way to Go: Adventures in Search of God's Will*. Burbank, CA: Pooh Stix Press, 1992.

Braden, Charles Samuel. *These Also Believe*. New York: The Macmillan Company, 1949.

Brown, Philip Marshall. *The Venture of Belief.* New York: Fleming H. Revell, 1935.

Buchman, Frank N. D. *Remaking the World.* London: Blandford Press, 1961.

―――― and Sherwood Eddy. *Ten Suggestions for Personal Work* (not located).

――――. *The Revolutionary Path.* London: Grosvenor, 1975.

Bundy, David D. *Keswick: A Bibliographic Introduction to the Higher Life Movements.* Wilmore, Kentucky: B. L. Fisher Library of Asbury Theological Seminary, 1975.

――――. "Keswick and the Experience of Evangelical Piety." Chap. 7 in *Modern Christian Revivals.* Urbana, IL: University of Illinois Press, 1992.

Campbell, Paul and Peter Howard. *Remaking Men.* New York: Arrowhead Books, 1954.

Cantrill, Hadley. *The Psychology of Social Movements.* New York: John Wiley & Sons, Inc., 1941.

Clapp, Charles, Jr. *The Big Bender.* New York: Harper & Row, 1938.

――――. *Drinking's Not the Problem.* New York: Thomas Y. Crowell, 1949.

Clark, Walter Houston. *The Oxford Group: Its History and Significance.* New York: Bookman Associates, 1951.

Crothers, Susan. *Susan and God.* New York: Harper & Brothers, 1939.

Day, Sherwood Sunderland. *The Principles of the Group.* Oxford: University Press, n.d.

Dayton, Donald W., ed. *The Higher Christian Life: Sources for the Study of the Holiness, Pentecostal and Keswick Movements.* New York: Garland Publishing, 1984.

Dinger, Clair M. *Moral Re-Armament: A Study of Its Technical and Religious Nature in the Light of Catholic Teaching.* Washington, D.C.: The Catholic University of America Press, 1961.

"Discord in Oxford Group: Buchmanites Ousted by Disciple from N.Y. Parish House." *Newsweek.* November 24, 1941.

Driberg, Tom. *The Mystery of Moral Re-Armament: A Study of Frank Buchman and His Movement.* New York: Alfred A. Knopf, 1965.

du Maurier, Daphne. *Come Wind, Come Weather.* London: Heinemann, 1941.

Eister, Allan W. *Drawing Room Conversion.* Durham: Duke University Press, 1950.

Entwistle, Basil, and John McCook Roots. *Moral Re-Armament: What Is It?* Pace Publications, 1967.

Ferguson, Charles W. *The Confusion of Tongues.* Garden City: Doubleday, Doran Company, Inc., 1940.

Foot, Stephen. *Life Began Yesterday.* New York: Harper & Brothers, 1935.

Forde, Eleanor Napier. *The Guidance of God.* Oxford: Printed at the University Press, 1930.

Frank Buchman-80. Compiled by His Friends. London: Blandford Press, 1958.

Gordon, Anne Wolrige. *Peter Howard: Life and Letters.* London: The Oxford Group, 1969.

Grensted, L. W. *The Person of Christ.* New York: Harper & Brothers, 1933.

Grogan, William. *John Riffe of the Steelworkers.* New York: Coward―McCann, 1959.

Hamilton, Loudon. *MRA: How It All Began.* London: Moral Re-Armament, 1968.

Hamlin, Bryan T. *Moral Re-Armament and Forgiveness in International Affairs.* London: Grosvenor, 1992.

Harris, Irving. *An Outline of the Life of Christ.* New York: The Oxford Group, 1935.

———. *Out in Front: Forerunners of Christ. A Study of the Lives of Eight Great Men.* New York: The Calvary Evangel, 1942.

———. *The Breeze of the Spirit: Sam Shoemaker and the Story of Faith at Work.* New York: The Seabury Press, 1978.

Harrison, Marjorie. *Saints Run Mad.* London: John Lane, Ltd., 1934.

Henderson, Michael. *A Different Accent.* Richmond, VA: Grosvenor Books USA, 1985.

———. *All Her Paths Are Peace: Women Pioneers in Peacemaking.* CT: Kumerian Press, 1994.

———. *Hope for a Change: Commentaries by an Optimistic Realist.* Salem, OR: Grosvenor Books, 1991.

———. *On History's Coattails: Commentaries by an English Journalist in America.* Richmond, VA: Grosvenor USA, 1988.

Henson, Herbert Hensley. *The Group Movement.* London: Oxford University Press, 1933.

Hicks, Roger. *How to Read the Bible.* London: Moral Re-Armament, n.d.

———. *Letters to Parsi.* London: Blandford Press, 1960.

———. *The Endless Adventure.* London: Blandford Press, 1964.

———. *The Lord's Prayer and Modern Man.* London: Blandford Press, 1967.

Hofmeyr, Bremer. *How to Change.* New York: Moral Re-Armament, n.d.

———. *How to Listen.* New York: Moral Re-Armament, n.d.

Holmes-Walker, Wilfrid. *New Enlistment* (no data available).

Howard, Peter. *Frank Buchman's Secret.* Garden City: New York: Doubleday & Company, Inc., 1961.

———. *Innocent Men.* London: Heinemann, 1941.

———. *That Man Frank Buchman.* London: Blandford Press, 1946.

———. *The World Rebuilt.* New York. Duell, Sloan & Pearce, 1951.

Hunter, T. Willard, with assistance from M.D.B. *A.A.'s Roots in the Oxford Group.* New York: A.A. Archives, 1988.

———. *Press Release.* Buchman Events/Pennsylvania, October 19, 1991.

———. *AA & MRA: "It Started Right There": Behind the Twelve Steps and the Self-help Movement.* OR: Grosvenor Books, 1994.

———. "The Oxford Group's Frank Buchman." July, 1978. Founders Day archives, maintained by Gail L. in Akron, Ohio.

———. *The Spirit of Charles Lindbergh: Another Dimension.* Lanham, MD: Madison Books, 1993.

———. *Uncommon Friends' Uncommon Friend.* A tribute to James Draper Newton, on the occasion of his eighty-fifth birthday. (Pamphlet, March 30, 1990).

———. *World Changing Through Life Changing.* Thesis, Newton Center, Mass: Andover-Newton Theological School, 1977.

Hutchinson, Michael. *A Christian Approach to Other Faiths.* London: Grosvenor Books, 1991.

———. *The Confessions.* (privately published study of St. Augustine's *Confessions*).

Jones, Olive M. *Inspired Children.* New York: Harper & Brothers, 1933.

———. *Inspired Youth.* New York: Harper & Brothers, 1938.

Kitchen, V. C. *I Was a Pagan.* New York: Harper & Brothers, 1934.

Koenig, His Eminence Franz Cardinal. *True Dialogue.* Oregon: Grosvenor USA, 1986.

Laun, Ferdinand. *Unter Gottes Fuhring*. The Oxford Group, n.d.

Lean, Garth. *Cast Out Your Nets*. London: Grosvenor, 1990.

―――. *Frank Buchman: A Life*. London: Constable, 1985.

―――. *Good God, It Works*. London: Blandford Press, 1974.

―――. *On the Tail of a Comet: The Life of Frank Buchman*. Colorado Springs: Helmers & Howard, 1988.

―――, and Morris Martin. *New Leadership*. London: William Heinemann, Ltd., 1936.

Leon, Philip. *The Philosophy of Courage or the Oxford Group Way*. New York: Oxford University Press, 1939.

"Less Buchmanism." *Time*, November 24, 1941.

Macintosh, Douglas C. *Personal Religion*. New York: Charles Scribner's Sons, 1942.

Mackay, Malcolm George. *More than Coincidence*. Edinburgh: The Saint Andrew Press, 1979.

Macmillan, Ebenezer. *Seeking and Finding*. New York: Harper & Brothers, 1933.

Margetson, The Very Reverend Provost. *The South African Adventure*. The Oxford Group, n.d.

Martin, Morris H. *The Thunder and the Sunshine*. Washington D.C.: MRA, n.d.

―――. *Born to Live in the Future*. n.l.: Up With People, 1991.

Mowat, R. C. *Modern Prophetic Voices: From Kierkegaard to Buchman*. Oxford: New Cherwel Press, 1994.

―――. *The Message of Frank Buchman*. London: Blandford Press, 1951.

―――. *Report on Moral Re-Armament*. London: Blandford Press, 1955.

Moyes, John S. *American Journey*. Sydney: Clarendon Publishing Co., n. d.

Murray, Robert H. *Group Movements Throughout the Ages*. New York: Harper & Brothers. 1935.

Newton, Eleanor Forde. *I Always Wanted Adventure*. London: Grosvenor, 1992.

Newton, James D. *Uncommon Friends: Life with Thomas Edison, Henry Ford, Harvey Firestone, Alexis Carrel, & Charles Lindbergh*. New York: Harcourt Brace, 1987.

Nichols, Beverley. *The Fool Hath Said*. Garden City: Doubleday, Doran & Company, 1936.

Orglmeister, Peter. *An Ideology for Today*. Pamphlet, 1965.

Petrocokino, Paul. *The New Man for the New World*. Cheshire: Paul Petrocokino, n.d.

Phillimore, Miles. *Just for Today*. Privately published pamphlet, 1940.

Pollock, J. C. *The Keswick Story: The Authorized History of the Keswick Convention*. Chicago: Moody Press, n.d.

Raynor, Frank D., and Leslie D. Weatherhead. *The Finger of God*. London: Group Publications, Ltd., 1934.

Reynolds, Amelia S. *New Lives for Old*. New York: Fleming H. Revell, 1929.

Roots, John McCook. *An Apostle to Youth*. Oxford: The Oxford Group, 1928.

Rose, Cecil. *When Man Listens*. New York: Oxford University Press, 1937.

Rose, Howard J. *The Quiet Time*. New York: Oxford Group at 61 Gramercy Park, North, 1937.

Russell, Arthur J. *For Sinners Only*. London: Hodder & Stoughton, 1932.

―――. *One Thing I Know*. New York: Harper & Brothers, 1933.

Sangster, W. E. *God Does Guide Us*. New York: The Abingdon Press, 1934.

Selbie, W. B. *Oxford and the Groups*. Oxford: Basie Blackwell, 1934.

Sherry, Frank H., and Mahlon H. Hellerich. *The Formative Years of Frank N. D. Buchman*. (Reprint of article at Frank Buchman home in Allentown, Pennsylvania).

Smith, J. Herbert. *The Meaning of Conversion*. N.p., n.d.

Spencer, F. A. M. *The Meaning of the Groups*. London: Metheun & Co., Ltd., 1934.

Spoerri, Theophil. *Dynamic out of Silence: Frank Buchman's Relevance Today*. Translated by John Morrison. London: Grosvenor Books, 1976.

Streeter, Burnett Hillman. *The God Who Speaks*. London: Macmillan & Co., Ltd., 1943.

Suenens, Rt. Rev. Msgr. *The Right View of Moral Re-Armament*. London: Burns and Oates, 1952.

The Bishop of Leicester, Chancellor R. J. Campbell and the Editor of the "Church of England Newspaper." *Stories of our Oxford House Party.*, July 17, 1931.

The Layman with a Notebook. *What Is the Oxford Group?* London: Oxford University Press, 1933.

Thornhill, Alan. *One Fight More*. London: Frederick Muller, 1943.

———. *The Significance of the Life of Frank Buchman*. London: Moral Re-Armament, 1952.

———. *Best of Friends: A Life of Enriching Friendships*. United Kingdom, Marshall Pickering, 1986.

Thornton-Duesbury, J. P. *Sharing*. The Oxford Group, n.d.

———. *The Open Secret of MRA*. London: Blandford, 1964.

"Calvary's Eviction of Buchman." *Time Magazine*, November 24, 1941.

Twitchell, Kenaston. *Do You Have to Be Selfish*. New York: Moral Re-Armament, n.d.

———. *How Do You Make Up Your Mind*. New York: Moral Re-Armament, n.d.

———. *Regeneration in the Ruhr*. Princeton: Princeton University Press, 1981.

———. *Supposing Your Were Absolutely Honest*. New York: Moral Re-Armament, n.d.

———. *The Strength of a Nation: Absolute Purity*. New York: Moral Re-Armament, n.d.

Van Dusen, Henry P. "Apostle to the Twentieth Century: Frank N. D. Buchman." *Atlantic Monthly* 154 (July 1934).

———. "The Oxford Group Movement." *Atlantic Monthly*. 154 (August 1934).

Viney, Hallen. *How Do I Begin?* The Oxford Group, 61 Gramercy Park, New York., 1937.

Vrooman, Lee. *The Faith That Built America*. New York: Arrowhead Books, Inc., 1955.

Walter, Howard A. *Soul Surgery: Some Thoughts on Incisive Personal Work*. 6th. ed. Oxford: at the University Press by John Johnson, 1940.

Weatherhead, Leslie D. *Discipleship*. London: Student Christian Movement Press, 1934.

———. *How Can I Find God?* London: Fleming H. Revell, 1934.

———. *Psychology and Life*. New York: Abingdon Press, 1935.

Williamson, Geoffrey. *Inside Buchmanism*. New York: Philosophical Library, Inc., 1955.

Winslow, Jack C. *Church in Action* (no data available to author).

———. *Vita! Touch with God: How to Carry on Adequate Devotional Life*. The Evangel, 8 East 40th St., New York, n.d.

———. *When I Awake*. London: Hodder & Stoughton, 1938.

———. *Why I Believe in the Oxford Group*. London: Hodder & Stoughton, 1934.

Books by or about Oxford Group Mentors

Bushnell, Horace. *The New Life*. London: Strahan & Co., 1868.

Chapman, J. Wilbur. *Life and Work of Dwight L. Moody*. Philadelphia, 1900.

Cheney, Mary B. *Life and Letters of Horace Bushnell*. New York: Harper & Brothers, 1890.

Drummond, Henry. *Essays and Addresses*. New York: James Potts & Company, 1904.

———. *Natural Law in the Spiritual World*. Potts Edition.

———. *The Changed Life*. New York: James Potts & Company, 1891.

———. *The Greatest Thing in the World and Other Addresses*. London: Collins, 1953.

———. *The Ideal Life*. New York: Hodder & Stoughton, 1897.

———. *The New Evangelism*. New York: Hodder & Stoughton, 1899.

Edwards, Robert L. *Of Singular Genius, of Singular Grace: A Biography of Horace Bushnell*. Cleveland: The Pilgrim Press, 1992.

Findlay, James F., Jr. *Dwight L. Moody American Evangelist*. Chicago, University of Chicago Press, 1969.

Fitt, Emma Moody, *Day by Day with D. L. Moody*. Chicago: Moody Press, n.d.

Goodspeed, Edgar J. *The Wonderful Career of Moody and Sankey in Great Britain and America*. New York: Henry S. Goodspeed & Co., 1876.

Guldseth, Mark O. *Streams*. Alaska: Fritz Creek Studios, 1982.

Hopkins, C. Howard. *John R. Mott, a Biography*. Grand Rapids: William B. Erdmans Publishing Company, 1979.

James, William. *The Varieties of Religious Experience*. New York: First Vintage Books/The Library of America, 1990.

Meyer, F. B. *The Secret of Guidance*. New York: Fleming H. Revell, 1896.

Moody, Paul D. *My Father: An Intimate Portrait of Dwight Moody*. Boston: Little Brown, 1938.

Moody, William R. *The Life of D. L. Moody*. New York: Fleming H. Revell, 1900.

Mott, John R. *The Evangelisation of the World in This Generation*. London, 1901.

Pollock, J. C. *Moody: A Biographical Portrait of the Pacesetter in Modern Mass Evangelism*. New York: Macmillan, 1963.

Smith, George Adam. *The Life of Henry Drummond*. New York: McClure, Phillips & Co., 1901.

Speer, Robert E. *Studies of the Man Christ Jesus*. New York: Fleming H. Revell, 1896.

———. *The Marks of a Man*. New York: Hodder & Stoughton, 1907.

———. *The Principles of Jesus*. New York: Fleming H. Revell Company, 1902.

Stewart, George, Jr. *Life of Henry B. Wright*. New York: Association Press, 1925.

Wright, Henry B. *The Will of God and a Man's Lifework*. New York: The Young Men's Christian Association Press, 1909.

Publications by or about Samuel Moor Shoemaker, Jr.

Shoemaker, Samuel Moor, Jr. "A 'Christian Program.'" In *Groups That Work: The Key to Renewal . . . for Churches, Communities, and Individuals*. Compiled by Walden Howard and the Editors of *Faith at Work*. Michigan: Zondervan, 1967.

———. "Act As If." *Christian Herald*. October, 1954.

———. "And So from My Heart I Say . . ." *The A.A. Grapevine.* New York: The A.A. Grapevine, Inc., September, 1948.

———. *. . . And Thy Neighbor.* Waco, Texas: Word Books, 1967.

———. *A Young Man's View of the Ministry.* New York: Association Press, 1923.

———. *Beginning Your Ministry.* New York: Harper & Row Publishers, 1963.

———. *By the Power of God.* New York: Harper & Brothers, 1954.

———. *Calvary Church Yesterday and Today.* New York: Fleming H. Revell, 1936.

———. *Children of the Second Birth.* New York: Fleming H. Revell, 1927.

———. *Christ and This Crisis.* New York: Fleming H. Revell, 1943.

———. *Christ's Words from the Cross.* New York: Fleming H. Revell, 1933.

———. *Confident Faith.* New York: Fleming H. Revell, 1932.

———. *Extraordinary Living for Ordinary Men.* Michigan: Zondervan, 1965.

———. *Faith at Work.* A symposium edited by Samuel Moor Shoemaker. Hawthorne Books, 1958.

———. *Faith at Work* magazine, frequent articles in.

———. *Freedom and Faith.* New York: Fleming H. Revell, 1949.

———. *God and America.* New York: Book Stall, 61 Gramercy Park North, New York, n.d.

———. *God's Control.* New York: Fleming H. Revell, 1939.

———. *How to Become a Christian.* New York: Harper & Brothers, 1953.

———. "How to Find God." Reprint from *Faith at Work* Magazine, n.d.

———. *How to Help People.* Cincinnati: Forward Movement Publications, 1976.

———. *How You Can Find Happiness.* New York: E. P. Dutton & Co., 1947.

———. *How You Can Help Other People.* New York: E. P. Dutton & Co., 1946.

———. *If I Be Lifted Up.* New York: Fleming H. Revell, 1931.

———. *In Memoriam: The Service of Remembrance.* Princeton: The Graduate Council, Princeton University, June 10, 1956.

———. *Living Your Life Today.* New York: Fleming H. Revell, 1947.

———. *Morning Radio Talk No. 1, by Reverend Samuel M. Shoemaker,* American Broadcasting Co., one-page transcript of program for October 4, 1945.

———. *National Awakening.* New York: Harper & Brothers, 1936.

———. *One Boy's Influence.* New York: Association Press, 1925.

———. *Realizing Religion.* New York: Association Press, 1923.

———. *Religion That Works.* New York: Fleming H. Revell, 1928.

———. *Revive Thy Church.* New York: Harper & Brothers, 1948.

———. *Sam Shoemaker at His Best.* New York: Faith At Work, 1964.

———. *So I Stand by the Door and Other Verses.* Pittsburgh: Calvary Rectory, 1958.

———. *The Breadth and Narrowness of the Gospel.* New York: Fleming H. Revell, 1929.

———. *The Calvary Evangel, monthly articles in.* New York. Calvary Episcopal Church.

———. *The Church Alive.* New York: E. P. Dutton & Co., Inc., 1951.

———. *The Church Can Save the World.* New York: Harper & Brothers, 1938.

———. *The Conversion of the Church.* New York: Fleming H. Revell, 1932.

———. "The Crisis of Self-Surrender." *Guideposts.* November, 1955.

———. *The Experiment of Faith.* New York: Harper & Brothers. 1957.

———. *The Gospel According to You.* New York: Fleming H. Revell, 1934.

————. *The James Houston Eccleston Day-Book: Containing a Short Account of His Life and Readings for Every Day in the Year Chosen from His Sermons.* Compiled by Samuel M. Shoemaker, Jr. New York: Longmans, Green & Co., 1915.

————. "The Spiritual Angle." *The A.A. Grapevine.* New York: The A.A. Grapevine, Inc., October, 1955.

————. "The Way to Find God." *The Calvary Evangel* (August, 1935).

————. *They're on the Way.* New York: E. P. Dutton, 1951.

————. "Those Twelve Steps As I Understand Them." *Best of the Grapevine: Volume II.* New York: The A.A. Grapevine, Inc., 1986.

————. *Twice-Born Ministers.* New York: Fleming H. Revell, 1929.

————. *Under New Management.* Grand Rapids: Zondervan Publishing House, 1966.

————. *What the Church Has to Learn from Alcoholics Anonymous.* Reprint of 1956 sermon. Available at A.A. Archives, New York.

————. *With the Holy Spirit and with Fire.* New York: Harper & Brothers, 1960.

"Buchman Religion Explained to 1,000." *New York Times.* May 27, 1931.

"Campus Calls by Dr. Shoemaker Foster Chain of Religious Cells." *New York Tribune.* February 25, 1951.

Centennial History: Calvary Episcopal Church, 1855-1955. Pittsburgh: Calvary Episcopal Church, 1955.

"Church Ejects Buchman Group." *New York Times.* November 8, 1941.

"Crusaders of Reform." *Princeton Alumni Weekly.* June 2, 1993.

Cuyler, John Potter, Jr. *Calvary Church in Action.* New York: Fleming H. Revell, 1934.

Day, Sherwood S. "Always Ready: S.M.S. As a Friend." *The Evangel* (New York: Calvary Church, July-August, 1950).

Get Changed; Get Together; Get Going: A History of The Pittsburgh Experiment. Pittsburgh: The Pittsburgh Experiment, n.d.

Harris, Irving. *The Breeze of the Spirit.* New York: The Seabury Press, 1978.

————. "S.M.S.—Man of God for Our Time." *Faith At Work* (January-February, 1964).

"Houseparties Across the Continent." *The Christian Century.* August 23, 1933.

Knippel, Charles Taylor. *Samuel M. Shoemaker's Theological Influence on William G. Wilson's Twelve Step Spiritual Program of Recovery (Alcoholics Anonymous).* Dissertation. St. Louis University, 1987.

"Listening to God Held Daily Need." *New York Times.* December 4, 1939.

Norton-Taylor, Duncan. "Businessmen on Their Knees." *Fortune.* October, 1953.

Olsson, Karl A. "The History of Faith at Work" (five parts). *Faith at Work News.* 1982-1983.

Peale, Norman Vincent. "The Unforgettable Sam Shoemaker." *Faith At Work.* January, 1964.

————. "The Human Touch: The Estimate of a Fellow Clergyman and Personal Friend." *The Evangel* (New York: Calvary Church, July-August, 1950).

Pitt, Louis W. "New Life, New Reality: A Brief Picture of S.M.S.'s Influence in the Diocese of New York." *Faith at Work*, July-August, 1950.

"Pittsburgh Man of the Year." *Pittsburgh Post Gazette.* January 12, 1956.

Sack, David Edward. *Sam Shoemaker and the "Happy Ethical Pagans."* Princeton, New Jersey: paper prepared in the Department of Religion, Princeton University, June, 1993.

"Sam Shoemaker and Faith at Work." Pamphlet on file at Faith At Work, Inc., 150 S. Washington St., Suite 204, Falls Church, VA 22046.

Schwartz, Robert. "Laymen and Clergy to Join Salute to Dr. S. M. Shoemaker." *Pittsburgh Press.* December 10, 1961.

Shoemaker, Helen Smith. *I Stand by the Door.* New York: Harper & Row, 1967.

"Sees Great Revival Near." *New York Times.* September 8, 1930.

"Soul Clinic Depicted by Pastor in Book." *New York Times.* August 5, 1927.

"Ten of the Greatest American Preachers." *Newsweek.* March 28, 1955.

The Pittsburgh Experiments Groups. Pittsburgh: The Pittsburgh Experiment, n.d.

Tools for Christian Living. Pittsburgh: The Pittsburgh Experiment, n.d.

"Urges Church Aid Oxford Group." *New York Times.* January 2, 1933, p. 26.

Wilson, Bill. "I Stand by the Door." *The A.A. Grapevine.* New York: The A.A. Grapevine, Inc., February, 1967.

Woolverton, John F. "Evangelical Protestantism and Alcoholism 1933-1962: Episcopalian Samuel Shoemaker, The Oxford Group and Alcoholics Anonymous." *Historical Magazine of the Protestant Episcopal Church* 52 (March, 1983).

Spiritual Literature-Non-Oxford Group

Kempis, Thomas à. *The Imitation of Christ.* Georgia: Mercer University Press, 1989.

Allen, James. *As a Man Thinketh.* New York: Peter Pauper Press, n.d.

―――. *Heavenly Life.* New York: Grosset & Dunlap, n.d.

Darton, George A. *Jesus of Nazareth.* New York: The Macmillan Company, 1922.

Brother Lawrence. *The Practice of the Presence of God.* Pennsylvania: Whitaker House, 1982.

Carruthers, Donald W. *How to Find Reality in Your Morning Devotions.* Pennsylvania State College, n.d.

Chambers, Oswald. *Studies in the Sermon on the Mount.* London: Simpkin, Marshall, Ltd., n.d.

Clark, Glenn. *Clear Horizons.* Vol 2. Minnesota: Macalester Park Publishing, 1941.

―――. *Fishers of Men.* Boston: Little, Brown, 1928.

―――. *God's Reach.* Minnesota: Macalester Park Publishing, 1951.

―――. *How to Find Health through Prayer.* New York: Harper & Brothers, 1940.

―――. *I Will Lift Up Mine Eyes.* New York: Harper & Brothers, 1937.

―――. *The Lord's Prayer and Other Talks on Prayer from The Camps Farthest Out.* Minnesota: Macalester Publishing Co., 1932.

―――. *The Man Who Talks with Flowers.* Minnesota: Macalester Park Publishing, 1939.

―――. *The Soul's Sincere Desire.* Boston: Little, Brown, 1925.

―――. *Touchdowns for the Lord. The Story of "Dad" A. J. Elliott.* Minnesota: Macalester Park Publishing Co., 1947.

―――. *Two or Three Gathered Together.* New York: Harper & Brothers, 1942.

Daily, Starr. *Recovery.* Minnesota: Macalester Park Publishing, 1948.

Eddy, Mary Baker. *Science and Health with Key to the Scriptures*. Boston: Published by the Trustees under the Will of Mary Baker G. Eddy, 1916.

Fillmore, Charles. *Christian Healing*. Kansas City: Unity School of Christianity, 1936.

———, and Cora Fillmore. *Teach Us to Pray*. Lee's Summit, Missouri: Unity School of Christianity, 1950.

Fosdick, Harry Emerson. *A Great Time to Be Alive*. New York: Harper & Brothers, 1944.

———. *As I See Religion*. New York: Grosset & Dunlap, 1932.

———. *On Being a Real Person*. New York: Harper & Brothers, 1943.

———. *The Man from Nazareth*. New York: Harper & Brothers, 1949.

———. *The Manhood of the Master*. London: Student Christian Association, 1924.

———. *The Meaning of Prayer*. New York: Association Press, 1915.

———. *The Meaning of Service*. London: Student Christian Movement, 1921.

Fox, Emmet. *Alter Your Life*. New York: Harper & Brothers, 1950.

———. *Find and Use Your Inner Power*. New York: Harper & Brothers, 1937.

———. *Power through Constructive Thinking*. New York: Harper & Brothers, 1932.

———. *Sparks of Truth*. New York: Grosset & Dunlap, 1941.

———. *The Sermon on the Mount*. New York: Harper & Row, 1934.

———. Pamphlets: *Getting Results by Prayer* (1933); *The Great Adventure* (1937); *You Must Be Born Again* (1936).

Glover, T. R. *The Jesus of History*. New York: Association Press, 1930.

Gordon, S. D. *The Quiet Time*. London: Fleming, n.d.

Heard, Gerald. *A Preface to Prayer*. New York: Harper & Brothers, 1944.

Hickson, James Moore. *Heal the Sick*. London: Methuen & Co., 1925.

James, William. *The Varieties of Religious Experience*. New York: First Vintage Press/The Library of America Edition, 1990.

Jones, E. Stanley. *Abundant Living*. New York: Cokesbury Press, 1942.

———. *Along the Indian Road*. New York: Abingdon Press, 1939.

———. *Christ and Human Suffering*. New York: Abingdon Press, 1930.

———. *Christ at the Round Table*. New York: Abingdon Press, 1928.

———. *The Choice Before Us*. New York: Abingdon Press, 1937.

———. *The Christ of Every Road*. New York: Abingdon Press, 1930.

———. *The Christ of the American Road*. New York: Abingdon-Cokesbury Press, 1944.

———. *The Christ of the Indian Road*. New York: Abingdon Press, 1925.

———. *The Christ of the Mount*. New York: Abingdon Press, 1930.

———. *Victorious Living*. New York: Abingdon Press, 1936.

———. *Way to Power and Poise*. New York: Abingdon Press, 1949.

Jung, Dr. Carl G. *Modern Man in Search of a Soul*. New York: Harcourt Brace Jovanovich, 1933.

Kagawa, Toyohiko. *Love: The Law of Life*. Philadelphia: The John C. Winston Company, 1929.

Laubach, Frank. *Prayer (Mightiest Force in the World)*. New York: Fleming H. Revell, 1946.

Layman, Charles M. *A Primer of Prayer*. Nashville: Tidings, 1949.

Lieb, Frederick G. *Sight Unseen*. New York: Harper & Brothers, 1939.

Ligon, Ernest M. *Psychology of a Christian Personality*. New York: Macmillan, 1935.

Link, Dr. Henry C. *The Rediscovery of Man*. New York: Macmillan, 1939.

Lupton, Dilworth. *Religion Says You Can*. Boston: The Beacon Press, 1938.

Moseley, J. Rufus. *Perfect Everything*. Minnesota: Macalester Publishing Co., 1949.

Oursler, Fulton. *Happy Grotto*. Declan and McMullen, 1948.

——. *The Greatest Story Ever Told*. New York: Doubleday, 1949.

Parker, William R. and Elaine St. Johns. *Prayer Can Change Your Life*. New ed. New York: Prentice Hall, 1957.

Peale, Norman Vincent. *The Art of Living*. New York: Abingdon Press, 1937.

Rawson, F. L. *The Nature of True Prayer*. Chicago: The Marlowe Company, n.d.

Sheean, Vincent. *Lead Kindly Light*. New York: Random House, 1949.

Sheen, Fulton J. *Peace of Soul*. New York: McGraw Hill, 1949.

Sheldon, Charles M. *In His Steps*. Nashville, Broadman Press, 1935.

Silkey, Charles Whitney. *Jesus and Our Generation*. Chicago: University of Chicago Press, 1925.

Speer, Robert E.. *Studies of the Man Christ Jesus*. New York: Fleming H. Revell, 1896.

Stalker, Rev. James. *The Life of Jesus Christ*. New York: Fleming H. Revell, 1891.

The Confessions of St. Augustine. Translated by E. B. Pusey. A Cardinal Edition. New York: Pocket Books, 1952.

The Fathers of the Church. New York: CIMA Publishing, 1947.

Trine, Ralph Waldo. *In Tune with the Infinite*. New York: Thomas H. Crowell, 1897.

——. *The Man Who Knew*. New York: Bobbs Merrill, 1936.

Weatherhead, Leslie D. *Discipleship*. New York: Abingdon Press, 1934.

——. *How Can I Find God?* New York: Fleming H. Revell, 1934.

——. *Psychology and Life*. New York: Abingdon Press, 1935.

Werber, Eva Bell. *Quiet Talks with the Master*. L.A.: De Vorss & Co., 1942.

Williams, R. Llewelen, *God's Great Plan, a Guide to the Bible*. Hoverhill Destiny Publishers, n.d.

Willitts, Ethel R. *Healing in Jesus Name*. Chicago: Ethel R. Willitts Evangelists, 1931.

Index

A

A.A. General Services xiv, 3, 9, 71
AA of Akron 20-23, 209
   *A Guide to the Twelve Steps of
     Alcoholics Anonymous* 21
   *A Manual for Alcoholics
     Anonymous* 20, 21, 38, 97,
     209
   Akron AAs 19, 34, 72, 125,
     192, 193
   *Second Reader for Alcoholics
     Anonymous* 22
   *Spiritual Milestones in Alcoholics
     Anonymous* 23, 192
Abandon yourself 182
Absolute honesty 83, 148-50, 174
Absolute love 84, 97, 148-50
Absolute purity 148-50, 174
Absolute unselfishness 84, 96, 148-
   50
Acts 1:4 116
Acts 1:8 75, 86, 171, 185
Acts 2:46 36
Acts 2:47 37
Acts 3:13 59
Acts 3:19 147, 183
Acts 4:7-12 79
Acts 4:31, 33 171
Acts 5:42 36
Acts 9:6 167, 182, 207
Acts 11:23 87
Acts 14:15 51
Acts 17:11 36
Acts 17:28 147

Acts 22:10 168
Acts 26:22 173, 179
Acts 28:24 37
Agapē 93
Agnostics 39, 56, 59, 60, 68, 69,
   77, 194, 203
Agree with thine adversary quickly
   120, 159, 183
Air (two-way prayer) 4
Akron Beacon Journal 10
Alcoholism
   100% hopeless, apart from divine
     help 2, 56, 193
   18-and-a-half million are addicted
     1
   financial costs of 1
   seventy-five million American
     lives are impacted 1
Alexander, Jack 8
Allen, James (*As a Man Thinketh*)
   43, 94
Almond, Harry xiii, 30, 151, 154,
   160, 164, 172, 174, 175, 205
Amends 84, 120, 121, 153, 158,
   159, 161, 183
Amos, Frank B. 6, 29, 44
Anger 99, 102, 120, 122, 124, 169,
   175
Anonymity 89-91, 121
Anxiety 209
   take no thought for [be not
     anxious about]--Matt. 6:25-34
     169
   thou wilt keep him in perfect
     peace (Isa. 26:3) 170

227

Art (Soul Surgery) 77, 110, 115,
   152, 155, 159, 208
As Bill Sees It 3, 58, 61, 64, 200
Ask, seek, knock 126
Asking amiss for selfish ends 108
Atheist(s) 3, 5, 24, 25, 24-26, 64,
   68, 69, 70, 78, 194
Austin, H. W. (*Frank Buchman As I
   Knew Him*) 3, 42
Awakening 51, 69, 78, 86, 88,
   125, 135-137, 141, 144, 146,
   156, 158, 163, 167, 170, 184,
   203

B

B., Jim (A.A. oldtimer) 26, 70, 71
B., Mel (A.A. member—*see also
   New Wine*) xiv, 4, 31, 55, 62,
   63, 116, 122, 183, 205
Barrier(s) 182, 183
Basic ideas (A.A.'s) xii, 4, 7, 16,
   17, 28, 79, 178-180, 186
Be still, and know that I am God
   146, 167
Beatitudes 117-119, 118, 119, 205
Begbie, Harold 17, 83, 136, 152
Belden, K. D. 161, 167
Belief, lack of 77
Beliefs xi, 74, 180, 190, 194
Believer 113
Believing 24, 51, 78, 79, 101, 103,
   144, 210
Bible
   best-selling book 6, 95
   Christian (Sam Shoemaker) 31
   Dr. Bob's own 29
   Gideon (Jim B.) 26, 72
   how to read the 163, 172
   King James Version 15, 33, 54,
      81, 82, 93, 96, 107, 114, 118,
      145, 146
   Moffatt's 33, 103, 146, 182
   principles came from 17
   reading of scripture 28

source book xii, 5, 27, 46, 168,
   206
stressed as reading material 14
study 4, 25, 29-31, 41, 47, 79,
   190, 193, 205
use of, at A.A. meetings 19, 28,
   29
"Big, Big Book" 30
"soaked in the" (Frank Buchman)
   30
Biblical beliefs (Frank Buchman's)
   180
Biblical roots of (A.A.) 6, 7, 16,
   18, 45, 54, 87, 88, 99, 132,
   135, 151, 155, 207
Big Book (*Alcoholics Anonymous*)
   First Edition x, xii, 3, 32, 39,
      41, 60, 61, 63, 67, 80, 98,
      137, 170, 179, 209, 210
   story portion (First Edition) 32
Block (to God) 15, 71, 77, 111,
   112, 124, 148, 152, 181
Book of Acts 36, 192
Book of James x, 5, 19-21, 28, 88,
   93, 96, 98-100, 104, 105, 109,
   111, 116, 162, 165, 173, 175,
   200
Born again 80, 156, 157, 180, 181
Breeze of the Spirit, The (W. Irving
   Harris) 17, 31
Brother Lawrence (*Practicing the
   Presence of God*) 43
Brown, Philip M. (*The Venture of
   Belief*) 83, 143
Buchman, Frank N. D. (founder of
   the Oxford Group) 17, 19, 30,
   44, 86, 119, 140, 143, 147,
   150, 157, 158, 164, 165, 172,
   205, 208
Bushnell, Horace (*The New Life*)
   66, 205

C

Calvary Church xi, 17, 44

D

G

H

I

J

M

N

O

P

Dick B.'s Historical Titles on Early A.A.'s Spiritual Roots and Successes

Dr. Bob's Library: Books for Twelve Step Growth   (Revised Paradise Edition)
Foreword by Ernest Kurtz, Ph.D., Author, *Not-God: A History of Alcoholics Anonymous.*
A study of the immense spiritual reading of the Bible, Christian literature, and Oxford Group books done and recommended by A.A. co-founder, Dr. Robert H. Smith. Paradise Research Pub.; 104 pp.; 8 1/2 x 11; velo bound; 1994; $13.00; ISBN 1-885803-00-1. (Previous title: *Dr. Bob's Library: An A.A-Good Book Connection*).

Anne Smith's Journal, 1933-1939: A.A.'s Principles of Success   (Rev. Paradise Ed.)
Foreword by Robert R. Smith, son of Dr. Bob & Anne Smith; co-author, *Children of the Healer.*
Dr. Bob's wife, Anne, kept a journal in the 1930's from which shared with early AAs and their families ideas from the Bible and the Oxford Group which impacted on A.A. Paradise Research Publications; 176 pp.; 6 x 9; perfect bound; 1994; $14.00; ISBN: 1-885803-01-X. (Previous title: *Anne Smith's Spiritual Workbook*).

Design for Living: The Oxford Group's Contribution to Early A.A.   (Rev. Paradise Ed.)
Foreword by Rev. T. Willard Hunter; author, columnist, Oxford Group activist.
A comprehensive history of the origins, principles, practices, and contributions to A.A. of "A First Century Christian Fellowship" (also known as the Oxford Group) of which A.A. was an integral part in the developmental period between 1931 and 1939. Paradise Research Publications; 269 pp.; 8 1/2 x 11; velo bound; 1995; $18.95; ISBN: 1-885803-12-5. (Previous title: *The Oxford Group & Alcoholics Anonymous*).

The Akron Genesis of Alcoholics Anonymous
Foreword by former U.S. Congressman John F. Seiberling, Director of the Peace Center, Akron University, whose mother, Henrietta Seiberling, was instrumental in A.A.'s founding.
The story of A.A.'s birth at Dr. Bob's Home in Akron on June 10, 1935. It tells what early AAs did in their meetings, homes, and hospital visits; what they read; and how their ideas developed from the Bible, the Oxford Group, and Christian literature. It depicts the roles of A.A. founders and their wives, and of Henrietta Seiberling, and T. Henry and Clarace Williams. Good Book Publishing Co.; 290 pp., 8 1/2 x 11; velo bound; 1996; $17.95; ISBN: 1-885803-10-9.

The Books Early AAs Read for Spiritual Growth   (5th ed.)
An exhaustive bibliography and brief summary of all the books known to have been read and recommended for spiritual growth by early AAs in Akron and on the East Coast. Paradise Research Publications; 50 pp.; 8 1/2 x 11; velo bound; 1995; $10.00; ISBN: 1-885803-04-4.

New Light on Alcoholism: The A.A. Legacy from Sam Shoemaker
Forewords by Nickie Shoemaker Haggart, daughter of Rev. Sam Shoemaker; and Mrs. W. Irving Harris, friend of Sam Shoemaker and Bill Wilson; widow of Shoemaker's assistant minister, Rev. W. Irving Harris.
A comprehensive history and analysis of the all-but-forgotten specific contributions to A.A. spiritual principles and practices by New York's famous Episcopal preacher, the Rev. Samuel M. Shoemaker, Jr.—dubbed by Bill W. as a "co-founder" of A.A. and credited by Bill as the well-spring of A.A.'s spiritual recovery ideas. Good Book Publishing Co.; 412 pp.; 6 x 9; perfect bound; 1994; $19.95; ISBN: 1-881212-06-8.

That Amazing Grace: The Role of Clarence and Grace S. in Alcoholics Anonymous
Foreword by Harold E. Hughes, former U.S. Senator from, and Governor of, Iowa, and founder of SOAR.
Details of early A.A.'s spiritual practices—from the recollections of Grace S., widow of venerable A.A. pioneer, Clarence S. Paradise Research Pub.; 160 pp.; 6 x 9; perfect bound; 1996; $16.95; ISBN: 1-885803-06-0.

Good Morning!: Quiet Time, Morning Watch, Meditation, and Early A.A.
A practical guide to Quiet Time—a "must" in early A.A. Discusses biblical roots, history, helpful books, and how to. Paradise Research Pub.; 107 pp.; 8 1/2 x 11; velo bound; 1996; $15.50; ISBN: 1-885803-09-5.

Turning Point: A History of Early A.A.'s Spiritual Roots and Successes
Foreword by Paul Wood, Ph.D., President, National Council on Alcoholism and Drug Dependence.
Turning Point is a comprehensive history of early A.A.'s spiritual roots and successes—the culmination of six years of research. This title shows specifically what the Twelve Step pioneers borrowed from: (1) The Bible; (2) Sam Shoemaker's teachings; (3) The Oxford Group; (4) Anne Smith's journal; and (5) meditation materials. Paradise Research Pub., 776 pp.; 6 x 9; perfect bound; 1997; $29.95; ISBN: 1-885803-07-9.

Inquiries, orders, and requests for
catalogs and discount schedules
should be addressed to:

Dick B.
c/o Good Book Publishing Company
P.O. Box 959
Kihei, Maui, Hawaii 96753-0959
1-808-874-4876 (phone & fax)
email: dickb@dickb.com
Internet Home Page: "http://dickb.com"

About the Author

Dick B. writes books on the spiritual history of early A.A. They show how the basic and highly successful biblical ideas used by early AAs can be valuable tools for success in today's A.A. The religious and recovery communities are using his research and titles to work more effectively with alcoholics, addicts, and others involved in Twelve Step programs.

The author is an active, recovered member of A.A.; a retired attorney; and a Bible student. He has sponsored more than seventy men in their recovery from alcoholism. Consistent with A.A.'s traditions of anonymity, he uses the pseudonym "Dick B."

He has had eleven titles published: *Turning Point: A History of Early A.A.'s Spiritual Roots and Successes*; *Good Morning!: Quiet Time, Morning Watch, Meditation, and Early A.A.*; *That Amazing Grace: The Role of Clarence and Grace S. in Alcoholics Anonymous*; *The Good Book and The Big Book: A.A.'s Roots in the Bible*; *New Light on Alcoholism: The A.A. Legacy from Sam Shoemaker*; *The Books Early AAs Read for Spiritual Growth*; *Design for Living: The Oxford Group's Contribution to Early A.A.*; *The Akron Genesis of Alcoholics Anonymous*; *Anne Smith's Journal*; *Dr. Bob's Library*; and *Courage to Change* (with Bill Pittman). These have been discussed in news articles and reviewed in *Library Journal, Bookstore Journal, For A Change, The Living Church, Sober Times, NECAD Newsletter, Recovery News, Episcopal Life, MRA Newsletter, STEPS for Recovery*, and the *Ohioana Quarterly*.

Dick is the father of two married sons (Ken and Don) and a grandfather. As a young man, he did a stint as a newspaper reporter. He attended the University of California, Berkeley, where he received his A.A. degree, majored in economics, and was elected to Phi Beta Kappa in his Junior year. In the United States Army, he was an Information-Education Specialist. He received his A.B. and J.D. degrees from Stanford University, and was Case Editor of the Stanford Law Review. Dick became interested in Bible study in his childhood Sunday School and was much inspired by his mother's almost daily study of Scripture. He joined, and later became president of, a Community Church affiliated with the United Church of Christ. By 1972, he was studying the origins of the Bible and began traveling abroad in pursuit of that subject. In 1979, he became much involved in a Biblical research, teaching, and fellowship ministry. In his community life, he was president of a merchants' council, Chamber of Commerce, church retirement center, and homeowners' association. He served on a public district board and was active in a service club.

In 1986, he was felled by alcoholism, gave up his law practice, and began recovery as a member of the Fellowship of Alcoholics Anonymous. In 1990, his interest in A.A.'s Biblical/Christian roots was sparked by his attendance at A.A.'s International Convention in Seattle. He has traveled widely; researched at archives, and at public and seminary libraries; interviewed scholars, historians, clergy, A.A. "old-timers" and survivors; and participated in programs, panels, and seminars on early A.A.'s spiritual history.

The author has several works in progress. Much of his research and writing is done in collaboration with his older son, Ken, who holds B.A., B.Th., and M.A. degrees. Ken has been a lecturer in New Testament Greek at a Bible college and a lecturer in Fundamentals of Oral Communication at San Francisco State University. Ken is a computer specialist.

Dick is a member of the American Historical Association, the Maui Writers Guild, and The Authors' Guild. He is available for panels, seminars, talk shows, and interviews.

Catalog & Order Sheet

How to Order Dick B.'s Historical Titles on Early A.A.

Order Form

Send:

Qty.

____ Turning Point (comp. history of early A.A.) @ $29.95 ea. $_____

____ New Light on Alcoholism (Sam Shoemaker) @ $19.95 ea. $_____

____ Design for Living (Oxford Group & A.A.) @ $18.95 ea. $_____

____ The Good Book and The Big Book @ $18.95 ea. $_____

____ The Akron Genesis of Alcoholics Anonymous @ $17.95 ea. $_____

____ That Amazing Grace (Clarence & Grace S.) @ $16.95 ea. $_____

____ Good Morning! (Quiet Time) @ $15.50 ea. $_____

____ Anne Smith's Journal @ $14.00 ea. $_____

____ Dr. Bob's Library @ $13.00 ea. $_____

____ Books Early AAs Read (5th ed.) @ $10.00 ea. $_____

Shipping and Handling
Add 10% of retail price (minimum $3.00)

Shipping and Handling $_____

Total Enclosed $_____

Name: _____ (as it appears on your credit card, if using one)

Address: _____

City: _____ State: ____ Zip: _____

Tel.: _____ **Credit card**: MC VISA Exp. _____

CC Account #: _____ Signature _____

Special Value for You!

If purchased separately, the author's ten titles would normally sell for $175.20, plus Shipping and Handling. Using this Order Form, you may purchase sets of all ten titles for **only $149.95 per set**, plus Shipping and Handling. Please contact us for Shipping and Handling charges for orders being shipped outside of the United States. **Please mail this Form**, with your check, money order, or credit card authorization, to: Dick B., c/o Good Book Publishing Co., Box 959, Kihei, HI 96753-0959. Please make your check or money order payable to **"Dick B."** in U.S. dollars drawn on a U.S. bank.
If you have any questions, please phone or fax: 1-808-874-4876.